In the Presence of Many

Green Balloon Publishing

Vivian Broughton is a Gestalt Psychotherapist and Constellations Facilitator. She gained her accreditation in Person Centred Counselling and in Gestalt through the Metanoia Psychotherapy Training Institute, London, UK, and worked in private practice as a psychotherapist for twenty years.

Since 1995 she has focused on the work of Bert Hellinger, running a formal training in Systemic Constellations in the UK since 2000. She has introduced leading constellations facilitators to the UK, including Albrecht Mahr, Franz Ruppert, Ursula Franke, Guni Baxa and Jan Jacob Stam.

She has made a particular study of the process of working with constellations in private consultations, as well as running groups, teaching, consulting, supervising and promoting the work of constellations in organisations and larger systems including the political, environmental, social and voluntary sectors. She co-organised the first conference on Systemic Constellations in the UK (Unimaginable Solutions: Introducing Constellations at Work, 2005) and has edited two books on Systemic Constellations translated from German. In addition to being a Director of the training organisation Constellations Work Trainings, she is a partner in the publishing company Green Balloon Publishing.

Vivian Broughton is one of the foremost practitioners of constellations in the UK and has made a considerable contribution to the furtherance of the work in that country. She also works in the USA. She lives in Bristol, UK.

In the Presence of Many

Reflections on Constellations Emphasising the Individual Context

Vivian Broughton

I can of mine own self do nothing.
John 5: 30

For Jennifer

Green Balloon Publishing

First published in the United Kingdom in 2010
by Green Balloon Publishing

© V. Broughton 2010

Green Balloon Publishing
An imprint of Constellations Work Trainings Limited,
Frome, Somerset, BA11 5DG
www.greenballoonbooks.co.uk
info@greenballoonbooks.co.uk

ISBN 978-0-9559683-1-0

Book production by Action Publishing Technology Ltd, Gloucester
Printed and bound in Great Britain

Contents

Contents

Appendices

Foreword

I have the pleasure of having known Vivian Broughton for more than 15 years, and of having witnessed the unfolding of her loving commitment and passion for constellation work. Vivian has certainly become one of the most experienced and distinguished constellation practitioners in the field, the proof of which you, the reader, are now holding in your hands.

On entering this book you should take a good breath because Vivian has written a challenging book in the very best sense.

Constellations work when developed in the 80's by Bert Hellinger was first received in Germany and then world-wide as if evolution was eagerly waiting for it; as if a revolutionary new understanding of intimate and large scale human relationships was needed and finally ready to be born. Constellations work both in groups and individual settings *is* indeed revolutionary, does indeed, in many different human contexts, allow for "unimaginable solutions", which is the title of the first UK conference on constellations work initiated by Vivian and colleagues in 2005.

However, this book stays very well grounded while introducing the reader into the mind- and heart-opening world of a deeper understanding of human nature and human possibilities through constellations work.

First of all the reader gets all the very well edited and clearly structured information that is needed for an in-depth understanding of current theory and practice of constellations work. A rich theoretical and experiential knowledge of constellations is thoroughly presented and illustrated by numerous graphic examples from the author's practice.

This in itself makes the book one of the very best introductions to the work currently available, not just for the individual setting but for the whole of constellations work.

What I equally appreciate is the cutting edge perspective of Vivian's book. Throughout the text the author gently and persistently challenges the notion of individualism, separateness and the narrow we-them divide that are still the prevailing worldviews underlying so much human-made suffering and destruction. Consistently when dealing with central topics such as conscience, soul, healing, representative perception or phenomenology the author stresses experiential and scientific evidence for our collective mutual interdependence and the fact of belonging not only to our family, to our people but to all people, even to all being. Constellations work as presented in this book develops a well documented path out of outdated postmodern narcissistic heroism and solitude – a path that Bert Hellinger, living with the Zulu people for 16 years, may have envisioned under the influence of the sub-Saharan African notion of Ubuntu: "I am because you are". Vivian does not demand that you believe this larger view of self and world, but she offers evidence from disciplines such as quantum physics, systems theory and current informational field approaches, in addition to rich clinical material that speaks for itself.

Out of the long list of topics supporting what has been said so far I want to mention just two prominent theoretical and clinical aspects of this book. The first is a central focus on recent trauma theory and practice as developed by Babette Rothschild, Peter Levine and Franz Ruppert in its application to constellations work. Trauma in its individual and multigenerational dimension has an enormous explanatory and therapeutic power to access the potential of a trans-personal understanding and healing of the all too often nameless confusion and suffering. Vivian's expertise and thorough devotion to that theme is one of the special gems of her book.

The second important topic is Vivian's special passion and

qualification: working with constellations in the individual context. And out of the vast experience and teaching that Vivian shares I want to emphasize but one crucial aspect. She gives a detailed explanation on how to support the client to become a useful i.e. reliable, representative in his own system. While stepping into another person's shoes or looking through the eyes of the other is a well known and most valuable approach, to fully become and embody another person's being through representation is a further essential step towards softening boundaries and opening up to inter-connectedness or even inter-being, as the Zen master Thich Nhat Hanh puts it. One of the revolutionary aspects of constellations work is exactly this: the stepping out of the prison of self-centeredness into the larger human field of many generations interacting and co-creating life as it is given.

Reconciliation with one's own and with our own people's life and fate is perhaps the single condition for healthy self-appreciation, loving compassion and, not least, humour in our life.

I think Vivian has done an excellent job in reminding us of and opening our eyes to these facts. Thus I wish her and her book well deserved success, and for the readers many beautifully challenging insights along the way.

Albrecht Mahr
Würzburg, October 1, 2009

The Journey

One day you finally knew
what you had to do, and began,
though the voices around you
kept shouting
their bad advice -
though the whole house
began to tremble
and you felt the old tug
at your ankles.
"Mend my life!"
each voice cried.
But you didn't stop.
You knew what you had to do,
though the wind pried
with its stiff fingers
at the very foundations,
though their melancholy
was terrible.
It was already late
enough, and a wild night,
and the road full of fallen
branches and stones.
But little by little,
as you left their voices behind,
the stars began to burn
through the sheets of clouds,
and there was a new voice
which you slowly
recognised as your own,
that kept you company
as you strode deeper and deeper
into the world,
determined to do
the only thing you could do -
determined to save
the only life you could save.

Mary Oliver

Preface

I hate long prefaces . . . I always want to get on with the book. After all, if I have taken the trouble to buy it, I want to get into what it has to offer me. And now, as an author myself I decided I didn't want to have a long preface. At the same time, I became more aware of the importance of my initial statement . . . most particularly the purpose of writing this book. Like many things one decides to do, I had no idea what I was getting myself into – the effort involved, personal challenge, horrible amounts of discipline, panic, fluctuations of confidence, resistance and rebellion (I became intrigued at the many, creative ways in which I could distract myself from the task) – would I have done it if I had known? Probably, but it probably was best not to know. Why take all the time and effort, all the inevitably confronting and challenging business of disciplining myself to do such a task? There have to be good reasons. So here are mine:

I have run a training programme in systemic constellations since 2000 and over these years I have often asked students how they intend to incorporate constellations into their work. Most students when asked have clearly stated that they do not intend to run groups. Their wish is to integrate the ideas and practice in some way into their current work, most of which is done on a one-to-one basis whether in psychotherapy or business consultancy. Since most of our witnessing and learning takes place in groups, it makes it difficult for many to conceptualise how to make the transition to private sessions. What do you do about the lack of group members to act as representatives? Year on year I was confronted with this question from my students, and because I was in private psychotherapy practice myself, it was an urgent question of mine as well. It therefore became an important part of my learning and experimenting, and I have endeavoured to put together here what I have learned in as comprehensible a manner as possible.

There is little literature on the subject of constellations in individual settings available as yet, the most important being: Ursula Franke's book "In My Mind's Eye: Family Constellations in Individual Therapy and Counselling" published by Carl Auer in English translation in 2003, and Eva Madelung and Barbara Innecken's book "Entering Inner Images: A Creative use of Constellations in Individual Therapy, Counselling, Groups and Self-Help" also published by Carl Auer in English translation in 2004. Other than that, anything written about individual work in the constellations field takes rather a back seat in books that are mainly focused on group work.

My intention is to reverse this, making individual work the main emphasis, with group work secondary. Having explored this area over a period of nine or so years, I find working with constellations in the one-to-one context intensely satisfying and productive – in many instances as much as working with groups. Whether working in one-off sessions (as I now generally do), or integrating the constellations approach into a professional practice of on-going client contact, the constellation can show all its power and clarity just as well in the one-to-one setting as in the group. For clients who have no experience of constellations (sometimes no experience of any kind of therapy), the individual consultation space offers a privacy and degree of personal attention in which to explore intimate issues about which they may feel shy, embarrassed or ashamed, with less fear of exposure and no need to worry about having to support other group members.

Another reason for writing such a book that deserves

mention is that to date almost all of the books that we have on the subject of constellations in general are translations from German. Quite naturally, since the work originated in Germany, the first wave of books were written by its first practitioner, Bert Hellinger, and by those who immediately followed him who, for the most part, are also German. Apart from Love's Hidden Symmetry, which was part translation and partly reworked in English by Hunter Beaumont, the exceptions to this library of German-to-English translations include two books by the South African John Payne, one by the Dutch Shamanist practitioner Daan van Kampenhout (translated from Dutch), a collection of essays edited by the American Gestalt therapist Ed Lynch and one by Svagito Liebermeister who although German by origin I believe wrote the book in English. There may be others, but I doubt many that I have missed. The main source of English-language writing to date has been The Knowing Field International Constellations Journal (formerly the Systemic Solutions Bulletin) which was started in 2000 by Barbara Stones and Jutta ten Herkel and has been under the editorship of Barbara Morgan since 2004.

It is likely that the lens through which a member of a different culture views constellations work may offer something new. Additionally, translated work tends to lose something, no matter how good the translation, whereas work written and read in its original language has an at-home feeling to those who speak the same language. I hope there is a fluidity to my writing that comes from the fact that English is my language, my home, the language of my heart and soul, without any mediation through translation. Over the past three years I have had the challenging experience of editing two constellations books translated from German into English.[1] This experience taught me a lot as I struggled to maintain the general tone and feel of the original authors, while at the same

---

[1] Insa Sparrer's *Miracle, Solution and System* and Franz Ruppert's *Trauma, Bonding and Family Constellations.*

time trying to find ways of bringing the text into a comfortable form for an English reader, that doesn't persistently remind you that you are reading a translation. I feel an additional responsibility to those who may choose to read this book whose primary language is neither English nor German. Since the work of constellations has travelled so well thoughout the world, any book on the subject in English is likely to be read by people of many nations, languages and cultures, in the absence of books written in their own language, English being currently the world's best attempt at an international common language. I feel a sense of humility and responsibility that this should be so.

My journey with systemic constellations has been particular. I believe I have followed a less than conventional route, taking an intuitive approach to my studentship. I have experienced many different teachers, styles and thinking within the field, and have been influenced to varying degrees by them all. Hellinger, while always present and a major influence through the experiences I have had of his presence and his work, and through his writings, has had less direct influence on me than Albrecht Mahr and Franz Ruppert. Others such as Franke, Beaumont, Stam, Baxa and Schneider I have had less direct contact with, but what I have had has affected me profoundly. I have also, through some direct contact and by the task of editing the English version of Sparrer's book, been influenced by the systemic structural work of Sparrer and Varga von Kibéd.

One result of this rather eclectic journey is that I have been constantly challenged by conflicting views espoused, and, with some tentativeness, I have attempted to find a place of my own, some synthesis that includes different views on aspects of constellations that may seem to conflict, but often have at their core a common truth. In addition, the process of writing has forced me to attempt to penetrate the words of Hellinger. It is not enough to re-phrase his words. I have endeavoured to take his ideas and those of others and find my own meaning from them. How successful I have been with this endeavour I am unsure, and so I view this book, and the ideas and meanings within, as a work in progress. There will be readers who dispute some of the things that I say, and while this is personally challenging, it also confirms to me that truth, theories and ideas are transitory, always under review and always in development, and this is as it should be. Theories can only really be theories of practice . . . practice must come first and theory must always be the servant of practice. To put theories first is to reify, and leads to attempting to fit reality to theory. This will never do. Theory must reflect reality not reality theory! Taking this stance relieves me of having to be right, allowing me to be tentative and exploratory, always knowing that no view is definitive, and all views will invite and stimulate the next book by another that takes the movement on. I feel supported in this by the words of the psychoanalyst John Bowlby: "When people start writing they think they've got to write something definitive . . . I think that is fatal. The mood to write in is 'This is quite an interesting story I've got to tell. I hope someone will be interested. Anyway it's the best I can do for the present.'" (Bowlby in Hunter, 1991) I think I have an interesting story to tell, and I hope someone will be interested . . . and it certainly is the best I can do for the present.

Terms and conventions

Taking a swift look through some of the currently available literature, it seems that the general convention is to use capital initials if we are talking about Constellations Work, or Family Constellations or Organisational Constellations, but not if we are talking about the "constellations process" or "setting up a constellation". In general I have followed this.

I use the term 'facilitator' to cover all those who work with systemic constellations in whatever capacity. Since the work of constellations is applicable in such a wide variety of settings and arenas I do not use the terms 'therapist' or 'psychotherapist' unless specifically discussing the work of psychotherapy, since to do so would imply that the work is primarily tied to these disciplines. The term 'facilitator' seems to me to allow the correct sense of freedom and non-alignment in terms of discipline, and in addition says what it is I think we do: facilitate – to 'assist the progress of (a person)'.[2] The word 'facilitator' also implies that our area of expertise is facilitation of a particular process, rather than that we are in any way an authority or expert on anyone else's life or business.

For similar reasons I use the term 'client' to indicate the person who brings an issue to the process of constellations.

I have mixed gender terms indiscriminately in an effort to balance the usage.

Case examples

All case examples are composites and/or inventions. It is never possible to convey properly the experience shared by facilitator and client as it was in its original moment, and I have taken the stance that to try to do so by insisting on 'authentic' and agreed renditions somehow diminishes that precious shared moment. As well, case examples are by their nature an attempt to illustrate something from the text, thus at times requiring manipulation to follow this purpose. This creates a situation that may be difficult for the actual client to agree to. Even in the detailed case examples in Love's Hidden Symmetry (Weber, Beaumont and Hellinger, 1998), which are I believe full verbatim transcripts, I imagine more is left out than is included of the subtleties of what actually happens. To create composites or inventions I think better serves the purpose. At the same time, of course, all 'inventions' come from my experience and practice over the past ten years and as such are never pure invention. I am indebted to all those whose work with me has contributed in some way to the writing of the case examples.

[2] Random House Unabridged Dictionary

Finally with regard to spelling: if this book comes into the hands of American readers, which I hope very much it will, I wish that my use of what I regard as 'proper' English spelling will not deter you! For me the word 'honour' is a word to honour! But 'honor' is also honourable!

There is a suggested reading list at the back of the book (Appendix 6).

Acknowledgements

Acknowledgements present a difficult task, especially for one interested in constellations, since everyone I have come into contact with in my life, as well as many whom I have never met, seem to have had some influence on who I am as a human being, constellations facilitator and writer. Indeed there are many unnamed, unknown or forgotten by me, who will have had some input into this work. I have felt during this process, truly in the presence of many.

Most particularly I acknowledge my family of origin, and particularly my mother, my father and my sister Jennifer, whose tragic death at the age of 34 has had an enduring impact on my life. My present family, my dearest partner John, whose consistent support, wisdom, love and challenge have kept my feet on the ground and provided a beautiful space for my growth. He has also been my editor, having spent many hours and careful effort in bringing this book to birth. His patient suggestions and creative ideas were a consistent help and inspiration to me.

Insofar as my teachers are concerned I want to acknowledge as most prominent influences on my work the following: the late Petruska Clarkson, who had a profound impact on much more of my life than just my work, and who I always found supportive and loving; Albrecht Mahr who is so dear to me as my first and most continual constellations teacher and friend; Franz Ruppert whose ideas and practice have had a major impact on my work, and who also has become a close and dear friend; Ursula Franke who reflected back to me my

Gestalt roots in her tender and loving work; Jan Jacob Stam who showed me how to combine a deeply spiritual nature with good business thinking; Matthias Varga von Kibéd who showed me magic and delicacy of touch, and helped me look under the surface of the constellations process; and Insa Sparrer who, not really knowing me, trusted me with the not inconsiderable task of editing her book in English, from which I learnt so much.

Other facilitators who have shown me new things and influenced my work and the person I now am are Guni Baxa, Gunthard Weber, Hunter Beaumont, Eva Madelung, Jakob Schneider, Sieglinde Schneider and Daan van Kampenhout. My greatest pleasure in this work has been to experience the many different styles of facilitation and personal under-standing of the work that these and other facilitators embody.

I have learned along the way of writing this book that probably no book is ever entirely the "author's" own. I owe much to my many colleagues and friends who read transcripts, had the courage to challenge me, disagree with me, offer suggestions and at times actual words to include, but I would add that in the end I am solely responsible for the content of this book and the interpretation of their contributions. Those who have supported and encouraged me throughout include: Jean Boulton who helped me extensively with understanding the complexities of systems theories and complex systems thinking; Susan Weil who helped me understand co-enquiry and reflexive learning, read and commented on the chapter on facilitator style, and with whom I had many exciting and stim-ulating discussions; Vanja Orlans for her persistent encourage-ment and belief in me; Barbara Morgan, Ty Francis, Yishai Gaster, Tony Glanville, Clare Kavanagh, Alannah Tandy Pilbrow and Jill White, all of whom gave me their support and encouragement, and were willing to grapple with me over different aspects of constellations thinking and practice and many other related subjects, suffering with me the pain of my doubts and feelings of inadequacy, always encouraging and optimistic. John McClean for his immaculate proof-reading and his friendship, and Miles Bailey of Action Publishing Technology for his great help in putting the book to its final form. And Pam Geggus ... a friend of the deepest spirit and love, whose opinion and support I value so much. Finally all my fellow students who have accompanied me on my journey, and who, knowing that I was writing, kept me on track by persistently asking me when the book would be coming out!

Bert Hellinger who, all through my growth since I first saw him work in the mid '90's, has been a constant presence and teacher. Without him I would not be doing this work that I love, nor writing this book. His insight is great and his work constantly touches my heart, continuously leading me on to greater understanding.

And finally, all those people who have permitted me to work with them, from whom I have learnt so much and whose lives have touched mine more deeply than they will ever know, I thank you.

Vivian Broughton, August 2009

"There's one important aspect of the spirit-mind. It never repeats itself. Everything is new. As soon as you rely on former experiences, then you rely on you, no longer on the spirit-mind. That is a big step to take, to trust something where you have no experience yet. Every insight coming from the spirit-mind is new and leads to something new. It's always creative and it always succeeds. And it can't be repeated."

Hellinger (2008)

Introduction

If thou wilt be observant and vigilant, thou wilt see at every moment the response to thy action.

Mevlana Jelaluddin Rumi

Family Constellations, as the work was originally called, is the development of Bert Hellinger, a family and group therapist and self-described empiricist and philosopher. Hellinger's childhood and adolescence were against a background of National Socialism and subsequent war in Nazi Germany, which he survived in part as a rebellious teenager, avoiding the Hitler Youth meetings, instead attending the then illegal Catholic Youth organizations, and then as a 17-year old drafted soldier in the German Army, captured by the allies and held in a prisoner of war camp in Belgium for the rest of the war. His later life includes some 16 years as a Catholic priest and committed missionary in South Africa working and living with the Zulu tribes, during which he engaged in an extensive training in interracial and ecumenical group dynamics. During his time with the Zulu peoples he learned from their traditional culture respect for one's ancestors, viewing them as having influence on the present, providing strength, support and wisdom that could be drawn on. He also learned the value of ritual from both the church and the tribal traditions of the Zulus, as providing ways of giving understanding, validation and acceptance. Subsequently he explored psychoanalysis, gestalt therapy, transactional analysis, primal therapy, hypnotherapy, NLP and family therapy, eventually leaving his ministry in the church. In the early '80's Hellinger began to combine his group and family therapy experience with the family re-construction work of Virginia Satir, who at the time

1

was working in Germany and Austria. Satir's method of setting up families using group members seems to have been catalytic in Hellinger's move towards the work he eventually called Family Constellations[3].

In the process of setting up group members as role-play representatives for a person's family (which had also been done by others in the field apart from Satir, most notably Jakob Moreno, who developed Psychodrama, and the German psychiatrist, Thea Schönfelder[4]), Hellinger seems to have begun listening to what the representatives were saying from a more existential and phenomenological base. By insisting on the representatives having little information about the person they represented, and that they refrain from taking up any sort of pose to indicate a certain attitude, Hellinger demonstrated a different approach from Moreno's Psychodrama, and even Satir's family re-construction work[5]. Hellinger thought that this helped the representatives in the constellation connect with deeper and more hidden dynamics and existential dilemmas. From his close observation of the subtle body and facial movements, impulses and other reported experiences of the representatives, he developed an understanding of what he later called the Orders of Love: that, as in all things, there is a certain order to relationships and living processes, particularly in closely bonded systems such as families, and disturbance to this order, disruption or non-observance of the principles of this order, have effects on system members, sometimes over many generations. This is not dissimilar to our understanding that if we go against the natural order in the environment, there will probably be consequences that may, over time, become devastating. We see this currently in our

---

[3] From Gunthard Weber's recollections in an interview with Barbara Morgan, The Knowing Field International Constellations Journal, 2009.

[4] Referenced in Sparrer, 2007.

[5] According to Sparrer (2007), the German psychiatrist Thea Schönfelder took a formidable step in this process by having representatives stand in their position "without making any statements, gestures or giving any specific details" in her work with psychiatric patients.

struggle with global warming, over-use of chemicals, exploitation of the great forests of the world, contamination of water sources and so on.

Along with this understanding of the principles of order in relationships, and the attendant principles of belonging and hierarchy, the constellations procedure developed. In general this involves: the defining of an issue of a particular person, the subsequent setting up of a relational patterning of that person's family system using other people (usually unknown to the person) to represent family members, and then including these representatives' experiences, cognitive, physical and emotional, as having relevance to the issue defined. This provides one of the basic assumptions of constellations work: that the experiences of the representatives provide valid information and can contribute towards some kind of resolution of the original issue for the client.

The advent of Hellinger's approach in Germany in the late 1980's and early 1990's seemed to fulfill a particular need in that country at that time. Many of the issues that would be brought to his groups (and his later large demonstration events) were issues to do with Germany's recent history: participants would often be descendants of the many people who had been persecuted in Germany during the second world war, holocaust survivors and their children and grandchildren, as well as those descended from the perpetrators of these events. The result was that the work of Family Constellations was often very dramatic, involving large numbers of people, often including representatives for people who had long since died, and frequently addressing profound social, political and historical issues along with the directly personal. Because the issues addressed commonly reflected back to the second world war, Hellinger's work very quickly became well-known in Germany, and gained a degree of notoriety in the German media. Hellinger himself tends to take a highly uncompromising stance on many sensitive and controversial issues. He was particularly outspoken on the subject of Germany's recent past, which the media in Germany were quick to exploit.

3

Hellinger has been invited to take his work to many parts of the world, and currently there are few countries where you will not find someone setting up constellations in some way. In some of these countries the controversy surrounding him has accompanied him and in others it hasn't. As with all new things, one has to take a balanced and informed stance that discriminates and draws healthily on what is good and useful and leaves the rest be.

The Group Setting

Most people first come into contact with constellations work in a group setting, and usually they are astonished at what they see and experience. Generally, the process is as follows:

A client who wishes to work sits with the facilitator and discusses his issue in the presence of the group. The facilitator may ask some questions or she may not. When the facilitator is clear about the issue and what the client wants, she will usually invite the client to choose group members to represent the necessary elements that relate to the issue. The client does so and places them in the room in a configuration that makes sense to him. The representatives then attend to their physical and emotional experience as they stand in their place, and to their sense of relationship with the other representatives through distance and direction. Usually the experiences that the representatives report are an acutely accurate portrayal of the person he or she is representing, regardless of the fact that he may not know the actual person or know anything about him. The experiences of the representatives are often very strong, may have an emotional component, and are informative for the client, either confirming what he knows or offering some new insight. Sometimes the representatives will feel a sense of movement in their body and, if invited to by the facilitator, may move, change position or allow their bodies to take up a particular pose, usually slowly and deliberately, as if they are in a trance or have been taken by a greater force. Indeed representatives often report feeling as if they are taken over

4

... as if they could not *not* do what their body wants to do. Depending on the style of the facilitator and the depth at which the constellation is working, the facilitator may leave the constellation to find its own resolution or she may intervene, moving representatives, suggesting words for the representatives to say, re-ordering the structure of the constellation in order to find a good resolution.

At the end of the constellation, the client dismisses the representatives who return to their seats.

There is, of course, much more than this to the process of constellations and their facilitation. There are many who, having seen a few constellations and read a bit about it think that they can do it. But of course it just is not so easy. Most of the leaders in the field of constellations facilitation have years of prior life and professional experience that support them, together with their willingness for continual, deep and challenging self-learning and exploration. This is not easy work no matter how simple it looks. At the same time, a facilitator can gain a perspective that she is not alone in the work; that she is in the presence of many beings, past and present. This can have an interesting effect on her self-opinion as a facilitator, inviting humility and a sense of service, as well as relieving her of the burden of having to be the important person who knows.

Constellations facilitation is an endeavour that challenges one's personal self-concept and one's concept of the Self, requiring a high tolerance of uncertainty, not-knowing, trust in greater forces and collective intelligence, and knowledge of one's own limits. The effectiveness of the constellation seems often to be directly related to the inner state of the facilitator. There are many other factors in the field that affect the success of a constellation, but the limits of the facilitator are perhaps the most crucial. These limits are not limits of knowledge about constellations, they are limits of being. They cannot be extended merely by reading about or even witnessing constellations. These limits can really only be addressed by personal experience as a client and a representative, by being immersed in the

5

constellations process, by practice as a facilitator and a continuing self-learning.

The Individual Session

The constellations process in the individual setting has its own challenges and rewards. The client and facilitator spend some time clarifying the issue, after which the client sets up a simple constellation using figures on a table or floor-markers for the representatives. The facilitator and client then may discuss what they see, finding good ways of connecting with the representational markers in turn and proceed generally in a similar way to the group constellation. Within the context of an on-going professional relationship, such as in psychotherapy, counselling or coaching, this can change the course of the work, providing great insight to the client and to the professional, often with a clearer understanding of where to go next.

Case example 1

A client came to me for individual psychotherapy with major issues of self-confidence and a diminished sense of self-authority. I asked her to set up her family on the floor, with pieces of felt as floor-markers, so that I could understand the complex web of relationships in her family, which included step-brothers and sisters from previous and later parental relationships. When she came to set up her mother as the last piece she sat and looked for a long time at what she had done, holding the piece for her mother in her hand. Finally she screwed up the piece of felt that represented her mother and threw it down in the centre saying: "that's what needs to happen to her."

Of course, we know that this will not be the end of this woman's journey of becoming a more self-authorising and effective individual, but for her at this time in her life it was absolutely formidable. It changed entirely her view of

6

herself and her mother, and during the following six months of counselling she repeatedly referred back to this moment as having been defining for her, as having for the first time given her a sense of separateness, enough to see things differently.

Aside from the deeper movements that may affect the client and her experience of her place in her family over time, the immediate change of perspective that constellations offer cannot be over-estimated. Take the instance of a grandmother who died when the client's mother was a small child and who became the subject of a story often told in the family, reified into a fixed idea - part of the family mythology. And then to bring the grandmother to life, in a sense, by giving her a place in the room by means of a person or a floor marker; giving her either through the experience of the representative, or the client herself standing on the marker for her grandmother, a voice and feelings, can be momentous for the client. Many times in such an instance I have sat with someone as she let this new lively experience of a grandmother, a mother, uncle or brother, someone she never met, permeate her body and psyche, while she says to me in a voice full of wonder something like: "I never knew her, and now she seems so real." If this were the most that one could expect from an individual constellations consultation, which it is not, then it would be enough. The embodiment of someone lost or never known by this kind of representation, the experience in the client at that moment, can truly startle one into a new state of being with a new perception of her place within the family.

The Facilitator

At the same time, some important distinctions need to be made. To set up something using either people or objects to represent those necessary elements is one thing. To approach what is set up with a broad perception of context, including a multi and trans-generational perspective, an understanding of the power of group and family loyalty, our over-arching need to belong and the price we are often willing to pay for that security, the sometimes devastating effects of trauma and exclusion on the system sometimes over many generations is quite another. Conversely, someone who has developed a personal experience and understanding of this complex nature of systems over many generations may never actually set up anything using objects or people, but would still be working within the domain of constellations insofar as this sense and understanding informs his thinking and work. In the end, the work stands by these understandings, which naturally deepen over time; it is never enough to understand intellectually, and yet, paradoxically, one cannot force this deeper understanding. One can only come at it obliquely, in the Taoist sense of the more you try the less is gained: "We do without doing and everything gets done." [6] Or in the words of Hamlet: "By indirections find directions out." [7]

On the other side of the coin, one cannot teach this work. All one can teach are skills, techniques and cognitive understanding, but this is not the work. One learns skills and understanding while the real work is going on in oneself at a much deeper level. This is the work I cannot make happen, I can only make space and time for it. The constellations facilitator must open himself to all, surrendering personal hypotheses to something bigger, continually moving into spaciousness, anonymity, emptiness and stillness, marvelling at the work, at the client, at the mystery that is the process of facilitator, client, group, constellation and system. He stands with humility in front of the wonder of life and its processes as portrayed in the constellation, where the past, present and future are found in a timeless space, in a place where, when asked: "who made this happen?", he cannot answer.

The most important thing I have learned, and perhaps the most important thing I can convey to you, is that the best way of learning and internalising this work is by participating in

[6]   *The Book of Runes*, Ralph Blum (1993).
[7]   *Hamlet*, Act 2, Scene 1. William Shakespeare.

constellations groups. The more you have experience of being a representative, the more you will understand the phenomenon of the representative experience, the way we can feel taken by a movement that is not ours, the way we can feel so different after having been chosen and placed as a representative, to how we had been feeling before. With this as a familiar embodied experience, you are more able to attend to such possibilities in the individual session. The client in the individual session may never have experienced constellations before, and my responsibility as the facilitator is not, in my opinion, merely to move the representative markers around to a better sense of order according to my hypothesis of the situation. There may be rare occasions when the facilitator does choose to do this, but in general, this misses the point of the constellation, and is likely to skip over needed processes. We have to find out how to allow movement to be there of its own accord in the individual context, sensed and felt in either the client or myself. This takes skill, experience and practice. Attending many professional learning and personal growth constellations groups and seminars, being a representative in others' constellations as much as you can, being a client, witnessing and being part of the process: these will be your best learning for your individual practice. To start at the individual end and expect to come to a greater understanding of the processes involved puts cart before horse. It is *only* by understanding the representative phenomenon in oneself that one can hope to understand how to recognise and allow it effectively in the individual setting. It is not just cognitive information that is available in the individual setting (some of which may be confused with long-held ideas by the client), but the client can himself experience the physical and emotional urge to movement that we see so often in the group constellation. It is our job as facilitator to enable our client to become aware of these subtle resonances when standing on a marker or during a visualisation, and we do this best by knowing it with great familiarity in ourselves.

At his best Bert Hellinger is an innovator who allows

himself to be led by the process, trusting that more than anything; and in turn he makes himself open to the insights offered. It is this that is the aspiration of the constellations facilitator: to allow oneself to be taught by the constellation at hand. I hope that this book holds this aspiration as a constant and central focus.

Complex Systems

Constellations work is rooted in complex systems thinking: an interacting, interrelating and evolutionary web of relationships. Elements can only be properly understood in relation to their context, where the whole is reflected and replicated in the part. The present is consequent on a myriad of scarcely perceived influences, constantly self-organising, evolving and responding to newly emergent information. To extract and isolate the family system level from these larger contexts is illusory; however, in the constellations process, as in any attempt at understanding, a momentary isolation is useful, providing that the boundaries of the system are held lightly and are allowed permeability. Many of the constellations that begin with what one might term 'the family system' call to our attention, during the progression of the work, the larger contexts of events such as wars, forced migrations, great societal shifts, political and governmental actions; activities such as slavery, national, industrial and technological revolutions; national or racial origin; and the myriad of other historical and present day circumstances that shape and influence our lives. The reality of life is that we are inseparable from each other and from the greater whole and its forces.

Box 1: A brief look at the similarities with Gestalt psychotherapy

I am by origin a gestalt psychotherapist, and for those interested I give here a brief digression into the similarities and concurrences of gestalt with constellations thinking. In part this demonstrates that many of the ideas within constellations were already there in the thinking and practice of many therapies and disciplines, and just needed to be let free into a different frame. Gestalt is my discipline, but much of what follows may well apply to other disciplines.

There is so much in the thinking and practice of constellations that concurs with gestalt thinking: holistic notions of completion, wholeness, integration and assimilation; a primarily phenomenological existential approach requiring an empirical primacy, interpretative abstinence and a creative, interested and empathic impartiality; an understanding of the greater context of the individual as addressed in 'field theory' – not in itself that far from the constellations concept of the 'knowing field' and the 'representative experience'.

Gestalt 'field theory' as a contextualising theory is only constrained by the practitioner's and theoretician's perception of the field as confined to the individual, his life and the influence of his parents and maybe his grandparents. In effect, Gestalt 'field theory' can easily expand its perception to include trans-generational phenomena. It is the therapist's perception that makes it what it is. In addition, Gestalt therapy has always had the methodology of the constellation in its two-chair experiment . . . only constrained by not including the representative experience phenomenon, insisting instead on the interpretation of what happens as a 'projection' of the client's view of things onto the other.

Above all Gestalt fosters the notion of life as a continual experiment, experience as the persistent possibility of engagement with the novel. Most of us spend much of our time repeating, re-hashing and re-living experiences and situations that we already know only too well, in spite of the

continued

reality that each and every situation in the present moment offers novelty and possibility. We are exploratory and experimental beings, and yet often we seem precisely the opposite as we tell ourselves the same old stories. The experiment is central to the gestalt process, maintaining an insistence on the present moment as imbued with potential, novelty and emergent possibility. The constellation as a process offers us this same vital possibility of experiment. Each intervention, suggestion and proposal, every movement, contact and touch, whether by facilitator, client or other representative is an experiment, offering information as to the next step. It is the moment when intervention becomes didactic, when the resulting information is dismissed as irrelevant, unimportant or wrong, when inflexible assumptions are made about the meaning or status of the emerging information that the work is in danger and loses its relevance for the client. In the group, and in the individual session, the constellation is an ongoing collaborative experiment between facilitator, client, representatives and the emerging truth of that moment. This notion of experiment allows the facilitator to move into the constellations procedure with an attitude of openness, wonder and humility, to be truly who he is in the face of the experiment of life as given before him right now.

Family & Organisational Systems

Generally speaking the work of constellations is divided into what is known as 'family constellations' and 'organisational constellations'. By 'family' we are talking about the personal, present day and ancestral domain. By 'organisational' we are talking about the more community, social and work-related domains, involving areas such as coaching and organisational consulting. This domain also includes exploration and intervention in larger systems such as businesses, voluntary, charitable, social and governmental organisations, environmental and ecological systems and so on. We could think of a spectrum of concerns that might look like the diagram on the next page:

Figure 1

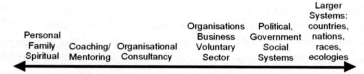

| Personal
Family
Spiritual | Coaching/
Mentoring | Organisational
Consultancy | Organisations
Business
Voluntary
Sector | Political,
Government
Social
Systems | Larger
Systems:
countries,
nations,
races,
ecologies |

Diagram showing the spectrum of domains which Constellations can address.

However, when looking at a diagram like this it is well to remember that the reality is more a matter of what is figure at this moment, everything else being in the ground but, as such, available and informing of what is figure. The personal and spiritual are always present whatever the focus of our interest is at the time; if we are focusing on the more personal, all those other domains that influence our lives are also present in the ground. Many of those who work in the area of organisa-tional consulting and executive coaching may, at times, find themselves inevitably touching on very personal and spiritual concerns. Thus another way of showing these domains as fields of interest and existence might be as follows:

Figure 2

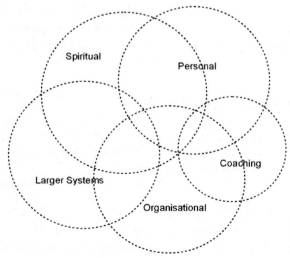

As practitioners of any work it is important to ensure that the contractual boundaries initially agreed between client and facilitator are adhered to, or only modified after careful consultation with the client. In order to respect the privacy of the organisational client the contract usually does not permit explicit transition into the personal domain, and the consultant has the responsibility of safeguarding her client from any such deviation. This could be different in the coaching contract, which may straddle both domains to an extent. There is no such need for such safeguarding in the opposite direction since it is in the personal frame that the contract assumes our willingness to be emotionally expressive and vulnerable. Organisational consultants are rightly sensitive to this issue, even though they are aware that the personal domain is always present; it becomes a matter of where you retain your focus, the nature of the consultant's relationship with her client, the setting and other factors.

I would consider that most of what follows in this book is applicable to all domains of practice, taking specific issues to do with the particular contract and context into consideration. There are constellations facilitators currently working in the field of politics and governmental agencies, in which they find very specific issues pertaining to the best means of practice in those settings. In time we will have more literature informing us of the findings of those who are working in these specific areas.

The Ideal Approach To 'Order'

"... great art is deeply ordered ... within the order there may be enormously instinctive and accidental things, nevertheless ... they come out of a desire for ordering ..."
Francis Bacon in *Sylvester (1975)*

Life is a tension between order and chaos; Nature's 'order' does certainly at times seem chaotic and yet her particular ordering is always there. It is the 'accidental' within the cradle of order that fosters the emergent novelty of insight, shifts in consciousness and an ability to transcend the known into a new knowing. We tend to yearn for order and fear its opposite; when given a certain framework of order we feel safe and comfortable, whereas chaos, uncertainty and confusion tend to make us feel unsafe and uncomfortable. And yet it is from within confusion and uncertainty that clarity comes.

Over the years of learning how to offer constellations thinking to students, I have found in myself a certain resistance to making rules about anything. The sentence "in most cases this is so, and often it is not" goes some way to illustrating my current approach. And yet, learning requires a certain framework that one can absorb, scrutinise, question and experiment with. So I would encourage the reader to move into this book with a questioning attitude, to hold lightly everything I and anyone else tells you about order, principles, systems, constellations and what you are likely to experience; to value your scepticism and doubt, to scrutinise your experience and follow the "authority in your own soul". (Hellinger, 1998) That is the only way you can find the unique constellations facilitator in you. The only truth is in the moment, and each client and each constellation tells a different story. I urge you always to be prepared to be surprised, to stay open and naïve in the face of such mysteries.

> "When people hang on my every word, I must be very careful of what I say. On the other hand, when I'm certain that the participants will carefully check everything I say against their own inner experience and not just swallow it uncritically, then I can risk a lot. When the other is my partner in investigating experience, a dialog [sic] between equals can emerge."
>
> *Hellinger (1998)*

Further Interests

There are some areas of interest that you will not find in other books on Constellations, or which have been addressed only peripherally. I think that this is because, in the newness of the work we have collectively been more interested in getting out there and doing it. It takes time for the more subtle aspects of practice to come under scrutiny. There are a couple of these that I have attempted to make a start with. One area that I have taken a particular interest in is the preferred stance and style of the facilitator (Chapter 12). I have attempted to address differences in style that I have witnessed, experienced and practised, primarily in terms of a spectrum of greater or lesser degrees of directiveness and intervention, with an eye on efficacy and efficiency, and attempting to assess the likely challenges, difficulties and dangers. This chapter may be of interest to experienced facilitators as well as students of this work, and tries to bring this subject to a more central position of consideration. In the excitement and rush of the initial emergence of constellations, the primary focus has been on the work itself, the constellations processes, theories and ideas, and much less focus has been given to the stance and style of the facilitator other than to talk about an inclusive, phenomenological attitude and peripherally some references to good practice. The sensitivity of touch of the facilitator, whether by temperament, attitude, concept or preference, has not been discussed much ... except by our clients, and those who fulfil representative roles, who do indeed discuss, analyse and criticise our styles. The subject also has a bearing on the work in the individual context particularly as, in the absence of actual people as representatives, the temptation in the individual session is to veer towards the more directive, didactic style, which has consequences that the facilitator should understand.

Another area that I find interesting is the relationship between the so-called "traditional" or "classical" constellations notion of entanglement (the unconscious identification with another, earlier system member) as the mechanism of systemic disturbance, and the notion of trauma as underlying all systemic disturbances (Chapter 5). These two views are not that different in themselves: in the traditional view of a present person "identified" with an earlier person in the system who has been "excluded", it is always the case that the earlier person has experienced or been involved in some traumatic event. It is the trauma reactions in the earlier person that is unresolved (excluded) in the system, and picked up by the later person. The sense of identification comes through the replication of the trauma reactions in the later person as their personal experience, in some cases influencing their actions which may also replicate the former events (for example a present-day person who suffers from suicidal ideation identified with a former system member who actually committed suicide or died in tragic and traumatic circumstances). In practice as a facilitator it probably makes no difference which perspective one prefers provided one knows the implications of the presence of trauma reactions in the present client.

A third area that I consider to have been given insufficient attention to date in the current literature is the business of understanding trauma processes sufficiently to be able work with people who have suffered trauma either personally or through inheritance with safety and confidence. Working with trauma, personally experienced or as a systemic legacy, requires an up-to-date understanding of trauma theories and processes, an ability to recognise traumatisation in others (and in ourselves), and an understanding and recognition of re-triggered trauma (re-traumatisation). Even larger systems such as businesses, social service organisations and governments, suffer from unconscious systemic trauma issues; personally inherited traumas of influential individuals (e.g. management) and large scale organisational trauma from events such as criminal acts, redundancies, sackings, mergers and so on, are major factors in systemic disturbance. In my view trauma, its dynamics and processes, and the across-generation nature of post-trauma phenomena, will be the important developments of the future. For example, if we really understand the unconscious, multi-generational impact and consequences of war trauma, rape, persecution and revenge, we might discover a strong enough impulse to further our search for other ways of effecting international and global negotiation. In constellations we see not just the effects of trauma on the descendants of victims, but also on those of perpetrators, witnesses and other collaterally traumatised individuals. More than any other method I have come across, the constellations process allows for such inherited trauma effects, sometimes involving countless generations, to be seen and understood, offering the possibility of finding some new way to resolution.

I do believe that the constellations process and ideas of emergence, self-organisational ordering and a trans-generational perspective are an important and timely contribution to our need to move beyond our late 20th century focus on individualism and modernist, reductionist, mechanical perspectives. As we face collective global issues that we struggle to comprehend, the necessity for transcendence of our current consciousness, a next evolutionary step, in order to reach beyond our current limits is inevitable. This must be towards a more connected understanding and embodied experience of our inter-dependence, not just on each other and everything in our current world, but on our connection with our history, the actions and experiences of our ancestors. The very soil from which we have sprung, everything that we are, is the bedrock from which we must take our next evolutionary step.

The book is in two main sections:

Part 1 covers a basic framework of constellations thinking, the methodology of the constellations process along with other considerations such as understanding and working with trauma, notions of what it means to be a helper, styles and preferences of the facilitator. All of this is broadly applicable to groups and the individual context, while at times I will make a particular reference to one or the other where there is a difference. Part 1 is a mix of established thinking and my reflections on this thinking, sometimes drawing on sources outside of the present constellations consciousness. In order to keep this distinction clear I have occasionally placed particular areas of thought as they are generally presented in separate boxes, while my reflections and discussions remain in the main text.

Part 2 is more practical, and looks specifically at the individual and small group context. I discuss different forms of practice and how one may successfully introduce the work within these different forms. I include many practical suggestions and process interventions to help the starting out facilitator, such as how best to conduct the initial issue-clarifying process, understanding relationship pictures, and detailed consideration of working with floor and table-top markers and visualisations. I specifically attend to ways of helping the client become a useful representative in his own constellation, the essential component in the individual session. Section III in this part discusses some special interest areas such as structured constellations, working with very small groups, couples, and supervision issues.

The appendices include details of the official symptomatology for Post Traumatic Stress Disorder and a section of further notes on working with trauma, a diagram that shows the pros and cons of two extremes of constellations facilitation, a suggested reading list and a brief look at the historical roots of systemic and transgenerational psychotherapeutic work and the methodology of constellations. I also include a brief comparison of the practice of systemic constellations with the established common practice of psychotherapy. This may assist those many psychotherapists who, in their adoption of systemic constellations into their practice, have discovered some discomfort in integrating the two. This discomfort may involve feelings of guilt towards our former group: a deep commitment to systemic constellations may test our loyalty to our prior views and professional paradigm, and present us with a lively challenge as to how to integrate the two.

Part 1

Reflections on the Work of Constellations

Soul receives from soul that knowledge, therefore not by
book nor from tongue.

If knowledge of mysteries come after emptiness of mind, that
is illumination of heart.

Mevlana Jelaluddin Rumi

Section I
Underlying Concepts and Principles

Chapter 1

Belonging and Conscience

"Conscience is a perceptual organ for systemic balance that helps us to know whether or not we're in harmony with our reference system." Hellinger (2001)

Perhaps, contrary to Freud's original ideas, the most influential and defining forces in our lives are to do with our need to belong. The regulation of the security of our belonging as a child, our sense of discomfort when our belonging is under threat, and comfort when our belonging seems secure, often unconsciously dominates our lives, influencing our actions, our thinking and our sense of wellbeing, confidence and authority. Closely tied to our compulsion to protect our belonging comes a kind of loyalty; not a fully conscious choiceful loyalty, but one that serves to protect our belonging, and arises from the wellspring of our systemic membership. This loyalty seems born out of love and alignment with those most important to our initial survival, but at the same time can drive us to actions that limit us, are often self-destructive and at times destructive of others; are at times in fact against our natural movement to evolve as healthy, autonomous and fulfilled beings. Hellinger has called this loyalty 'blind love'; it is a love that lives in a dark and murky illusory space, where the daylight of clarity and reason does not penetrate; a love that colludes with the unconscious requirements of the group, the urge to maintain the status quo and not question or challenge.

Think for a moment of the many times you have felt caught between a desire to do something for yourself, that would further your own aspirations as an adult, and a gripping feeling of guilt and obligation, combined with a fear that to do what you would will bring you disapproval and castigation, hurt and accusation from your family. The underlying threat is one of banishment and exclusion, a fall from grace too terrible to contemplate. We do not usually even allow these experiences to full conscious awareness. The urge to comply, to reconcile, to agree is so strong, and so unconscious and so utterly linked to our fears of annihilation and death that we usually react and give in. It is often an automatic reaction, something we cannot properly bring to thought and discrimination.

Think, perhaps, of the daughter who, abused by her father, remains silent well into adulthood. It is not just the shame and sense of worthlessness, or guilt at her perceived collusion. How does she point towards her father? What does this accusation cost her in terms of her belonging? How in the safe holding of a therapeutic alliance does she make sense of her feelings of loyalty, even love, for her father who abused her? How does even the therapist manage to hold this paradox?

'Personal Conscience':[8]

> Can we even talk about God here? Such a God, who chooses and abandons, is frightening, because even those chosen live in fear of being cast out at any time. *Hellinger (2001)*

[8] The use of the word 'personal' here may be confusing for some, being applied to a function whose purpose is regulation of group norms and membership. I retain it as part of the accepted terminology of constellations. For clarity, where I am discussing a more individual and differentiated set of values, I have used the term 'individual' conscience.

Hellinger calls the conscience that regulates our sense of secure belonging our 'personal conscience'.

All the groups to which we belong have requirements of their members that, so long as we adhere to them, keep us safe within that context. These requirements are termed as what is 'right' and what is 'wrong' within that group context. They *group rules* may be conscious within the group, and clearly stated, but often they are less so, and may even be completely unconscious. Provided we are congruent with what is deemed 'right' in a particular group our belonging is secure, and if we behave according to what is deemed 'wrong' in this group our belonging may then be in jeopardy. When the requirements are unconscious we still know. We can tell by the responses and reactions of those we are close to . . . we sense it in our body.

We experience these effects quite clearly. When we follow the requirements of the group we feel, as Hellinger has put it *innocent,* meaning safe and secure in our belonging. If we transgress any of the group requirements we immediately feel uncomfortable, troubled, even scared, and our sense of belonging feels in jeopardy; we experience a strong need to address this discomfort. Hellinger terms this experience as feeling *guilty.* Therefore, our sense of innocence would be an indicator that our place within a particular system is secure, and our sense of guilt would indicate that our place may be in jeopardy for some reason.

Our sense of belonging is a most primitive and primary need and comes into being through the intimate process of bonding, the initial feeding, touching and sensing. As a baby and young child we would not survive outside of a family group; our belonging helps to guarantee our survival. Bonding is a physical, psychological and emotional process, and happens at a profound and unconscious level, involving all our senses as we interact with our parents and our world. A healthy bonding process supports our social abilities, and our increasing sense of separateness, individuality and autonomy. In this initial phase of our life, belonging is exactly co-equal with surviving; beyond the need for nourishment and contact, many of the requirements and rules of the family are in the beginning for our protection and survival. As we grow from a healthy bonding we grow in power and independence, and in this way there is confidence and space for the ties of the 'personal conscience' to the primary rules and requirements of the family to relax. In this atmosphere, we can feel supported to challenge the boundaries of our group, and our parents feel supported to let that happen and to let us go. Through this healthy process of support for increased experimentation and exploration in time we are able to develop an autonomous individual conscience that may, at times, challenge the group conscience, and not feel as though our survival is at stake.

If, on the other hand, due to entanglements and unresolved traumas within the family, we do not feel supported to become more separate and autonomous, we will remain dependent and weak, and we will stay obedient to the requirements of the group and continually constrained by our feelings of guilt at our desire to move beyond these boundaries. Our parents, for many reasons, may not feel able to support our independence and separation, in which case the experiences of our 'personal conscience' will hold us within the confines of the group's culture and requirements in a stagnant and rigid way.

However it is, we are bonded to this first group, our family, for life. Nothing replaces this deep bonding experience in later life. The only other bonding that comes as close is the bond we develop with our children and their father or mother. All our later bondings will to some extent reflect the nature of our initial bonding; if this initial bonding is unsatisfactory, it is difficult for us to move beyond the sense that any threat to our belonging is also a threat to our very survival and all of our relationships will feel perilous and unsatisfactory. Many of the relationships we make as adults may continue to have a dramatic quality, persistently requiring us to take whatever action necessary to relieve the feelings of a perceived threat to our survival. This action is usually a movement of reconciliation towards the person or group we feel we have offended.

There is always a tension within any relationship between protecting our sense of belonging and safety, and our desire to grow beyond the constraints of the relationship. For the parents there is also the tension between wanting to keep their child by their side, and wanting to let him go, between wanting him to be their child, within the constraints, and recognising that for him to grow he needs to transcend these constraints.

And then there is the complexity of different requirements in different relationships. What secures our relationship with our mother, for example, may endanger our relationship with our father; what helps us keep safe in our peer group may endanger our sense of safe belonging at home. We know very well how to be with the one group, and with the other. . but sometimes to do both is impossible. In extreme cases this can develop into serious emotional and psychological disorder as we try to reconcile the irreconcilable within ourselves. How, in the absence of a self-authority to live my life in my own way, do I please the contradictory wishes of each of my parents? If I live according to the dictates of the one, what do I do with my feelings of guilt towards the other?

In my work with people, I see that in order for a person to grow she must be willing to experience her guilt at stepping outside of the boundaries of her group . . . each step of challenge to the requirements of the group invokes a moment of guilt. Bearing this moment of guilt, without collapsing back into the constraints of the group, enables us to develop a sense of order and individual[9] conscience that allows for a certain independence of thought and action.

The 'personal conscience' is intimately bound up with the group's boundaries, and in a collective sense dictates who belongs to the group and who does not, who is held and who is excluded. Within the family, of course, no one can actually

---

[9] By 'individual conscience' I refer to a more mature sense of values informed by experience and choice as opposed to 'personal conscience' as described above.

be excluded, but they can be overlooked, ignored and psychologically annihilated, effectively banished. Because the 'personal conscience' is so completely tied up with the group's requirements and identity it has little to do with any kind of absolute morality. The values and views of the group are required to be the values and views of its members. As Hellinger has put it:

> "A clear or a guilty conscience has little to do with good and evil; the worst atrocities and injustices are committed with a clear conscience, and we feel quite guilty doing good when it deviates from what [important] others expect of us." (*1998*)

And:

> "Genocide ... is committed with a good conscience for the benefit of one's own group. From the outside, we say they are murderers but for themselves, they feel they are serving their own group ... they acted in good conscience. It's not our good conscience; it's theirs." (*2006*)

This tells us crucially about the limits of the 'personal conscience': if we follow it blindly and do not move beyond it, we will always function within this limited framework, and to that extent never from any kind of more autonomous base. In this way we may take actions that, were we able to transcend a particular group framework, we might not take. At the same time it is not possible for us to exist as beings outside of such groupings. Even as the human species there are requirements and constraints that we adhere to. All mass movements, ideological collectives, cultures and social communities are such groups, thereby having clear and not-so-clear boundaries on what is and what is not acceptable for their members. To this extent, it is interesting to consider consciously every choice and decision I make, as to how much it is based on these forceful pressures. It is not so easy to step outside and choose independently ... the forces of the groupings to which we belong are great and our consciousness of these is always limited.

The 'Systemic Conscience'

The 'systemic conscience' is what we call the collective conscience of the group, not the more conscious requirements of membership but the more unconscious conscience of the whole as an entity in itself. This is akin to Jung's collective unconscious except in as much as each grouping operates its own collective conscience in addition to its own membership of greater wholes. It is sometimes referred to as the systemic soul, indicating its integral and essential nature. Its scope is wider and deeper than the 'personal conscience', operating over many generations and placing the system first and the individual system member second. It works in service of the integrity of the system, and in that way may 'sacrifice' individual members for the greater systemic need. As such, the two consciences (personal and systemic) in one person can create an unbearable conflict, where for example our systemic identification with an excluded ancestor prompts us to behave in a certain way that is in conflict with our 'personal conscience' as it relates to our current family.

The impulse of the systemic conscience is continually towards maintaining the integrity of the system, including what the group has on the more conscious level attempted to exclude, trying to redress disturbance and move towards more harmony. The dynamics that disturb systems are primarily those of exclusion, often precipitated by the impact of traumatic events on the system, which remain unresolved and disturbing, persistently pressing for resolution and completion.

The 'systemic conscience' is our unconscious connection with all other system members. We do not experience the 'systemic conscience' as a conscious physiological and emotional experience as we do our 'personal conscience', but it becomes evident by the behaviour and actions of systemic members across generations. In the constellations process, the representatives of these identifications and alignments report experiences of great love combined with a strong sense of

Box 2:   Exclusion

It is worth discussing briefly the notion of exclusion to understand better how the two consciences ('personal' and 'systemic') operate together. Acts of exclusion usually seem to originate at the level of the personal conscience, where the price of a secure membership is to collude with the exclusion of the person/event that does not 'fit' with the group's current requirements and identity. This exclusion is usually due to a traumatic event or series of events that overwhelms the ability of the person or group to assimilate the experience, and it is at the level of the systemic conscience that the effect is held and the consequences of the exclusion are activated.

For example, the exclusion may originate in the loss of a child and the unbearable feelings of grief of the parents. In order to continue with their lives they may put the lost child and the unresolved feelings aside, perhaps having another child to replace the lost one. The group then says "we will not mention this again, we will forget and move on", this becoming the requirement of all group members, transgression of which may threaten their belonging. The subject becomes forbidden, and over time, forgotten. The lost child is not mentioned and therefore, in constellations' thinking, is deemed to have been excluded from the system. The appropriate emotional expression (in our example, the expression of grief) is also excluded. All this is then held at the unconscious level of the systemic consciousness as an unassimilated component: the person/event/emotional expression.

However, the system cannot tolerate such 'forgetting': the unresolved event/person/emotional expression is held suspended, affecting to an extent the whole system. This unconscious systemic 're-membering' (literally re-instating the excluded member) seems often to be taken up particularly by one system member in a later generation. Sometimes this is carried by a person in each of a number of subsequent generations, like a thread running through the systemic history, each generation nominating someone to carry on the unconscious memory. The later person embodies the systemic attempt at rebalancing by his actions and attitudes to his life. These behaviours and actions of the later person are always self-limiting in terms of the possibilities of the actual person, and may even extend to being self-destructive, addictive and dangerous to the self and sometimes to others. The person may even be moved to sacrifice their life in the process, which Hellinger has termed "following another into death" (Hellinger, 1997). This might be the background of a person with persistent suicidal ideation or who makes repeated suicide attempts. It may also be the life of a person who persistently seems to encounter life-threatening situations. Ruppert (2008) has proposed that most serious mental illness (often without clear causality in respect of the person's own life experience) is founded on the across generation impact of traumatic events (See Chapter 5). The French psychologist, Anne Ancelin Schützenberger, in her book The Ancestor Syndrome (1998), provides in detail many instances from her work of recurrent events in families across many generations, often involving serious accidents, deaths by accident, suicide or even murder, sometimes occurring on the same day in a later year or in very similar circumstances as an original event.

commitment and loyalty. It is therefore possible to think of this loving and committed loyalty as the systemic energy for the attempt at rebalancing systemic harmony. This loyalty has also been termed 'blind love' (see above), indicating that the action taken is out of a non-aware loving compulsion that is blinded to the realities of the situation, a kind of 'magical thinking' that believes that identification and replication of another's fate may help that person. In the clear light of the constellations process this can be seen for the illusion that it is. The death or self-destruction of a later system member can in no way help someone who has gone earlier in avoiding his fate.

It has also been observed in the constellations process that a perpetrator of a serious crime, rather than being excluded from the system, must be consciously *included* in his own system, and *also* in the system of his victim. If this does not happen a sense of discomfort persists among the representatives in the constellations[10]. Extreme acts of one person against the life and integrity of another create a kind of bonding, as do extreme acts of bravery on behalf of another, such as saving another's life or losing one's life in the act of saving another.

As in the case of the 'personal conscience', since the 'systemic conscience' is only concerned with prompting the increased harmony and preservation of the integrity of the system, it also is no indication of any absolute morality. Notions of what is right and what is wrong are moderated by the requirements, and therefore by the limits, of the 'systemic conscience' as much as they are by the 'personal conscience'.

Movements in the Constellation

In the constellations process, if the representatives are free to move according to their experience, the quality of their movement is often an indication of what level of conscience is at play. Movements that are quick, superficial, from the mind more than the body and without deliberation are usually seen to be at the level of the more conscious 'personal conscience', while the movements at the level of the 'systemic conscience' are slower and more considered. They come primarily through the body, but may also appear in the cognitive realm as intuitive knowing. The experience of the representatives is of having no choice, the movement moves them rather than them moving themselves. If all the necessary elements are included these movements may well enable the representatives to come to a resolution without intervention by the facilitator.

---

[10] This relates to the general thinking that as the systemic urge is towards a more balanced and harmonious relational situation, so the representatives by their experience in the process of the constellation show whether this is possible or not. This is one of the indicators as to whether the constellations process is on a path towards a more harmonious healing possibility.

A Greater Conscience

Within constellations thinking there is also a greater conscience, an integrating and integral conscience, that, for example, Hellinger calls the spirit-mind and what we might recognise as transcendent consciousness, non-duality, oneness, the Tao, God, Atman or Brahman. This is that which transcends notions of 'right' and 'wrong' and is the movement of life as it is, the unfolding of things as they are. There is no judgement here; no sense of what is right and what is wrong. It is the oneness that thinks all thought and moves all movement. It is mysterious to us, embedded as we all are in our constructs of truth and justice, good and evil. Here all notions of what is good and what is evil meld into *isness*. There is no more that can be said about it. As the Bible has it: "... for he maketh his sun to rise on the evil and on the good, and sendeth rain on the just and on the unjust"[11].

Or the poem by Rumi:

> Out beyond ideas of wrong-doing and right-doing,
>   there is a field. I'll meet you there.
> When the soul lies down in that grass,
>   the world is too full to talk about.
> Ideas, language, even the phrase 'each other' does not make
>   any sense.
> *Mevlana Jelaluddin Rumi*

Movements of the spirit-mind

The movements of the spirit-mind according to Hellinger are those movements in the constellation that are motivated by a greater force that operates beyond notions of right and wrong, beyond the limitations of the personal and systemic conscience, and so are free to find a resolution that is in tune with that greater cosmic unity. At unique times this does

---

[11] *King James Bible*, Matthew 5:45.

33

indeed happen and seems collectively as a moment of grace, beyond words.

A Final Note

It is useful for us as facilitators to remember that we too are bound by our own personal and systemic conscience, our own group memberships and forces. Our notions of what we consider 'right' and 'wrong' come from these, and the extent to which we work from within these frames is the extent to which we ourselves are limited in our facilitation. This provides us with the impulse to continue in our own personal journey of inclusion and understanding.

Below is a diagram that attempts to show the relationship between these three levels of conscience, and the process by which exclusion occurs and the effect that it has.

Figure 3

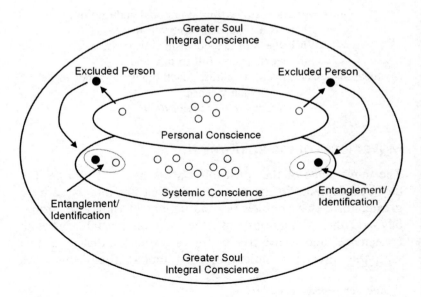

- The small circles represent system members.
- The value system of the group as to what is 'right' and what is 'wrong', the requirements and 'rules', decides at the level of belonging who belongs and who will be excluded.
- The **systemic conscience** does not tolerate the exclusion, and someone later will take up the re-membering of the excluded person, the entanglement/identification. The system requires the re-inclusion of the excluded person/event.
- Sometimes the systemic urge for completion causes later members to commit crimes or suffer serious mental or physical illness in order to 're-member' the excluded person/event.
- The excluded person/event is an unintegrated element of the system.
- What is excluded always involves a person tied to an event and unexpressed feelings. The re-membering of the person includes the event and the unexpressed feelings.

Chapter 2

Systems and Principles

For that which continues decays; and that which has the
power to renew itself is eternal.
Krishnamurti (1995).

"Without an interest in these formative, long-range, vertical
family relational laws of function, the therapist will remain
handicapped in dealing with pathogenicity and health in
families." *Boszormenyi-Nagy & Spark (1984).*

Introduction

The work of constellations was founded on the notion of the
family as a system. This view is not new and forms the basis
of most family therapy disciplines. Systems in this sense are
the organised and self-organising collections of entities that
make up all life forms (see Box on Systems & Complexity
Theories)[12]. Life comprises collections of entities, and every
collection belongs to larger collections. We do not and cannot
exist outside of such groupings. We are in ourselves a collection of dynamic groups of atoms, cells, bacteria and
functioning systems, and in turn we belong to and are part of
many larger collections: our family, our community, our

---

[12] Due to the fact that Constellations Work has adopted the term 'system' for its
own use, I have continued to use it. However, as you may see if you read the
box on Systems & Complexity theories, a more correct terminology might be
to use the form 'holon' for the grouping that one is discussing (such as the
family) and complexity terminology for the theoretical discourse, thus
distancing ourselves from conventional systems thinking that really doesn't
do justice to the forces we are working with in the constellations process.
However I am not for now interested in re-writing constellations thinking, I
am more interested in helping you learn the practice!

Systems

school, workplace, profession, our race, culture, society, political system, global and solar system, our galaxy. All things belong, that is to say are in relationship, affected by and affecting other belonging entities. Such a view shows us a rich, dynamic, self-organising web of interactivity and inter-connectedness. We are potentially affected by everything and potentially can affect everything. Our actions are at the same time context-oriented acts that do not come just from our isolated intentions, and yet are awesome in the possibility of their unknown consequences to others. We are at the same time an integral part of the whole and a small, fairly insignif-icant part of that whole.. crucially important and crucially unimportant. We are an individual and yet not, one entity and an element of larger entities. It then becomes clear that where we begin and where we end becomes indefinable.

Box 3: Systems and complexity theories ... and holons

In fact conventional systems theories do not sit well with Constellations work, and the sense in which we use the term 'systemic' is far more in line with complexity and chaos thinking, and the holonic theories of Ken Wilbur (2000). The term "holon" to mean a whole/part, something that is at the same time a whole in itself and also a part of something else, was first termed by Arthur Koestler .

These ideas allow more for the natural, spontaneous process of self-organisation in the present - this is what we see the representatives doing if allowed to move spontaneously in the constellation, even if the movements cannot find a resolution, the representatives attempt to with what is available in the moment. Such ideas include the dynamic whole/part, emergent, evolutionary, non-goal oriented nature of the constellations process - the fact that when something different/new is seen in the present it changes everything. However, the consequences of change are never

continued

37

predictable. The notion of the butterfly flapping its wings in Tokyo causing a tornado in the Caribbean has often been misunderstood - there is no possibility of predicting the effect of the butterfly's flapping wings - one can only say that it will have an effect. Complexity thinking views this 'seeing the emergent in the present' as presenting the opportunity to capture the moment of emergence, allowing for a creative act of seeding and nourishing new attractors (potent stimulations). The inclusion in a constellation of some element that has been missed or forgotten can be seen as an act of seeding providing it comes on the surge of the self-organising process of the constellation, i.e. in response to the call from the representatives' sense of something missing – hence the notion I will discuss later of the facilitator's approach as ultimately needing to be experimental (see chapter 11).

At the same time, complexity thinking acknowledges the pointlessness of fighting with what are called chaotic attractors, what we might call 'resistance', understanding such behaviour as revealing the self-organising nature of complex dynamics in the present. To fight self-organisation is to lose. The notion of 'seeding and nourishing new attractors', or stimulating insight and moments of transcendence and evolution, is carried on the wave of present self-organisation. Albrecht Mahr in his work makes a point of suggesting that the client evolve a meditative practice that they do for a while after the workshop based on the emergent information from the constellation. This I would see as nourishing what has been seeded; it doesn't have any goal orientation, but supports continued emergence and flow.

Where conventional systems theories fall down is in their more mechanistic and linear view, seeing the whole as something more than the sum of the parts rather than all as whole/parts (holons); holding that intervening in a particular way will automatically have a beneficial and predictable affect on the whole. We can never know this; as facilitators we can only seed and nourish what seems to support harmony in the moment, and for ourselves as clients, stay present to what emerges. Complexity and holonic thinking see the macrocosm as a reflection of the microcosm, like a hologram, not more than but the same; the same dynamics and forces that form and inform our galaxy, pulse similarly through every cell in our bodies. Systems theories see the parts of the whole in a hierarchical ascendancy where the lower affects the upper and the upper the lower, but not as the same, and this hierarchical "ordering" indicates a precedence of importance which invites the imposition of power and authority, and so the potential for the abuse of power.

Systems in the Constellations Process[13]

For the purposes of our work with constellations, the following properties describe what we mean by a system:

- At its simplest a system is two or more elements that are in relationship (e.g. people, intra-psychic elements or groups of people)
- Change in one part is a change in the whole
- Change to the whole is a change in the part
- All systems reflect larger and smaller systems
- All systems interconnect
- All systems are naturally self-organising, emergent and evolutionary (can change)
- At the same time systems are committed to maintaining and sustaining their nature however they can, sometimes if necessary at the expense of part of the system (for the greater good) – what we call "entanglement"
- Systems do not have fixed boundaries and are in a constant state of flux and change
- Relational dynamics in systems are dependent co-arising; all things are mutually co-creative, the chicken and the

---

[13] I am indebted to my colleague Jean Boulton for help in understanding the scientifically stated properties of systems and their relevance in complexity theory. What I have written here is my understanding from discussions with her and other readings, and as such may not concur with her views.

egg co-arise. The questioner asks his question in relation to the answerer and so asks the question the answerer requires; the answerer answers the question in relation to the questioner and so answers the questioner his question. Whose question? And whose answer? Both question and answer belong to both.

It is useful to remember in our work that the term 'system' is a convenience. It helps us in our discussion of and thinking about our work, but in reality there are no such clearly boundaried things as systems. We speak of the 'family system', but if I ask you what the family system is you may come up with a different definition and set of boundaries than I. For example, do you include cousins, second cousins and second cousins once removed? Do you include ancestors back over 1,000 years? Do you include future, as yet unknown descendants? Do you define the family system as comprising those who are alive (usually the case in family therapy), or do you include the dead? If I am a system in myself where do I end and 'other' begin? I breathe the air around me in and out, at what point does the air I breathe cease to be part of the environment and become part of me? A notion of 'soul' is that 'me' that includes all that I am dependent on and comprised of . . .

> "If you are a poet, you will see clearly that there is a cloud floating in this sheet of paper. Without a cloud, there will be no rain; without rain, the trees cannot grow; and without trees, we cannot make paper. The cloud is essential for the paper to exist . . . if we look . . . even more deeply, we can see the sunshine . . . without sunshine the forest cannot grow . . . we can see the logger who cut the tree . . . we see wheat . . . the logger cannot exist without his daily bread . . . The logger's father and mother are in it too. When we look in this way, we see that without all of these things, this sheet of paper cannot exist . . . We cannot point out one thing that is not here – time, space, the earth, the rain, the minerals in the soil, the sunshine, the cloud, the river, the heat." *Thich Nhat Hanh, (1991)*

In the constellations process the *boundaries of the constella-* *tion are defined by the issue at hand, the client's issue.* The constellation itself is a particular collection of elements relative to the presented issue, whose boundaries must be permeable in order to include that which has previously been excluded, allowing new information and emergent insight to arise.

Principles that Sustain Relational Systems

From his experience with constellations Hellinger formulated what he called 'The Orders of Love' as principles that sustain the flow of loving relationships within family systems. This laid down ordering can present us as facilitators with a significant challenge: we are persistently working with the tension between honouring the self-organising, emergent nature of life as represented in the constellation and the desire to re-order things as we may believe they should be according to these "orders". One way of holding this tension is to understand that self-organisation finds its own order and, given time, it is likely that such self-organisation will indeed following certain understood and recognised patterns such as Hellinger outlined. In my view this is what Hellinger saw in the constellations process: that self-organised order does indeed follow certain principles. But to reverse the process and impose order according to dictates does not in the end respect the creative potential of the constellations process.

'Order' can be understood as recognisable patterns, of the kind that we see in nature, in the seasons; an order that imbues all life, that is beyond human intervention. The patterns to which we are referring are those that are in a sense obvious, and yet often we live as if they are unimportant, we could say, in an illusionary state of ignorance. For example, we know very well, if pointed out to us, that our mother is the only mother we can have, and yet we often behave as if we could change her; we bemoan our fate of having this mother instead of the kind of mother we should have had. And yet, if we had another mother we would not be who we are. It is as simple as that. The implication is that we are better off agreeing to the mother we have, than spending our lives complaining in bitterness and resentment that she should have been different. More gracious and less wearing over time is to feel gratitude for the life that we have received, agreeing to be creative with what we have and leave it at that.

Generally speaking, the force of this natural ordering operates at the level of the systemic conscience, beyond our conscious awareness. If ignored or compromised by illusion and ignorance (which are of the nature of the 'personal conscience', driven by the need to conform and comply rather than by the desire to see clearly), or by a collective decision to exclude a member/memory, these forces will cause disruption and distress at that unconscious level. This disruption shows as destructive or damaging behaviour, serious illness, and distressing feelings such as depression, anxiety and despair, sometimes two or three generations after. It is when the disruption is included and seen in the constellations process that spontaneous change is possible.

The primary principles concern the inclusion of those who have been excluded, forgotten or mis-remembered, the recognition of temporal hierarchy, the respect of another's fate and the balance of exchange.

1. **Principle of inclusion:** All members of a system have an equal right to belong and to a 'place' within the system regardless of their seeming importance or unimportance. It is not possible to exclude anyone who is a member without adverse consequences. Within families, one's membership can never be revoked or resigned. 'Excluded' members or events hold great systemic power, acting somewhat like a black hole where, even though not seen, the effect is massive, sometimes paralysing the whole system.

   Within organisations, unlike families, system members may resign, leave, or be dismissed. However, the hidden dynamics may indicate that, even though a 'member' has voluntarily resigned, their presence still has influence, and in that sense they remain a member until something is done that allows the system to recognise the resignation and move on. The same may be true if an employee is discharged, particularly if unfairly, or if it involves feelings of guilt and hurt that are not included and recognised. Consciously the organisation may consider the employee not a member, but the deeper dynamics of the group may disagree, with difficult consequences.

The sense of 'place' reflects the member's relationship with all the others of that system The experience of this 'place' simply described is as if he is in is a 'good' place (ie feels comfortable, has autonomy and movement in his life) or a not good place (the person feels uncomfortable, trapped and unable to move forward in his life).

2. **Principle of precedence:** Precedence is in terms of temporal hierarchy and held responsibility. An aspect of a person's 'place' has is to do with where they are in the flow of time from past through present into the future. This simple truth can be stated as: those who came first come first, and those who came later come later. Grandparents take precedence in time over parents and grandchildren. The elder sibling takes precedence over the younger. This is not saying anything about importance or value, it is stating a respectful fact: this person came before that person and there are certain implications in this. These implications emerge strongly in situations where this precedence is not observed, for example if a child, for whatever reason, is drawn to treat her mother as if her mother is a child. The child becomes the mother of the mother. This is a reverse flow of energy, does not acknowledge the reality of precedence and keeps both mother and child trapped. This most commonly happens when the mother has not received mothering from her mother, and looks to her child to supply what she lacked, but since it is a reversal

child
mothering
mother

43

of the natural order, in the end it will not work and does not succeed in resolving the difficulty. It is also often disruptive when a younger sibling for whatever reason takes on or is required to take on the authority and precedence of the elder position. The relationship between the actual older child and the actual younger child is unlikely to be easy.

Precedence also refers to the responsibility required of the person. An elder sibling has a responsibility that is different from that of her younger sibling. In an organisation someone who has more responsibility takes precedence over someone who has less. This does not say anything about the merit of each, it merely recognises who comes first in terms of burden of responsibility.

In certain situations these orders are reversed. For example: even though earlier system members have precedence over later members, new members will, for a while, take precedence over the older, as in a new born child who initially needs very careful nurturing, or the new organisation that needs particular care and attention in the beginning.

It is helpful to the system if length of membership is positively acknowledged, recognised, valued and respected. We see this typically in many tribal cultures' honouring of the elders in the community and the tribe's ancestral precedents.

3. **Principle of personal fate:** Each person has her own fate and responsibility for herself in her life. No one can relieve another of her fate or take responsibility for another's life. It is an illusion to think that we can relieve another of her fate no matter how painful it may seem to us. This principle is particularly relevant to those in the so-called 'caring' professions, for example counsellors, psychotherapists, social workers and those in the medical professions. The ability of a counsellor to respect the reality of his client's fate is the extent to which he can

stay out of entanglement with his client while at the same time empathising with her. It is important to our understanding here to know the difference between 'fate' and 'destiny'. Fate comprises the unchangeable givens of myself and my life ... for example it is my fate to be white, English, middle-class and female, and to be part of the family in which I was born and reared. Destiny we can change by the choices and actions we take, but these are always mediated by our fate. These are the things of life that are beyond the realm of our responsibility and control, that just *are,* and it is best for us if we agree to these rather than live under the illusion of blindness to them. For example my mother is the only mother I can have ... to spend valuable energy and time wishing for another is futile and illusory.

Fate

Destiny

4. **Principle of balance:** there are different types of taking and different types of giving, and all need to be recognised, valued and in some circumstances reciprocated. For example the giving of a mother to her child is not the same as the giving of a woman to a man; and the taking of a child from his parents is different from the taking of a child from his elder sister. The gift that a mother and father give to their child by giving birth to him is never returnable and cannot be reciprocated. The best one can do is act with gratitude and pass the benefit on by giving to our children or giving in some way to others and to the world. On the other hand, what the child in turn does for his parents when they are nearing the end of their life is also a particular gift, which cannot be reciprocated by the parent except with gratitude and acceptance. Within organisations, the balance of exchange is discharged, for example, by appropriate remuneration and recognition for a job done. I once read of an organisation that charged its employees with the task of deciding what the appropriate remuneration for their particular job was. The organisation involved said that it was entirely satisfied with the results, stating that all employees were

45

proven to be conscientiously responsible in their estimations of their value to the organisation.

Our sense of justice and injustice as related to how we feel seen for our contribution and who we actually are, is crucial inasmuch as it affects our sense of well-being, personal value and right to be in the world. Injustice as in the non-seeing of the intrinsic value and status of another is the breeding ground for intolerance, prejudice, revenge and ultimately persecution, terrorisation and war.

The Physical Representation

The ordering or patterning of relationships seems to have a physically represented pattern of 'place' as well as 'time' which is so often revealed in the constellations process. The physically represented ordering has two principles:

1. There is a past, a present and a future, where those in the past have a temporal precedence over those who come later, and the constellation will generally move to a configuration where this is obvious. It will be indicated by the movement of those who are older (i.e. parents, grandparents or other ancestors) into a space which one can assume is the past (their 'place'), while the representatives for the children may all go together into what one can then assume is the future (their 'place'). If allowed by the facilitator these can be spontaneous movements by the representatives, occurring over the time of the particular constellation. When the facilitator sees these movements she knows where the ancestors will be and where the children will be.

Figure 4   Diagram showing the timeline orientation of a constellation.

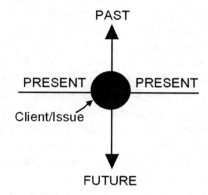

2. There is a precedence of 'place', which might reflect time, contribution or responsibility dependent on the issue at hand, and generally will follow a clockwise direction. The person to the right generally takes precedence over the person to the left (where everyone is facing into the middle of the circle). ie the person standing on one's right has a certain precedence.

Figure 5   Diagram Showing the Precedential flow.

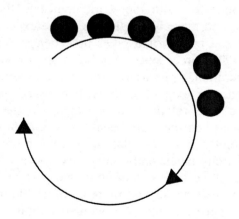

If there are only three or four people in the constellation this will usually be represented by a straight line, but if there are more they will often form a crescent in the clockwise direction, sometimes configuring into a complete circle. This ordering may happen as a spontaneous urge by the representatives in their movement towards a better 'felt situation'. However, a facilitator who knows this patterning may also use it in particularly intractable situations to help the constellation find a good-enough new positioning. This is often useful in organisational work with very large systems - such as social services systems - where a 'resolution' as such is unlikely, but insight emerges from seeing the complexity and listening to the representative information.

An interesting exercise to do in a group, or in an organisational situation, is to invite participants to form a semi-circle that allocates precedence according to a particular group interest. For example, in training programmes it is always interesting for new students to form a semi-circle according the length of time of their individual connection to the work being taught, how long they have known about it or how long they have been learning. So the person who has had the longest connection (or who connected first) has a certain precedence over all the others and would position herself at the beginning of the semi-circle, and the person who has most recently connected with the work comes at the end of the semi-circle, and there is a rightness to the experience of all.

The person to the right takes precedence over the person to the left. This precedence may be in age (as with siblings), in the generational hierarchy, in terms of responsibility (in organisations for example), or with husband and wife. The man in a couple relationship is usually to the right of the woman, former partners are usually to the right of the person who is currently in a later relationship and so on. Experiments in constellations persistently show that more often than not, the representative for the husband/male partner in a relationship usually feels easier and more comfortable to the right of his female partner, and the woman seems to feel more comfortable to the left of her male partner. This is as reported by the representatives, who often know nothing or very little about constellations thinking, as an experience of being 'in the right place'. The elder child usually feels more 'right' to the right of his or her younger sibling.

Hellinger has said, particularly of the husband/wife places, which, needless to say, has often caused controversy (why should the man take any kind of precedence over the woman?), that it is to do with the primary roles and the different responsibilities of the man and the woman in a couple relationship. The man has traditionally had the role of protector and hunter while the woman traditionally has needed protection for herself and the children. In the relationship between a man and a woman both are equals with differences, a "difference among equals". It is interesting to note that in the Christian marriage ceremony this is how the man and woman stand, the man to the right of the woman. Many constellations facilitators who have worked in other cultures, have seen that this is generally the same in most cultures. I have facilitated many constellations with people who know nothing about the ideas behind constellations where spontaneously the representative for a man in a husband-wife relationship moves from the left side of his 'wife' to the right. When questioned he usually will say: "it just feels better". As I have said before I suggest you make no rules but persistently approach the constellations process in an exploratory and open way.

When working with same-sex couples, the representatives will usually know which way round feels better, and I find that this usually tallies with the actual couple's sense of themselves in terms of the roles that they take up within the relationship.

This also informs the tradition in constellations work in the group of the client sitting to the right of the facilitator, the client thereby having precedence over the facilitator. I like to do this since it reminds me of who is important now, and accentuates my role as the servant to the client and the client's system. In the individual session I will arrange the chairs so that we are not directly facing each other (as perhaps in a conventional counselling setting), but angled towards an open space in front of us, where the client is to my right, but we are not sitting completely side by side as I might in a group.

It is possible as a facilitator, and tempting at times, to use this ordering notion to re-order a 'dis-ordered' constellation. This is a direct move to a supposed 'solution picture', and in the doing must miss out many processes that might actually be needed for the client to get to this result in her life, however useful it might prove at times. In applying the generally observed order to a particular constellation, it is important to have in mind that it does not always apply. An example where it might not be the case is if a woman comes to her relationship with a man, with a large amount of power as in property ownership, or where she comes to the relationship to take care of a man who is an invalid. Both of these situations include a particular kind of inequality over and above the normal partnership relationship. In both of these instances the woman takes on a particular responsibility, and in the constellation it may well feel better for the representatives to be the other way round. There may also be a deviation from the basic patterning if a second sibling had to assume the responsibilities of the eldest because his elder sister was disabled or otherwise not fully able to be the elder sibling.

So it is well to remember with this physical representation of the systemic principles that each situation must be observed in its own right, and it is of questionable use to apply the 'orders' indiscriminately. In the truly experimental nature of the constellation, nothing should be taken as an absolute, but instead always in the spirit of 'usually it is so and sometimes it's not'. The constellations process energetically dies as soon as we attempt to impose any order according to our ideas rather than allow what needs to emerge to do so freely. The relationship between the facilitator and the constellation (that is all of the representatives in the constellation) is always a continually negotiated process of what is possible in this moment, respecting the spontaneous and creative self-organising nature of emergent and evolving systems.

A final note here is that understanding the physical representation of the systemic principles can help the facilitator, in the group and in the individual context, in a diagnostic fashion. If, for example, in the initially set up constellation, an eldest daughter stands next to her father a facilitator would notice this and wonder what compensatory action this might represent . . . why is the mother not able to be there? What did this mean for the eldest daughter, to have what may have been a confusing relationship with her father? What does this say about the relationship between the mother and the father? For more understanding of this see Chapter 21, Understanding Relationship Pictures.

Common ways in which the above principles are compromised:

1. **Exclusion:** By the attempted exclusion of members, either wilfully or by forgetfulness, particularly ancestors/founders, those who die young or in tragically 'out of time' circumstances, do wrong, or cause shame to the system. Exclusion in its various forms is the single most common systemic entanglement and in a sense underlies all the other principles. For example, to disregard a person's appropriate 'place' according to their temporal precedence in effect is an act of exclusion.

   An exclusion always involves a person, an event connected with that person, and an emotional counterpart (the appropriate unexpressed emotions). For example, if a young son who is killed in a war and is 'forgotten' by the survivors as a way of coping, it is the son, his death and the accompanying feelings of grief that are excluded. The event involved is always traumatic, having an impact on both the person or people involved and on those closely bonded with those people.

2. **Disregarding the elders:** Not acknowledging, or forgetting, the precedence of those who came first e.g. forebears/founders, leaves one adrift and without any strong basis in the reality of one's own place. We see this when someone sets himself up as superior to those who came before without acknowledgement of the prior contribution: for example, a man who makes himself superior to his father by judgement and criticism, forgetting his father's achievements and contribution to his own life by being his father. This is not to say that the father is faultless in his actions, but to focus on these faults rather than the more profound givens of his relationship with his father, as his father, is in the end a distraction. Or this may happen in an organisation if an employee attempts to usurp his boss's job, seeing himself as better than him and does not include the contribution made by his boss and the reality of the current situation.

3. **Illusion and hubris:** Not facing and taking responsibility for the facts of one's life as one finds it, one's fate. For example, we can never have another childhood, and the illusion that a different childhood would allow us to succeed in our lives distracts us from the truth. The best we can do is agree and accept what gifts we have from our childhood and get on with our life. Our western individualistic late 20th and early 21st century culture and world view have fostered extreme notions of narcissistic self-responsibility and self-possibility, resulting in our losing sight of our interdependency on each other and the rest of the world, which has currently put us in great danger.

4. **Imbalance and injustice:** persisting only in giving or only in receiving, or in insisting on giving more than one has, or on receiving more than one has a right to. It is also shown in experiences of not feeling seen and valued for who we are, feeling mistreated and misjudged. This may arise from the unconscious identification with the 'excluded', the unseen person or event, that fuels distur-

bance, rage, reaction and reciprocal violence, and is most commonly manifest in the perpetrator-victim-perpetrator cycle (see Chapter 5 on entanglement). For example, it is persecutory to the other to always need to be the giver and never succumb to the complex feelings of being in debt to another. It is also persecutory to the other to maintain a view of the other that devalues, misinterprets and mis-judges.

While knowledge of these principles can help one live one's life more easily, systemically speaking they are compromised unconsciously due to the forces of belonging, loyalty, and unconscious systemic attempts at rectification of prior wrong-doings and traumas.

A word of caution here: it is a mistake to use any of this in an accusatory fashion, for example in stating to someone that they are getting it wrong by transgressing one of the above principles. These principles by their nature relate to the whole system, and while that does not leave individuals blameless for their acts, it is useful to understand everything as signalling some systemic disruption: individual actions point to the deeper dynamics of the system. So in the facilitation of constellations it is never helpful to try and force a representative (or a client) to act in accordance with these principles. Our job as facilitators is to help the constellation show what the client is reflecting by their actions, how the client literally represents in their issue the deeper disruption of the system. It is this 'allowing to become visible' that creates the conditions for clarity, insight, understanding, compassion and transcendence.

One of the beautiful aspects of constellations in my view is that, if one considers the whole context of included events and people, everyone's behaviour, no matter how abhorrent, becomes part of the fabric, colour and texture of this particular system. No event or action can ever be seen as merely an aberration or malicious intent. It is my view that acts that we might consider abhorrent can only be properly understood within a context that may cover many generations, where persecution and revenge become the currency by which that system repeatedly attempts to maintain its integrity. Everything has a deeper context that helps our understanding, which in turn leads to the possibility of compassion. Not pity, which diminishes, but compassion which sees, understands and is not compelled to act, but can transcend the past and evolve in the present.

It is best if we become very familiar with these principles by our experiences in our own lives, so that they become part of our perception of ourselves, our world and our clients. This takes time and exposure to the work, but in the end helps us to be able to hold them in the ground of our awareness as facilitators. We are then able to engage with the constellation as it is and as it emerges in the moment, and our understanding of what we see comes into dialogue with our experience of these principles.

Common Dynamics

There are various common dynamics that occur as a result of disturbance. In all cases they are an unconscious, group-motivated attempt by someone later in the system to redress disturbance. The manifestation of this attempt is usually costly to the person, often requiring him to replicate in some way the fate of the excluded person. This is the basis of what we call 'entanglement' (See Chapter 5), and the process of the constellation is in one sense to reveal these acts of 'blind love' so that they may become instead acts of enlightened, unentangled love.

To recapitulate the process of entanglement as it occurs:
- An event happens that offends or disturbs the group as in:
  - An unacceptable/unbearable death (child or youth, young mother or father, young sibling)
  - Other form of disappearance (mother or father leaves children for whatever reason)

- Personal trauma (near-death, witnessed horror or perpetrated act[14])
- Other act that goes against group requirements such as committing a crime or other gross non-conformity. This may be the refusal to commit an act deemed appropriate by the group, such as an act of terror by a member of a terrorist group.

– The group requires that the event/person is forgotten, ignored or otherwise excluded from the group.

– Continuing membership of the group requires compliance with this exclusion by the remaining members.

– The deeper 'systemic conscience' cannot tolerate this challenge to its integrity.

– The excluded element sits within the systemic memory as an unintegrated part of the whole.

– This affects all system members to some extent, but will eventually take up residence, so to speak, in one particular member usually a generation or two later.

– This person will 're-member' the forgotten person, most often by replicating their situation, behaviour or destiny, at the cost of their own freedom and fulfilment. This usually takes one or more of the following forms.

1. Someone later in the system aligns herself with an 'excluded' person by:
   – Living a similar life or replicating some aspect of the person's life, eg living a self-destructive existence, or having accidents, illnesses or addictions.
   Carrying the emotional and psychological burden, e.g. depression, which is the unresolved/unexpressed grief of someone earlier
   – Following him to death as in suicide or similar kind

---

[14] It is an interesting fact that in terms of our growing understanding of trauma processes, it seems that people recover more quickly from natural trauma such as the Tsunami, than they do from human to human perpetrated traumatic acts.

of accident. Sometimes the events are uncannily similar to that experienced by the excluded person.[15]

2. Someone places herself in a superior place by:
   - Taking up a seemingly vacant place, e.g. if a child becomes the parent to her mother because her mother's mother was unavailable (perhaps through early death).
   - By critically judging someone who came earlier without understanding (eg by criticism of a parent without knowing the history behind their behaviour) thereby becoming illusorily superior.
3. Someone tries to prevent another from following his own chosen path/destiny, commonly a child who sees unconsciously that his parent is in danger of leaving by committing suicide or becoming ill.

These dynamics are the basic ones and have many variations. The resulting 'symptoms' also are many but can be categorised briefly as follows:

- Lack of strength and commitment to one's life
- Persistent emotions that seem not to be based in any event in the person's own life
- Lack of success and fulfilment in one's life
- Persistent illness either physical and psychological
- Persistent conflict and unrest within the system
- Persistent and repetitive unsatisfactory life patterns, such as similarly failed relationships

Consequent to these are many distinguishing principles pertaining to different relationships within the family or other system which make up what is known as the 'Orders of Love'. I have put these in a box rather than including them in the main text because they are all implied in the above basic principles, and while they may be of interest for the student, my

---

[15] See the work of Anne Ancelin Schützenberger *(1998)*

view is that the more definitive one becomes with these principles, the less phenomenological one is likely to be in practice. The constellations process is the primary source for information on how things are, not more rules and principles.

Box 4:   'Orders of Love'

To fulfil curiosity about the more detailed principles that Hellinger called the Orders of Love, I have included the main ones below as taken from Hellinger's writing (Insights, 2002):

"And there's another thing to consider. *The Orders of Love aren't rigid structures* [my italics]. They're always changing; they're different from moment to moment. There's something richly varied in them, a profound abundance that we can glimpse for only a brief moment. That's the reason why every family constellation is different, even when the issues in the families are similar... some people who are accustomed to thinking in terms of "true and false" or "right and wrong" have a tendency to hear what I say as a statement about a general truth. It's not! It's only *a recognition of the truth that could be glimpsed in a certain moment.* [my italics] It applies only to that moment, and in that moment, it has its full truth." (Hellinger, 1998)

It becomes clear that relationships of the same nature are subject to the same laws, and relationships of a different nature follow different laws.

Man and woman:
- A man is attracted to a woman because, as a man, he lacks 'the feminine'.
- A woman is attracted to a man because, as a woman, she lacks 'the masculine'.
- To be a man, the man needs a woman.
- To be a woman, the woman needs a man.
- The masculinity of the man and the femininity of the woman are fulfilled in the child.

continued

- It is only as a father that a man becomes a man in the fullest sense.
- It is only as a mother that a woman becomes a woman in the fullest sense.
- The one gives to the other what the other lacks.
- The order usually requires that when a man and woman come together, the woman leaves her family and follows the man into his, into his language and culture and religion.
- A second partnership can only be successful if the bonding that occurred in the first is fully acknowledged and honoured.

Parents and Children:
- Parents give and children take. The gift is life.
- Parents give to their children what they have taken from their parents.
- Children pass on, especially to their children, what they have received.
- Children accept their parents as their parents and everything their parents give them.

Siblings:
- Whosoever is first gives to those who follow. The first gives to the second and so on.
- Whoever follows must accept from whomever was before. The second accepts from the first and so on.
- The oldest child gives more and the youngest takes more.
- In return the youngest looks after the parents in old age.

Father's son; Mother's daughter:
- In order to become a man, a son has to give up his first love, his mother.
- A son must leave the sphere of influence of his mother and enter the sphere of influence of his father.
- In order for a daughter to become a woman she must first leave the sphere of influence of her mother and go to her father, then she must return to her mother's sphere of influence again.

- Under the sole influence of his mother, a son often only manages to reach adolescence.
- Remaining under the influence of her father, a daughter stays in adolescence.

Chapter 3

Concepts of Soul

"The great malady of the twentieth century, implicated in all
of our troubles and affecting us individually and socially, is
'loss of soul'. When soul is neglected, it does not just go
away; it appears symptomatically in obsessions, addictions,
violence, and loss of meaning."
Moore (1992)

"A true and complete understanding of the soul is probably
beyond the grasp of our intellect, just as it is not possible to
really understand the nature of the power that created
our universe."
Van Kampenhout (2001)

The notion of 'soul' is central to most constellations facilitators' thinking in their work. Since constellations originated in
Germany, where the word 'seele' (soul) is commonly used,
we in the English-speaking world have adopted the use of the
word soul, often without a clear idea of what we mean. There
is a difference in meaning between the German word 'seele'
and the English word 'soul'. As I understand it, 'seele' incorporates that essential aspect of soul that we would understand
as soul (no matter that it is very difficult to define) along with
what we would call the 'psyche'. The Greek 'psukhe' from
which we derive the word 'psyche' does, in fact, mean "soul,
spirit, mind"[16], but it is now more widely understood in the
English language to mean "the mental or psychological structure of a person".[17]

Psychotherapists and counsellors (perhaps not those who
work from a more transpersonal perspective) who read a book

[16] *Concise Oxford Dictionary*
[17] ibid

60

about constellations may feel uncomfortable with references to 'soul', but it is an essential aspect of this work, and so I think it deserves some discussion to understand what we are talking about. Indeed as Thomas Moore has indicated (see quote at the beginning of this chapter), it may be that our lack of interest in and familiar use of the term soul, what it actually means for us in our lives, underlies much of our present day more narcissistic and materialistic world view.

According to the philosopher Emanuel Levinas (quoted in Suurmond, 1999) "The Greek term for 'soul' *(psukhe)* originally conveys our fundamental dependency on the other . . . For my existence, I depend on the life and love of my parents, my family and my friends. Also, I cannot live without the farmers who grow my food, the language developed and spoken by my community . . . Life essentially is a gratuitous gift to me from others and this is expressed by the word 'soul'." (Suurmond, 1999) That is, 'everything other' as it is in ourselves; our interdependency with everyone and all things, our very collectivity, without which we would not exist.

Constellations facilitator Hunter Beaumont has proposed a working definition as: "a realm or dimension of human experience subjectively distinct from both mind and body." (2006) He adds that this is "a phenomenological definition and makes no metaphysical claims about its [the soul's] state of salvation or damnation after death." He is talking about that in us that feels such things as longing, compassion, heartache, hope and yearning, these experiences being neither wholly of the mind nor wholly of the physical, asking the question: "are they human experiences of a third kind inhabiting an inner space between body and mind?" (by which I understand he means 'soul').

Hellinger has said: "In religion, just as much as in psychotherapy, there is a myth that the soul is believed to be something personal. When we look objectively . . . it becomes clear that it is not we who possess a soul but rather a soul which possesses us; and that the soul is not there to serve us but rather that we are in the service of the soul." (2003a)

Dan Booth Cohen, also a constellations facilitator, discusses the history of the term "soul" in the western cultures, with particular reference to the use of the term in systemic and family constellations[18]. He says: "Unlike the theist who believes in immortal soul, the atheist who denies it and the seeker of spirituality who connects it to universal consciousness, in a Constellation the human being does not exist as an 'I'. . the inner soul of the individual is attuned to a larger field of systemic intelligence." (2008) This is the essence of systemic constellations: being part of the greater whole. We talk about the 'family soul' or the 'systemic soul', and "this includes everything that makes a family a particular family over space and time . . . [including] all the family members, the events and experiences, memories, decisions . . ." (Schneider, 2007). I would include in this all the particular events and traumas that happened to individuals, and the greater socio-political events that affected whole families, tribes and nations. As an individual I am all of that. The systemic soul is who we are, and who we are is the systemic soul.

The core of constellations work is recognition of the true source of our life, our parents as the gateway through which we gain life; that we would not be in this world, but for the life that is born in us through the coming together of our parents. That through our parents we are connected with ". . . all those who have lived and will live, and those living now, as if we were all part of one life and one soul. Therefore soul reaches beyond us into another space: into our families, into larger groups and into the world as a whole." (Hellinger, 2002) By 'soul' we mean that deepest level of ourselves that in choosing knows no choice but movement towards truth and the whole. When talking about the 'family soul', the 'tribal soul', the 'national soul' we are talking about a collective essential aspect that moves us; that we may not experience consciously but that holds us and calls us into movement and action.

---

[18] *The Knowing Field Journal* (2008).

Chapter 4

Concepts of Healing

"Family Constellations aim to startle the soul into recollection." Dan Booth Cohen (2008)

Introduction

Traditionally constellations work has oriented itself around the notion of 'a good resolution for the client', which has a broad range of definitions. So what do we actually mean by a 'good resolution'?

The word 'resolution' has a reified feel to it that, in the beginning of constellations work concurred with the view that one constellation could sort out your life. This was an attitude that rode on the crest of the exciting wave of possibilities of the constellations process back in the early '90's. We are, generally speaking, now more pedestrian in our aspirations as constellations facilitators. This in no way diminishes the extraordinary outcomes and effects that do occur in this work, but we also realise that for the most part a constellation is a step on the way, a step amongst many. To attribute the constellation with the ability to resolve someone's life difficulties in one session sets one as a facilitator on a rocky course of irresponsible claims that will not be fulfilled, making us and our client vulnerable to disappointment, confusion, helplessness and even despair. Better to keep our aspirations modest and allow space for the seemingly miraculous to unfold and emerge if it is possible in that moment.

For the person who belongs to a highly traumatised family, sometimes over many generations, it is not realistic to suggest that there is one resolution that takes care of the multitude of issues she carries. Of course the notion of honouring the life that I have received, the parents and ancestors through whom life came to me, and moving on to make something good of my life without wasting energy on regrets, bitterness, recriminations and accusations, is not without truth and merit, but it is fantastical and illusory to think that for many it is as easy as that. Current research in neuroscience makes it plain that many of our actions and reactions are indeed hard-wired so to speak through the effect of the environment and atmosphere of our early childhood. The effect of an incomplete and interrupted attachment process as a child on the potential neural connections that are made in those first years will influence profoundly our ability to make relationships, understand things clearly and succeed in our lives. We do not yet know how a process such as a constellation, the resulting possible enlightened clarity, embodied experience and transcendent shift, affects or changes our neural connections, or helps to increase the neural connections made. We do know that sometimes experientially we engage in something that 'changes our life'; that in all of the time of ongoing therapy, or repeated constellations there may be one or two such moments that truly 'change everything'. We are also beginning to understand better that our childhood is profoundly affected by the childhoods and lives of our parents, their parents and even their parents.

Healing, becoming whole or integrated, has a certain process. The experience of fragmentation, dissociation, disintegration (or non-integration), confusion and helplessness is familiar to all of us at times, but for some it is a more persistent, pervasive and consistent life experience than for others. Over a wide spectrum of mental and emotional difficulties we see evidence of the process of a splitting of the sense of self – fragmentation – that, in the different degrees of severity is sometimes more and sometimes less conscious, or even totally unconscious. In Franz Ruppert's book on trauma and family constellations (2008) he makes a focus on the split that happens in the event of a trauma, between that part of ourselves that holds all the emotional experiences and potential expressions of the trauma, (e.g. shock, terror, fear, grief etc) that cannot be experienced and expressed at the time, and the part of ourselves that puts all its energy into surviving. This split becomes reified and unconscious over time. (For more on this see chapter 5)

Confusion is the experience of the undifferentiated fragmentation, which usually feels like a mess. Often I have sat with a person who describes many things that she experiences as affecting her life, touching on different topics that seem somehow connected but also do not seem to make sense or give any clarity. Perhaps for a moment she says "it feels like a mess", and I may suggest that she take a cushion to represent all of this 'mess' and place it somewhere in the room. When she returns to her seat she instantly experiences more clarity and often will tell me how much better she feels just being able to put the 'mess' outside of herself for a while and sit and look at it. This is a process of differentiation, of making the fragmented parts of oneself separate from the self that feels the confusion. From here we can personify the 'mess' by a representation (marker or person), and we can then further differentiate the 'mess' as appropriate, by adding more representations. This process allows the person to come more into the present reality of full awareness of themselves and their here and now experience. This is presence – being fully in his or her present experience with awareness, without being immersed in the 'mess'.

Differentiation is useful when on the road to integration. The extreme of differentiation is dissociation, or even psychosis, where the differentiated boundaries become reified and intransigent; from within a dissociated state integration is not possible. Integration happens when the splits have been differentiated, seen, understood and processed in whatever way necessary in the present moment (speaking, being heard, being seen, allowing the hidden, complex dynamics to emerge, emotional expression). In the constellations process we find that the client holds within herself the splits endemic in the family; she is in fact the present representation of the systemic processes and reactions to traumas, as shown by her identification with an excluded or forgotten person/event/experience. We differentiate these splits by setting up the constellation with representatives or markers for the relevant people (and/or events, qualities etc).

Integration is a spontaneous process that cannot be forced, created or predicted. It involves fully present embodied experience and awareness - rather than just cognitive thinking, analysis, interpretation and working out. It comes from seeing something truly for what it is, involving a spontaneous transcendence of what was seen and known before. Integration and transcendence are primary factors in the growth and evolution of consciousness, what Hellinger has called 'bringing together what appeared to be separate before' (2008) and Booth Cohen calls the soul being startled into recollection (2008). These experiences occur in those moments when we step out of the historical and familiar patterns of our system[19], relinquishing the illusion that we are helpless and trapped in the web of causal connections, and become fully present to ourselves and our current experience.

So we could say that a resolution in the widest sense is that moment of seeing that causes the integration of new understanding, clarity and insight and the resultant possibility of transcendence. At the same time it helps us to have a framework within which to formulate a process that may create a space for this possibility, and what follows are different ways in which we can think of this process towards integration in the constellation. These are not discrete from each other and we may subscribe more to one or another in different circumstances, and all of them in a broad sense.

1. The constellations process as a movement from tension to relaxation. The existence of an issue as presented by the client indicates an energetic tension in the system. It is evident

[19] What Ruppert calls coming out of symbiotic entanglement (verbal exchange).

in the client in their physical tension, diminished breathing and lack of fluidity. In the constellations process it is indicated in the initial phases by the representatives' reports of discomfort and disturbance, a feeling best described as "not right" or "not good". It is also shown in the individual session by the degree of disconnection between the representative markers in the initially set up patterning, i.e. no two markers face each other directly, so cannot be in full contact. The tension is created by two conflicting energetic movements: one towards freedom and vibrant liveliness, and the other towards maintaining the fixity of not facing what has to be faced. The movements in the constellation that occur, or are prompted by the facilitator, are always a proposal towards increased relaxation. Sometimes this involves a heightening of the tension as the dilemma becomes clearer. In gestalt therapy we have the notion of the "paradoxical theory of change" which says that if you take something to an extreme, making it really vibrantly clear, the result will be a spontaneous flip to something new, often what seems to be the opposite from the original position. This is illustrated in the yin/yang symbol below (Figure 6) where the seed of a thing's opposite is always present in the thing itself; at its greatest expression it shows its opposite embedded within. So we could say that the seed of the new situation is always in the old, and if we increase the tension of the old to a high degree, then by force of the tension the new must emerge.

The movement towards a more harmonious and balanced energetic state in the constellation is indicated by the responses of the client and the representatives, reports of feeling better, easier, more at peace, or feeling "right" or in the "right place", often accompanied by a deep out-breath or sigh and an easing of physical tension. There is usually a feeling in the room of relief and quiet.

Figure 6

2. Finding 'a good resolution' for the client: this makes
the client a more figural component. A 'good resolution for
the client' does not mean that we have to make the constellation fit the client's wishes; after all, the client's wish is based
on an insufficiency, otherwise he would already have been
able to resolve it for himself, and he comes to the facilitator
in the main hoping for something unknown to emerge. This
'unknown' by its nature cannot be foretold, and so, while the
client's stated wish is integral, at the same time the facilitator
needs to hold it lightly, thereby keeping the constellations
space fresh and fertile. Indeed the client's initially stated
wishes are often imprecise and vague, sometimes even impossible or impractical. It is in the process of the initial interview
that the facilitator and client move towards a more precise and
possible issue, sometimes stated as 'a possible good outcome'.
This, the facilitator and client can use as a guide. In a more
solutions-focused view as espoused by Insa Sparrer (2007),
this process of defining a goal or 'good outcome' is a very
precise art, and shows its effectiveness most strongly in a
more problem-solving context particularly suitable within an
organisational or coaching relationship, and in the clarifying
process of the 'miracle question' (see Sparrer, 2007 for a

detailed description of this process). At the same time it is remarkable how, even though seemingly vague and unrealistic, the client's initial few statements do indeed hold the seeds of what is to come in the constellations process. More often than not, when we are coming to the end of the constellation, when clarity is flowing, those initial sentences do indeed reflect and resonate with what we have been doing and where we have arrived.

However, it is well to remember that blindly following the notion of what is a good resolution for the client can lead the facilitator down some tricky paths. One such path is trying hard to get a result that feels good for the client and thereby missing another more crucial issue.

3. Finding a resolution for the system as a whole: this allows one a greater scope in that what may be a resolution for the system may not be what the client's stated want is. Even so, one may assume that what helps the system also helps the client and what helps the client also helps, in some way the system. In this way we are following the view that the client is in fact always the system as represented in himself. He is and cannot *not* be his system, like a hologram where all is represented in each fragment. As the West African writer, Malidoma Patrice Somé, says: "the young ones are the future of the old ones" (1993).

In the end, as we shall see from what follows (see item 1 below), as a facilitator we have no charge over how the client uses what emerges from the constellation, and what he chooses to hold as important. Psychotherapy and counselling continue to be among the hardest disciplines to evaluate, and I certainly have had situations where, on meeting someone later with whom I have previously worked, they relate to me a constellation that I barely recognise, at the same time as telling me how useful it was. Perhaps the best testimony to the effectiveness of such work could be the numbers of people over a period of time who find their lives enriched in some way by what we do.

In traditional psychotherapy, sometimes over some years, we spend time attempting to make sense of our relationship with our parents, trying to understand our feelings of resentment, rage and disappointment, often clinging to the notion that if we work hard enough at it we will sort the whole thing out. In so doing we are often likely to stay entangled. As Dan Booth Cohen has asked, what if instead our starting point was: 'It does not matter how our parents are. It makes no difference. Life, and all that comes with life, comes to us through them ... There are no more accusations, no blaming. We just take what is given and we turn and let the flow of life pass through us onto the next generation ... Then we are in true harmony.' (Hellinger, 2002, quoted by Booth Cohen, Knowing Field Journal, 2008).

This re-orientation of our view of our parents takes us beyond recriminations and blame, takes us to the depth of what it means to be alive, asks the question: would you rather not be here?, confronting us with the reality that our parents are our parents and that we cannot have other. We either agree to our parents as the gateway through which we have received life or we stay caught in the unhelpful, blind and blinding world of blame and resentment. We maintain the dynamics of our life by our view of our life; if we change our view then we release not only ourselves from the constraints of our view, but we also release the other from the difficult dynamics in which we hold him or her, for as we are truly systemic beings we, too, can hold the system in its fixity.

Case example 2

A client of mine who had been for a number of sessions came one day with the clear and upsetting admission that he thought he had never loved his mother. We sat with this for a while, set up a constellation and worked with it a bit. Finally I suggested to him that he experiment with saying to his mother in the constellation: "I have never allowed myself to realise just how much I love you." He hesitated and looked at me with reluctance. "Come on" I said, "it's just an experiment, see what happens if you let the muscles in your face and your tongue make the words!" As he looked in the direction that we had positioned his mother tears came to his eyes. As he said the words he broke down into sobs.

At the end of the session I suggested he not do anything different in his life, but live with the experience and see how it was. The next session (some two months later) he came and said that his relationship with his mother had completely changed. He hadn't said anything about the session to her, but the relationship had changed anyway. And then one day he had told his mother how much he loved her.

This kind of step often does not happen just like that . . . along the way there may be many stages, which may include the need to express anger and frustration. In our facilitation, it is always a question of doing what is possible in the moment, and this is mediated by what the stated intention of the client is. In the organisational and coaching domain for example, the stated intention of the client may be of a problem-solving or enquiry nature where notions of 'soul' and 'reconnection with the source' are in the ground. The level at which we work varies according to the context of our work. Even so, it is likely that what is possible at any given moment is influenced, and at times limited, by a number of factors, which are all interrelated and reciprocally affecting:

- What the client has the resources to take
- What the client-system can allow
- What the context can hold
- What the facilitator can be

1. What the client has the resources to take:
I have had many experiences, particularly in individual settings, where I may see the possibility of a resolution for the system-as-a-whole, but it was clear that the client had finished her constellation at some earlier point of important insight. If

I ask such a client what has been important for her in the work we have done, she is likely to mention something that happened halfway through as having had the most profound effect, and in my view it is best to leave it at that. Even so, a constellation that arrives at a useful conclusion according to the reported experiences of the representatives, even though it may be beyond what the client can consciously take at present, nevertheless may have some effect on the client and on the system-as-a-whole in time.

I am of the opinion that there is a safety and reliability in the constellations process that I, as the facilitator, can trust; this is that the constellation can only really show what the client has the resources consciously and unconsciously to see. I have seen Franz Ruppert in practice say to a client, when a constellations process seemed to have become stuck, "Are you ready for what needs to be seen and stated to be so?" or similar words. This can bring the client in a grounded way to a consciousness of her own authority in what we do, clearly stating where that authority for the work lies. A client who answers this question too quickly needs to be encouraged to slow down and consider the question seriously. In this instance I have on occasion worked with a client who, when asked such a question, has been clearly able to say "No I am not", and we both accept this as the present truth.

As facilitators we can agree to meet the client where she is while at the same time holding the space for something deeper and wider. For one person, a transcendent shift of perspective that helps her feel freer and more peaceful in her life is what she consciously seeks, for another to be able to hold his ground in negotiating day to day activities with his partner and children may be his goal and currently the most helpful thing for him. One person's interest may be at the existential or spiritual level while another's is more practical. It is not helpful to make judgements about the one or the other. As practitioners, we are not in charge of our clients' lives and, providing we work with them with respect and integrity it is entirely up to them what they are inter- ested in addressing and what they do with the results.

2. What the client-system can allow:

The client comes with an issue that is to do with her own life, at the same time expressing the system-as-a-whole. Effecting some change in the client's expressed issue will affect the system. Usually this does not present any difficulty since the experiences of the representatives generally indicate a benign wish from those who have gone before for the happiness and fulfilment of those who come later. However, in some families the systemic issues are such that the client's experience is that she is held back by the system. This is most common when the family holds secrets that, if brought to light may threaten the integrity of the family, requiring members to experience shame and guilt.

Franz Ruppert, in his exploration and work on trauma as the underlying factor in systemic entanglements (see chapter 5), has proposed a particular category of trauma, termed 'bonding system trauma', in which the whole bonding system is collectively and persistently traumatised (Ruppert, 2008). By 'bonding system' he is referring to the family as an inter-linked system, where unresolved traumas are transmitted through the bonding process between parents and child down through the generations. The bonding system trauma then is when the whole family system is traumatised, and seems to originate in persistent traumatising experiences such as perse-cution, systemic violence or sexual abuse, or the committing of an act of major impact on the whole system, usually expe-rienced as shameful or criminal such as murder within the system. In such cases, the main systemic energy is consoli-dated around keeping the act secret, thereby protecting the system against having to deal with feelings of shame and guilt, and the effect on its relationship with the outside world.

It is in instances of a bonding system trauma that the process of a constellation may get stuck, and the question then has to be whether the client/system can allow the secret to be spoken. The energetic forces of the system to keep the silence, and protect itself from exposure, are in conflict with the client's reach for freedom by proposing to set up a constellation. In this case, the constellation in its impasse, is generally ruled by what the system-as-a-whole will allow. To make the whole thing more complex the system also has a need for peace and harmony and so is split between wanting success for the client and wanting to hold the secrecy, while the client is split between wanting liberty and peace, and his sense of loyalty to the system. Almost all constellations that get 'stuck' are likely to be fuelled by these dynamics.

3. What the context can hold:
When I started running groups and working in individual sessions, if I did a constellation that didn't seem to get to the depth and resolution I thought it should, I usually thought it was because I was not up to the job. I have since realised that, while I have my limits and that may be part of the problem, there may be other issues at play. There are many contextual factors that influence the possibilities aside from my competence. One group I ran was particularly interesting in that, although I perceived many likely symptoms of trauma in the group members, none of the constellations seemed to quite hit the mark. On later reflection, I realised that the group as a whole just had not felt safe enough to venture into the painful areas. The room was nice and airy but there was often quite a lot of noise outside; at one point there was a chanting group across the way that was quite invasive. At the same time, the venue was set in an area of the town that was definitely not safe at night; it was rather run-down and a known trouble spot in terms of drug-trafficking and violence, many of the residents being minority groups who were struggling in their lives. While the building of the venue itself was lovely and welcoming there were no decent places to have lunch or a cup of coffee outside, and while the immediate surroundings had the potential of being beautiful, there was a definitely slightly derelict feel to it. In addition, everyone in the group was slightly on edge, because they all sensed the imminent trauma in the others. This, together with the physical environment, meant that it was not possible to engage at a greater depth.

4. What the facilitator can be:

What the facilitator can be in any situation obviously is influenced by all of the above, together with his own qualities, experience, understanding and personal resources. However, the most crucial factor is how effectively he can find an empty centre in himself, and from that empty centre influence and hold the space in the face of the other factors discussed above. Our most conscientious efforts are required in our own personal and professional development in order to create within us the capacity to hold a good space for the client. To do this we need to be able to to tolerate uncertainty, confusion and ambiguity, resisting our need to understand and maintaining respect for the emerging process.

Healing Potential of the Constellations Process:

A helpful view of the assumptions of the healing potential of the constellations process is as follows:

- If someone wants to work with a constellations facilitator, then she has an issue. . she may not be clear about what that issue is, but she has an issue.
- If someone's experience is that she has a personal issue, it is always an issue of the system as well.
- If there is an issue in the system that the system cannot resolve for itself, it implies that the dynamics are stuck.
- Dynamics are stuck around a disruption of the principles outlined in Chapter 2.
- If we set up a constellation, it will show us the stuck dynamics.
- This allows the client and facilitator to see and understand the disruption, and allows the system as represented by the constellation to experience the stuckness.
- We are then better able to include some element that has been missing, or re-order that which has been disordered (which in itself means including that which has been

missed). Such a re-ordering may happen spontaneously, especially when the vital excluded factor is re-included.

- Any such movement changes the constellation, and thereby to some extent the system as a whole.
- Such movement once made and witnessed by the client cannot in a sense be unmade or unwitnessed.
- Any resulting insight cannot be obliterated from the client's soul and may result in a spontaneous integration. It may however be consciously forgotten temporarily, and it can be helpful to support the client to find ways of holding the new image consciously by some ritual in his life.

The Stages Of Healing:

Healing is about change, and true change is an embodied experience of integration. To change one's thinking will have some effect on the whole, but the change is limited. This is why behavioural and cognitive therapies can only work to a certain extent, and within their own terms of reference. True change is a transcendent shift in the whole person. It may only take a split-second, but in that moment everything changes, for that person nothing is ever the same again. It is a moment of enlightenment, where the veil of limited perception is lifted. It cannot be made to happen, and often has many prior events and understandings that have contributed to being ready for it.

Along the way, there are stages of healing which need to be respected and seen within the context of the person's whole journey of change. Some of these movements on that journey may seem to take the person in the opposite direction. A client may need to vent his anger and fury about how his life was as a child, to experience disappointment, despair and hopeless-ness, before there is enough space within him to see beyond. If a client is angry, he is angry. If he does not move from that place eventually, then he is stuck. In the therapy world of the latter part of the last century, emotional expression, as in beating up cushions, was for a time considered an essential component of some forms of therapy. However, my experience, and that of many of my colleagues, was that in the end this focus was unhelpful and likely to trap the client in a continually unresolved process of cathartic acting out. The constellations process often shows very clearly the hidden gain of staying angry. . the grandiosity, self-righteousness and self-importance that remaining a victim can offer us. One of the most poignant ritual statements that Hellinger used in the early days was to invite the client to say to the representative of his mother: "I am just a child here. . you are big, I am small". For some people there is a wonderful relief in saying this and letting go of the burden of their sense of self-importance, and for others there is a terrifying loss of status that feels life-threatening.

The stages of one's healing unfold in a way that, on reflection later, one can often see has structure and form, intelligence and wisdom, even though in the moment this may not be clear to anyone. We could say that there is a certain order to the individual healing process of a person, and, if you listen carefully with the whole of your being, you may connect with that; and trusting, you may move together towards a collaborative moment of insight, where you may both be changed.

Chapter 5

Entanglement and Trauma: Causes and Symptoms

> In a way we are less free than we think we are. Yet we can regain our freedom and put an end to repetitions ... [living] "our own" lives, and no longer the lives of [those] whom we "replace," knowingly or not. *Schützenberger (1998)*

Entanglement

Entanglement is the term used to describe the way in which someone is unhelpfully bound at an unconscious level to the system, as represented by their identification with an excluded person/event. This entanglement has been described by Hellinger as 'blind love', meaning that our actions are motivated from a strong sense of loyalty and love, but because the tie is unconscious we are helpless and blind to find another way. The constellations process allows for these unconscious entanglements to become visible, thereby allowing us to make a different choice in our way of staying connected and being in relationship. The notion of 'enlightened love' is the awareness that enables us consciously and healthily to remember those to whom we are connected, thereby releasing ourselves from the unconscious binding into a more conscious and choiceful connection.

The term 'exclusion' is widely used among constellations practitioners, whereas 'forgetting', 'overlooking' or 'ignoring' better represents what actually happens. A systemic member cannot actually ever be excluded; that would be like saying that you never had a grandfather. This is manifestly not possible. But people do get forgotten, overlooked or ignored for many reasons, usually because to remember and include them as its price the experiencing of unbearable pain, shame, responsibility or guilt. The attempt to exclude is always unsuccessful, in that the 'excluded' person continues to have an influence on the family or organisation, entanglements being the unresolved disturbances suspended as unintegrated aspects of the system. This process could even be a kind of gradual 'losing' of the person.[20]

So long as this 'exclusion' remains unconscious the system will keep repeating a certain pattern of behaviour and experience.

The entangled person identifies at an unconscious level with the systemic disturbance, the person, event or emotion that has been overlooked or ignored, and this affects how he or she is able to behave and live their life. Another way of thinking of this is to ask what is it within this system that no one wants to look at, that everyone wants to avoid the pain or suffering of having to see and include? Systemically all actions and events have consequences and the system endeavours to perpetuate its own existence as best it can in the face of the unresolved consequences, and it does this by requiring those who come later to hold these effects. Those who do so, do so out of unconscious strong feelings of love and loyalty to the other system members. Their disturbing suffering, made visible through the constellations, is sometimes astonishing.

---

[20] In Barack Obama's autobiographical book "Dreams from my Father" he recounts on his first visit to Kenya, his father's homeland, his aunt whom he has just met for the first time saying to his sister on getting out of the car: "Make sure he does not get lost again." He asks his sister what his aunt meant by this and his sister replies: "It's a common expression here, usually it means the person hasn't seen you in a while. 'You've been lost', they'll say. Or 'Don't get lost'. Sometimes it has a more serious meaning. Let's say a son or husband moves to the city, or to the West . . . They promise to return after completing school. They say they'll send for the family once they get settled. At first they write once a week. Then it's just once a month. Then they stop writing completely. No one sees them again. They've been lost, you see. Even if people know where they are."

Trauma

Trauma as the basis of all entanglement – the work of Franz Ruppert[21]

Ruppert, in his work on trauma and family constellations (Ruppert, 2008), views all entanglement as originating with a trauma experienced by someone earlier in the system. He has proposed that the unresolved effects of traumatisation are transmitted down the generations through the intimate process of bonding, primarily between the mother and her child. This view is another way of understanding how events have their effect across generations, and is a further contribution to our understanding of systemic processes. Ruppert provides a full and fascinating account of his work and his thinking, which I propose merely to encapsulate here to help with understanding the role of trauma in the constellations dynamics.

The process of traumatisation renders the affected person completely helpless in the face of the trauma situation, where fight or flight may be inadequate or impossible, thereby requiring the more traumatic freeze and fragment response. This fragmentation constitutes a split in the personality of the person whereby the unexpressed and unresolved trauma feelings of terror, horror, rage or grief are split off and buried in the unconscious, while the other part of the person gets on with surviving and continuing their life. Energetically in the heat of the trauma moment, emotional expression would be a luxury that cannot be afforded or for which there is no discernible support. All effort and energy must go towards whatever is necessary to survive the threat. Whether this threat is a mortal threat or the threat of feeling the all-consuming pain of pure grief at the loss of, say, a child, or the experience of shock at witnessing some horror, the experience in the moment is as if one would die. This split that hives off

---

[21] This account in no way takes the place of a full reading of Ruppert's book for an understanding of the processes involved in trauma transmission across multiple generations.

the emotional response into suspension while all resources are put into survival then remains in place, and the trauma feelings remain suspended, unconscious and unresolved, resurfacing when the trauma situation is re-triggered at times by parallel or similar experiences later in life. The surviving strategies that worked in the moment become a fixed and habitual part of the personality, having as its function keeping the suspended traumatised feelings out of awareness.

The emotional/physical nature of the bonding process between parent and child (most particularly mother and child) means that the child bonds helplessly with the mother as she is, experiencing and absorbing both the more conscious feelings of the mother as well as the unconscious split off trauma feelings in the case of a traumatised parent. (Note that this parent may also have been in receipt of traumatic experiences from *her* parents – thereby creating a 'multi-generational transmission' (Ruppert, 2008).) Love and terror may come in the bonding as a combined package. Alternatively, the child experiences a distracted, absent love from her mother combined, for example, with grief over an unresolved loss. In the intimate bonding process neither the child nor the mother can do other than experience each other as they are. . the mother cannot protect her child from that which is unconscious in her, and the child cannot refuse any part of her mother. At its most serious, Ruppert calls this a "trauma of bonding", where the actual bonding between mother and child is a traumatic experience for the child (and sometimes for the mother as well[22]).

These conflicted emotional experiences in the mother will confuse the emotional life of the child, who, as an adult, will seek fulfilment in her relationships in both a replication of this initial familiar disturbed bonding relationship, and in an urge

[22] In the case of a mother who, for example, has already lost a child before the current bonding, or who lost her own mother when she was very young, when she holds her new child, the bonding process can re-stimulate a connection with death. This makes her emotional state as she holds her child confused, and perhaps terrifying for her and therefore for the child.

for completion of that which she did not have. This search is doomed by its conflicting and paradoxical nature. On becoming a parent herself, there is a re-stimulation of this primary bonding experience as she holds her own baby, which in turn is transmitted to the new child along with the taken-on systemic trauma in the mother. This results, in the third generation, in a diffuse, persistent, confusing and ubiquitous generalised experience that seems to have no roots. Ruppert has proposed that this kind of process lies at the core of most serious psychological and emotional disturbances such as schizophrenia, psychosis, bi-polar, suicidal ideation and chronic depression. The effects of trauma two and three generations down, where the original event has lost its presence and is unknown, results in many seemingly perplexing and misunderstood serious mental and physical illnesses that seem not to have any definable cause.

Ruppert's practical work with constellations focuses on the re-integration of the split within the person involved, and the disrupted connections with other important people in the client's life. He thinks in terms of a personality splitting into three discrete parts (or psychological clusters that have a specific function[23]) as a result of trauma: a traumatised part, a surviving part and a healthy part. The traumatised part holds the unresolved and unbearable feelings from the trauma in unconscious suspension, and only manifests when triggered by circumstances, resulting in feelings of extreme panic and anxiety and hyper-arousal symptoms (See Appendix 1 for details of these symptoms). The surviving part originally managed the initial trauma process and survived. In this sense, the surviving part is life enhancing. After the event is over the surviving part is involved in managing the boundary that keeps the trauma experience out of consciousness, thereby maintaining the split. Ruppert has said that it is impossible to work

---

[23] The term 'parts' tends to prompt a more fixed view, whereas complex systemic thinking, while understanding that sometimes things do become more 'fixed', includes the understanding they are processes that are also always potentially subject to change.

with a client who is only available in their surviving role because the sole function of the surviving part is to keep things under control and not allow the unresolved trauma any expression.[24]. The third part of the split is the healthy part: that in the person which knows something is wrong and attempts to take them towards help, e.g. into therapy.

Current thinking about trauma therapy includes the revisiting of traumatic experiences under supportive conditions as part of the healing process. Rothschild (2000) and Levine (1997) see this as involving a slow and safely supported process with a therapist who is trained and experienced in working with trauma. The risks of an unsupported re-traumatisation are considered severe and best avoided. (Current trauma theory focuses on working with people who have experienced trauma themselves, the notion of transmitted trauma being generally not much acknowledged in the field[25]. I call this personal traumatisation, while a transmitted traumatisation is the taking on of an unresolved systemic trauma that happened to someone earlier in the system.)

In across-generation systemic work, the client in front of us is likely to be carrying a transmitted trauma, even if they are also suffering from their own experience of a traumatic event or series of events. As discussed above, they may be suffering from a trauma of bonding. In this sense it is likely that transmitted trauma is ubiquitous: all of us to some extent are probably the recipients of some kind of transmitted trauma. This is particularly likely if we look at the world's history over the last hundred years: two world wars and many other smaller wars, the holocaust, various other genocides,

---

[24] Verbal communication.

[25] However, the effects of traumatisation on subsequent generations *are* acknowledged, and to an extent understood and worked with, in extreme cases such as with the children of holocaust survivors and of other severely war-traumatised people. Even so generally this is on a more behavioural level, ie how the traumatised parents treated and behaved with their children. For a fascinating personal account together with a well-researched study of this work read "*The War After*" by Anne Karpf *(1997)*.

mass migrations, millions of refugees, terrorism, extreme poverty and, with our late 20th century technology, the constant increasingly graphic imagery and news accounts that we are subject to. In order to be in a position to work effectively with people holding transmitted trauma, therefore, it is essential that we, the therapists and facilitators, and those others who work with people, be conscious of the presence of such trauma in ourselves. And even this is problematic, because of the nature of trauma. The burying of the initial experience in the unconscious with the attendant means of keeping it unconscious, means that our natural motivation is to avoid any chance of it surfacing.

While currently our understanding of how to work with post traumatic stress (PTSD – see Appendices 1 and 2) of personal experiences of trauma is developing,[26] working with bonding trauma and trans-generational trauma is in its infancy, and seems to present different issues. As yet, we do not know definitively what heals trauma (see footnote 26). The principle debate surrounds the argument between the view of a safe and supported, in-the-present, conscious 'revisiting' of the trauma event, involving techniques that allow the client to manage and control his experience and reactions, and a view that the client should be helped to manage his life in a way that prevents him from ever 're-visiting' the trauma, for fear of a terrifying re-traumatisation experience.

In the group, the constellations process may provide us with a unique technique for working with either inherited trauma or personal trauma, and that is the client's representative. It is possible for the client's representative to approach or revisit this trauma on behalf of the client. This is also

---

[26] Rothschild, in the preface to her book *The Body Remembers*, feels moved to include a 'disclaimer' in respect of the current developments in trauma thinking. I quote part of it: "The scientific study of . . . trauma, PTSD and memory is accelerating at such a . . . pace that it is impossible to keep up. There are . . . strong disagreements between scientific groups . . . What causes and what heals PTSD and how memory functions are subject to broad debate [and] dispute." *Rothschild (2000)*

possible in the individual session by using table-top markers or toys, which allows the client to helpfully dissociate to a degree from his own trauma experience and have it flow into the marker object. How complete either of these is for the client as a healing process is, as yet, uncertain. Is it sufficient for the representative to experience the trauma reactions on behalf of the client or must the client experience it himself? We are perhaps still too new to this work to know, and the whole business of representation is still too mysterious for us to fully understand.

From my personal experience as a client, and what I see in my work with clients, my current view on transgenerational trauma is this: the taken-on trauma resides in the client in a form similar to how it was in the original person, and the moment the client connects with the trauma issue of the previously traumatised person, he goes into an expression of the trauma feelings of that person pretty much as if it were his own. My own experience as a client was as if in that moment I and the previously traumatised person were one, as if his trauma was my trauma with no separation. After the experience I understood how deeply connected I had been with the traumatised person. It was not that I felt that I *carried* the trauma; it was as if in that place of the unconscious trauma he and I were not separate, we were one. I have also seen this in my clients, particularly in the individual session where there is no possibility of the client having a representative do it for him. I have been with clients who in that moment of connection with the traumatised person go into a trauma reaction and express the unexpressed feelings as if it were he or she who had been traumatised in the first place. However, unlike the original trauma experience, this expression is quick, sometimes not lasting more than a minute. I am convinced it is not a re-traumatisation; the person is not panicked and stays in touch with me; he or she does not dissociate or go into a hyper-aroused state. It is as if she is a vessel for expression, nothing more, she efficiently experiences the essence of what needs to be allowed and moves out of it. After all, even though she may experience it as if it were her own, it is not hers, she did not have the experience of the original event.

Ruppert categorizes four basic traumas:

1. **Trauma of existence:** the trauma of personal mortality such as a serious accident, attack on one's life or other life-threatening event.
2. **Trauma of loss:** the loss of a person with whom one is closely bonded which is "out of time", in other words before the natural time of a person's death. Typical examples might be the early death of a mother or father of a small child, or the death of one's own child in their youth (accident or war event). This could also include miscarriage, stillbirth and abortion.
3. **Trauma of bonding:** the trauma is to the child in the process of bonding with the mother, due to the traumatised state of the mother, therefore a form of compounded trauma (inherited trauma plus the trauma of the bonding process).
4. **Trauma of the bonding system:** the whole system is collectively traumatised, not just one or two people. It is to do with acts that are deemed shameful, criminal and 'against life' committed by someone in the system against another in the same system or, in some cases, against someone outside of the system. Acts of persecution, torture, verbal, emotional, physical and sexual abuse, murder and so forth fall in this category.

The first two types of trauma are simple and straightforward. They are events that happen to someone or some people and cause a trauma reaction in them. As such this is a personal trauma experience.

The second two types are more complex in that they are less clear, and not caused by simple events.

Particular issues with bonding trauma

The bonding trauma is experienced by the child in the bonding process with his mother, and is usually due to the mother having suffered a trauma herself. This kind of disturbed bonding finds an equivalent in the attachment work of Mary Ainsworth (Ainsworth, 1973), as 'insecure-ambivalent attachment' and 'insecure-avoidant attachment'.[27] So the child experiences a two-fold trauma. On the one hand the child takes on the residue of the mother's trauma, and on the other the child has to deal with an insufficient or interrupted bonding process himself, as a result of his mother's inability to be fully present because of her traumatisation. Since it is extremely likely that for some reason the mother may be traumatised (after all she may well suffer from a bonding trauma herself if her mother has suffered a trauma) then it is likely (but un-researched as yet) that the most common form of trauma is in fact the trauma of bonding[28].

Within the traditional family constellations practice this is present in the work of "the interrupted reaching out movement", where the movement of a child towards his mother and mother towards her child was interrupted due to the mother's unavailability. This is often worked with by the facilitator taking up the role of the mother, or using a representative to be the mother, while the client, as himself, is supported to make the movement towards the mother. However, in the constellation this simple practice is often confused because the representative for the mother may show her unavailability due to her own trauma, and the movement may only be possible by the facilitator forcing the issue and jumping over this

[27] It will be exciting when attachment theorists move to taking an across generation perspective into account, since it would seem that this could only enhance current attachment thinking.
[28] There is of course here the whole subject of birth trauma which I don't intend to go into, although I have experienced in constellations on occasion a client or her representative being stimulated into a re-birth process that, with the support of representatives and the group, can become a very positive experience.

important phenomenon. How effective this can be is open to question.

Bonding trauma often results in a multi-generational pattern of the child trying to be the parent to her parent, endeavouring to give the parent what she perceives her parent did not receive. It is common for a client, during the process of the constellation, to understand that her mother was incapable of being present for her because *her* mother had been unavailable to her, and this kind of insight allows the client to relinquish unrealistic desires of her mother. It invokes a compassion in the client where she feels more able to step back from her mother and be less blaming and frustrated.

Secrets, shame and guilt: particular issues with bonding system trauma

As I have said in Chapter 4, with reference to Ruppert's category of the traumatisation of the whole bonding system, the most difficult kinds of entanglement within a constellation involve events that the system sees as needing to be kept secret. Secrecy is often stimulated by complex feelings of extreme shame and guilt and usually involve serious infringements of socially acceptable behaviour, even criminal behaviour such as fraud, manslaughter or murder. It could also be something that at some time was socially unacceptable such as illegitimacy, even though it may not currently be deemed such a socially stigmatising issue. It may be something that within the particular system is regarded in a certain way that another system may see differently; for example, abortion in one system could be regarded as murder, whereas in another it could be circumstantially acceptable. Secrets also occur around events and actions such as sexual abuse and incest. Confusing relationships such as a daughter having a baby fathered by her father or brother likewise fall into this category. However, it is well, even with incest, to consider the perspective of the system in order to understand the effect, rather than assume the effect from one's own perspective.

Crucially in all cases, it depends on how the event is viewed within the system.

Secrecy mounts over time, even when the original events are long forgotten, the system having developed a culture of not speaking about such sensitive issues, avoiding painful feelings of shame and guilt. The essence of the secrecy syndrome is that the whole system colludes consciously or unconsciously in keeping the secret and, in so doing, members resist looking at the truth, at times without any understanding of why. The resulting systemic dynamics are contracted, limited and restrictive, often resulting in members only feeling safe within the confines of the traumatised family system, or only able to make relationships with others similarly afflicted. This then results in the creation of further situations in which the traumatisation is passed on to the next generation, not just as a transmitted trauma, but also in repetitive acting out of the original traumatising act. This is particularly so in cases of sexual abuse, incest and domestic violence, and in less overtly dramatic but still profoundly affecting instances of emotional and physical neglect. Children absorb from their parents the experiences of guilt and shame without any understanding of why they feel these feelings themselves, sometimes believing themselves to be guilty of some dreadful act. The energetic compulsion of this kind of systemic trauma is focused on keeping the secret. Later system members may know nothing about the original event, but always have a sense of something not being quite right. It is the most difficult kind of constellation to help move towards more harmony and balance since the representatives will reflect the limited and restricted experiences of not being able to speak. The energy of the constellation is likely to be turgid and dull although there may also be a collective feeling of sitting on a volcano that at any moment may explode. Sometimes it has to be sufficient in the moment, to reveal and understand that there is a secret, without going into what the secret is. This can often be very useful for the client as an affirmation of a long-held experience that has never been so defined. This kind of work is likely to require a number of constellations over time, the focus of which should not include trying to find out what the event was. This information may emerge in the process, but it is more helpful to the client to find a way of releasing herself from the bonds of helplessness and unconscious repetition, rather than embarking on an archaeological expedition to heal her entire family of many generations of suffering and destructive behaviour.

Case example 3

Following is what a client wrote to me after having done her first constellation in a group, which we simply set up and then listened to the experiences of the representatives:

"I found the constellation amazing, just to see the women from my past with the empty look and holding the secret of incest so tightly, which made them unable to function as women, silenced them all. They couldn't walk in their own shoes. They have walked in shoes handed down to them, thickly covered with silent screams of despair.

"They have the same story as me which they wanted to hand down to me, because this is the family inheritance, and I want to change this for me.

"I'm aware that one member on both sides of my family, my father's and mother's family, was aware of what was going on but felt unable to do anything. My mother's grandmother and my father's aunty, they knew."

Perpetrators and victims

There are traumatisations that do not seem to fit in any of the above categories and may require further consideration. For example, there is the trauma of the perpetrator, and the trauma of the witnesses, whether of acts in the privacy of the home or in such arenas as war. The victims can be seen as experiencing existential threat.

Hellinger has seen in constellations that perpetrators of

violent and life-threatening acts against another become part of the victim's system and vice versa. The fundamental personal nature of the act, for example, of taking another's life would indeed make that person extremely important in the other's system, as would the converse act of saving another's life. There is a kind of bonding that occurs between people in these circumstances that always requires special attention to understand what is needed.

Perpetrator-victim-perpetrator cycle

One of Hellinger's most important developments in his work was when he moved from sending the representative for the perpetrator of an event that had had a great impact on a system out of the room[29], and instead allowed him or her to stay present to the constellation. Subsequently he moved to setting up perpetrators and victims as part of the evolution of an individual's constellation that centred on someone in the constellation having been victimised as part of a collective brutality. He would set up, say, seven people as victims and seven people opposite them as perpetrators and then allow the dynamics to unfold with often very dramatic and moving effect.

Even later, he began to include the mothers of both perpetrators and victims in the constellation, finding that it increases the capacity for understanding and clarity, and thereby healing, when we can allow the unfolding contact and connection between all of these. We have more understanding of these extraordinary processes and connections from the Truth and Reconciliation work in South Africa, and subsequent work with Archbishop Desmond Tutu in Ireland; we have much to learn from this work and those victims and perpetrators who do take the step of meeting and connecting with each other.

[29] The thinking at the time was that, by his act, the person had forfeited his right to belong to the family system and so facilitators tended to send the representative out of the room. Now we understand that system members cannot be excluded in this way, and generally in the constellation it is better if he stays and is included along with recognition of his guilt.

Through the emergence of Hellinger's work with perpetrators and victims we now understand better the cycle that is likely to result from incomplete perpetrator/victim dynamics. If not resolved, in the end the victim is likely to turn perpetrator and take revenge on the original perpetrator, or more often on another person entirely. This dynamic is not unfamiliar to us, indeed we see it played out before us every day in our newspapers where terrorists, who often originally experienced themselves as victims, then turn perpetrators as suicide bombers, arbitrarily meting out their revenge on further innocent victims. A most tragic unfolding of this dynamic that we can see is in the ongoing and unending conflict between Israel and Palestine, where more often than not Israel is seen as the perpetrator having, in its very recent past been tragically victimised itself. The experience of the desire for revenge, the uncontainable outrage of the victimised, is one of our most powerful experiences and, if unchecked, can lead to a continual spiral of perpetration that may continue for centuries. Hence the recurrence of the historical feelings of outrage and fervour connected with the word 'crusade' in the years since 9/11. It has felt at times as if those ancient conflicts were just as current today.

Trauma across generations

Can the effects of trauma across generations dissipate? In some situations trauma effects worsen across generations – particularly if the original trauma keeps being re-enacted as in, for example, systemic violence, sexual abuse and incest. In these situations, where it becomes apparent that this kind of systemic behaviour has persisted over many generations, the original act and re-enactment come to define the systemic character. The abusive behaviour becomes the currency of the system. Extreme compensatory actions such as secrecy, paranoia, emotional absence and hyper-protectiveness also can become the character and currency of the system.

My own view is that it must also be the case that trauma

effects can dissipate over time, which might depend on various factors:

1. The severity of the original trauma combined with the resilience of the originally traumatised person and of those who follow to deal with the trauma.
2. The external and internal resources and support available to the originally traumatised person and to those who follow at the time of the trauma and in the present[30].
3. Whether the originally traumatised person had already suffered trauma.
4. Whether those who follow suffer other trauma themselves.

There is no doubt that we see in many constellations that parents try hard to transcend their difficulties in order to parent their children as best they can. These efforts may have the darker edge of unconscious entanglement, holding secrets, unresolved emotional traces, but nevertheless, it is also the case that families as systems do survive ... evidenced by the client in front of us, who may of course have children and even grandchildren of his own.

In Conclusion

Whether as a facilitator one chooses to work from the overt perspective of traumatisation as the origins of entanglement or with the notion of systemic identification with the missing person/element as the underlying cause is, to a certain extent irrelevant, in that they are not that different. For someone to be forgotten or otherwise 'excluded' is always connected with some traumatic event whether a loss, accident, war trauma,

---

[30] It is interesting to speculate on the fact that it is only in the last 30 or 40 years that we have had the resources of good counselling and psychotherapy for the many. As a resource this, and our growing understanding of trauma processes, must have and be having an effect on the potential parenting of future generations.

act of persecution or victimisation, the effect being severe enough for the remaining system members to turn away and 'forget'.

Schema for Healing Process

What follows is an attempt to put the process of the movement from entanglement to clarity and autonomy into a diagrammatic form for ease of understanding. As with all such attempts it is a simplification. At the same time it may provide a broad map of the natural process that a person follows in this movement with the support of a constellations facilitator.

Figure 7

1. Entanglement:

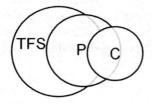

TFS - Traumatised Family System
P - Parent/Parent System
C - Client/Child

The child is almost completely merged with the parent who is almost completely merged with the traumatised or entangled family system of the parent. In effect everyone is too close to be able to gain any useful perspective and clear conscious contact is not possible.

2. Client's effort to move towards autonomy and individuation

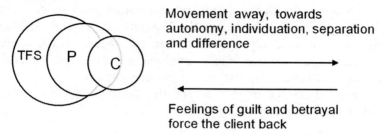

Movement away, towards autonomy, individuation, separation and difference

Feelings of guilt and betrayal force the client back

In this picture we see that the natural move towards autonomy is overwhelmed by the systemic pull of loyalty, which manifests in experiences of guilt and being traitorous and in unconscious beliefs such as: "My mother/the group could not survive my being different."

3. Step 1: The constellation facilitator supports the client to move away

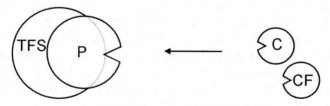

CF - Constellations Facilitator

With distance client looks back at parent and traumatised system

In the constellations process (or other kind of therapy that can work in this way) the facilitator supports the client to take as much of a step back as necessary, usually evidenced by the client feeling better and safer, and her breathing being easier. She is out of the immediate sphere of influence of the parent and the entangled family system and therefore less in the merged trauma experience. This 'stepping back' may involve a great distance. We may have to say in the session that a yard equals a thousand miles.

In the constellations process representatives can be used for the parent and the traumatised system. It is quite feasible to use just one representative for the whole traumatised system, or if it is clear who is involved, say the client's grand-mother, to have a representative for that person.

From here the client can see the situation more clearly, feel safer and breathe more easily.

Parent's representative steps back
and looks at traumatised system.
Client observes.

4.   Step 2: Parent steps back
Facilitator may facilitate a process between the parent's representative and the representative for the traumatised system if it is obvious what needs to take place. For example, if it is known that the parent's mother died when the parent was a small child, then the representative for the parent's mother may be included, or the representative for the traumatised family system (TFS) may spontaneously become the parent's mother.

5.   Step 3: Unknown missing trauma element included
TE – Trauma event/person.

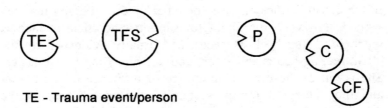

TE - Trauma event/person

96

In situations where the trauma is unknown or obviously several generations back (evidenced by representatives of several generations of members of the traumatised system (TFS) being unable to make real and full contact with the parent or the client), the facilitator can include a representative/marker for the assumed original trauma event/traumatised person.

Working in this way we assume that parents' natural instinct is to be present and available for their child, and that their inability to do so is due to some, perhaps unknown, trauma in the system that caused emotional and psychological disruption over several generations. In such a way we can represent, for example, "the trauma that happened in this family system that resulted in this client's mother not being able to be present to her child".

Other examples of how we can express this might include:

- "Whatever happened that the mothers in this system were unable to look at their children". This comes when we can see that there is a pattern of a certain behaviour across many generations.
- "Whatever happened that resulted in the current difficulties experienced by the client"

These kinds of representations are abstract but serve three purposes:

1. They invite the constellation to configure itself around a potential missing element. . often resulting in either the constellation or the client understanding at some point whom it is.
2. They get around the business of needing to know what actually happened by making a general assumption that something *must* have happened to affect people in the system so much as to result in the client's difficulties.
3. It expands the client's perspective to understanding a more complex and across generation context, thereby making her focus less intensely on her parent and more

on the context. This allows her to feel more understanding of, and perhaps compassion for, her parent.

6. Step 4: Including those before the trauma

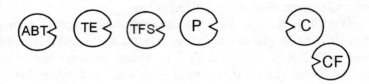

ABT: Ancestors from before the trauma.

Here we have included ancestors from before the trauma event
(ABT). This expands the client's perception even more, to
understanding that there was a time in her family's history
before this particular trauma event that has had effects on her.
If the other representatives are still unable to fully connect
with the client, she can have good contact and support with
this ancestor. Including this element also often has a good
effect on the whole constellation. Representatives of the
trauma event and the traumatised family system often report
feeling fixed as if frozen in time. The inclusion of someone
from before, who is not involved in this trauma often helps
free up the reified constellation.

Section II
The Methodology of Constellations

Chapter 6

The 'Knowing Field'[31] and the Representative Experience

" . . .suddenly they are taken by a movement they cannot resist and they feel exactly like the people they represent."
Hellinger (2006)

In a group, the representatives attend to their physical and emotional experience as they stand where they have been placed. Their attention is directed predominantly to their current awareness and their sense of relationship with other elements of the constellation represented by people. In the beginning, it is helpful for the representatives to attend primarily to their embodied experience, their physical and emotional awareness, rather more than to their thinking about their experience. Our thinking processes often move quickly into meaning-making, which may miss important physical and emotional information. A primary focus on the physiological experience allows space and time too for those seemingly

---

[31] I believe that the term 'knowing field' was first used in the context of constellations work by Albrecht Mahr.

random and spontaneous notions and images that seem to arise less from rational thought than from a more embodied awareness. The information that the representatives experience usually relates closely to the person represented, even if they know little or nothing about the person. This is often corroborated by the client, but in some instances may be beyond the client's current knowledge. There have been frequent occasions where, after the workshop a client may check on some information offered by a representative, and has found it to be correct. This phenomenon is known as the representative's experience or representative perception[32]. There are a number of ways in which we can understand this process:

A Spatial View

We are very sensitive to our physical positioning in relation to others. You only need to watch people and their body movements when they are near other people to see quite distinct patterns of physical-spatial relationship. It seems odd to us to talk to someone who is out of view, or while standing behind someone else. It might feel too confronting to be absolutely face to face with someone and we might find ourselves drawn to move back or turn away, and this may feel different to us in different situations and with different people. So it is entirely likely that representatives in a constellation are in the first place resonating at this physical-spatial level with their surroundings.

You can experiment with this with a friend or colleague. Without any notion that there may be an issue, simply place yourselves in different spatial configurations with each other and report your experience. From these reports you may then find that you move into more complex interpretations of the particular relationship. . and don't forget, we are not trying to focus on any constellated issue here. . it is just spatial relationships represented by distance and direction.

[32] This term was initially used by Matthias Varga von Kibéd and Insa Sparrer.

An Informational Or 'Knowing Field' View:

At the same time as representatives in a constellation may tune in to experiences that are to do with the spatial relationships around them, they also seem to tune in to more than this. Quite often the experiences representatives have are much stronger than one would normally attribute to mere positioning, and can also seem at variance with what one would expect from the positioning. Sometimes information reported by a representative is very physical, such as feeling fixed to the spot or feeling unbalanced as if on uneven ground, feeling tingly or heavy; sometimes it is an emotional experience, even quite powerfully so. Usually the experience is, for the representative, quite clear and unquestionable. When people are a representative for the first time, they are consistently startled by their experience, often reporting that they felt they could not do other than what their body willed, and that their experience was completely different from how they had been feeling before they were chosen as a representative.

These phenomena have been so consistent over the years during which facilitators have been working with constellations, that they are now the pivot around which the constellations process works. The phenomenon of the representative experience is so persistent, and often so uncannily consistent with the experience of the client, that experienced facilitators have come to trust it, even take it as an ubiquitous phenomenon of life[33]. There have been many attempts to make rational sense of what is going on that people can be chosen to represent someone else, and can so consistently represent her truthfully and accurately (as corroborated by the client). Any book that you pick up about constellations will have somewhere in it a version of the author's views of how this phenomenon happens.

There is considerable writing and evidence to support the

---

[33] Sparrer (2007) talks about "the difficulty of not performing constellations: constellations as a daily process." (p. 73)

view that there is an energetic field that carries information about nature, variously called a morphogenetic field[34], the zero point field[35], and the in-formational field[36]. To go with Ervin Laszlo's in-formational field for a moment, he postulates that, like the "gravitational field, the electromagnetic field and the quantum field, the in-formational field cannot be seen, heard, touched, tasted, or smelled. However, this field produces effects, and these can be perceived. This is the same in regard to all the fields known to science." (Laszlo, 2007) For example, we only can perceive the gravitational field effect on an object when we drop it, but we can never see the field itself. Laszlo continues "In the case of the field that could account for the presence of information in nature, the evidence is the puzzling, quasi-instant form of coherence that comes to light in the physical, cosmological, and biological sciences, as well as in consciousness research. These phenomena call for an explanation, and the simplest and most logical explanation is a field that links the entities that prove to be non-locally coherent." (ibid) In other words he is proposing a field that contains life information that accounts for such experiences as we find in the representative experience of 'non-local coherence'.

Another source that I find makes a useful contribution is the account by Jill Bolte Taylor, a neuro-anatomist or brain neuro-scientist, who had the extraordinary experience of having her entire left-brain temporarily knocked out by a blood clot. For a brain scientist, as she recounts, this was a most interesting experience, even if, for a while, she was unable to understand conceptually the danger she was in. She survived the ordeal and, although it took her a full 10 years to completely recover her left-brain capability, her account of what it was like to just be in her right brain has a particular interest for us.[37] She recounts that as her left

[34] Sheldrake *(1995)*
[35] Usefully written about in Lyn McTaggart's book *"The Field"* *(2001)*
[36] Ervin Laszlo *(2007)*
[37] Jill Bolte Taylor gives a video account at the following website: http://www.ted.com/index.php/talks/view/id/229

brain became more affected by the stroke she lost the ability to speak, to write, to remember anything about her life or her history, to process information in any kind of linear way. As she puts it:

> "Instead of finding answers and information, I met a growing sense of peace. In place of [the] constant chatter that had attached me to the details of my life I felt enfolded by a blanket of tranquil euphoria ... as the language centers [sic] of my left hemisphere grew increasingly silent and I became detached from the memories of my life, I was comforted by an expanding sense of grace ... my consciousness soared into an all-knowingness, a 'being at *one*' with the universe." [her italics]. She goes on: "I sensed the composition of my being as that of a fluid rather than a solid. I no longer perceived myself as a whole object separate from everything. Instead, I now blended in with the space and flow around me." *Bolte Taylor (2006)*

Jean Boulton[38], in an article in The Knowing Field Journal on the science behind the constellations process, finishes by saying:

> "I am not going so far as to say that quantum theory or complexity theory can explain constellations; it would be far too presumptuous to do so. What I am saying is that the characteristics of the new science are congruent with some of our experiences of constellations in particular and of other seemingly non-rational phenomena as well ... We ought to turn round our thinking and say, "Why wouldn't this be normal? Why couldn't it be the case that our family system has an energetic field that exists and can be both experienced by others and changed? Why shouldn't thoughts have the ability to influence events?" *Boulton (2006)*

The Representative Experience

When we are chosen to be a representative in a constellation we enter a kind of trance state that is more connected with our right

---

[38] Visiting Lecturer at Cranfield School of Management and Complexity Theorist.

brain than our left, and in that moment the boundaries of ourselves soften, and we are more available to this information-al field, to an experience of interconnectedness. Generally, we live our lives in an eternal dilemma, a constant paradox. In scientific terms we behave as if our world operates according to a Newtonian, linear, Descartian model where things bump into each other and operate rationally according to well-understood physical laws. This is the domain that confirms to us our separateness, our individuality, even our disconnectedness. This is the domain of our left brain hemisphere.

And yet at the same time we also know that there is a broader reality, where we experience things that do not comply with such linear and rational laws. The twilight world of modern physics: quantum physics, where light is "both wave-like and particle-like at the same time" (Zohar & Marshall 1994); where a particle is at times thought of as being a particular point in space, and at others is best considered as smeared right throughout the universe; where the effect of the observer shows that objectivity is impossible, and events are linked synchronously, defying our sense of separateness and individuation; where all possibilities are available until we open the box[39], when they collapse into one. We all have experiences of what we might call the "supernatural" or the "psychic". Who has not had the experience of the phone ringing and knowing, before we pick it up, who it is? Psychotherapists commonly have the experience of discussing a certain client in their supervision consultation, and then discovering at the next meeting that the client has shifted in some way that relates to the supervision discussion. Another instance is where someone in a client's life changes or does something relevant even though they don't know that they have been the subject of discussion in the client's therapy. These experiences in fact are not so alien to us as perhaps at first they seem.

Insa Sparrer states: "Constellations teach us that people do not exist separately from each other, as we tend to believe . . .

[39] Reference to Erwin Schrodinger's Quantum Cat. See *Zohar & Marshall (1994), p. 28.*

The common assumption that we exist separately from one another . . . must therefore be brought into question." (2007)

If we ask how a certain piece of information can be transmitted to someone else, Sparrer would suggest that this is the wrong question: "If, for example, we start from the assumption that there is a connection between people, the question then becomes: 'What is it that separates people? We are then forced to find out why we no longer have contact with each other." (ibid)

She adds: "We also learn from constellations that feelings and emotions do not belong to us as individuals in the way that we think. If new feelings and emotions can appear within us during the constellations process and then disappear equally quickly after de-roling, this tells us that bodily feelings and emotions are not stable attributes belonging to us – they visit us like fluttering birds and then leave us again." (ibid)

Hellinger has said: "My experience is that it's almost always safe to trust the representatives, to trust that they're providing useful information about the system." (1999) My own working assumption is that everything that happens once the constellation is set in train is in some way relevant to the issue. The constellation, as represented by those chosen, will very effectively decide what is relevant and what is not if I am willing to stand back and trust it. Albrecht Mahr talks about "radical inclusion"[40] by which he means both the inclusion of all those who have a connection to the system (ie those who have been excluded) *and* of all information that emerges during the constellation. Mahr illustrates this by an inclusive movement with his hand and the repeated sentence: "and this . . . and this . . . and this"[41] One could say that it is safer to include than risk missing something.

Some facilitators do not work in this way and will restrict what the representatives or those in the remaining 'holding' group may wish to say. In the particular moment they may have good reason to do so, but in general I tend to agree to

[40] Personal communication.
[41] Personal experience of working with Dr Mahr

everything as it arises, and so far have found this usually to be helpful, and rarely not. I prefer to hand back to the constellations process the authority as to what is and what is not important, and I usually find that this confidence is not misplaced. This requires the facilitator to be willing to abstain from the desire to assess and select what may or may not be relevant. (For more on this see Chapter 12.)

Unlike Psychodrama where the role-players are given instruction as to how to be and behave in the drama (which *is* role-playing), in the constellations process the representatives are given minimal, and sometimes no, information. They are merely placed, with no gestures or behavioural coaching – without 'attitude'. It may be useful to think of them as serving as resonators, available to receive and register information relevant to the constellation. We assume a kind of direct communication between the constellation as set up, and the people/elements represented. My experience of being a representative on countless occasions is that, at the moment of being chosen to represent someone a connection forms between myself and the person represented. I may know nothing about the person I represent and yet my experience in all cases has been that my intention is to represent that person as best I can whatever that means. The dedication and loyalty that arise between the person representing and the person represented are something that the facilitator is better honouring than disregarding or denying. As one prominent constellations facilitator has said "I can afford to lose a client . . . I cannot afford to lose a representative."[42]

The experience for the representative is that he is always himself, and yet he is also in some sense someone else. I was once on a workshop where one of the participants could see auras, and she said that the common auric effect when someone was chosen as a representative was that his personal aura shrank to quite small and that another aura came into place, presumably that of the person represented.

Representatives are frequently chosen to represent people

---

[42] Jan Jacob Stam

who have similar issues to their own even though they may never have met the client whose constellation it is before. Thus the representative may gain insight into his own issue by his participation, making the constellation an extraordinary collaborative, co-creative experience, where much more is healed than just the client's presenting issue. It can become a healing event for the whole group.

The representative experience is primarily physical and emotional. A common experience is that the sensations seem to rise up the body from the ground, being perceived first as physical sensation which then grows and intensifies into physical need, which may translate into movement, and sometimes feelings which may be expressed in statements or emotional expression. Some people as representatives will say what they experience, as in "I feel very sad", or "I feel rooted to the spot", and some will show in their body what it is they are experiencing. These differing types of expression may have to do with the facilitator's style - what they allow and what they do not (see Chapter 12 for more on this) - but also with what the actual person representing feels is more comfortable. For example, a person who is generally not very emotionally expressive in his own life will more likely describe his experience rather than express it, whereas someone who feels fairly free with emotional expression is more likely to go straight into the expression rather than describe her experience. Of course the style of expression may also be to do with the person represented, or even a fundamental part of the constellations dynamic. For example, in a constellation of a family that holds secrets and does not allow open and free expression, a representative may well feel restrained even if her natural inclination is towards expression.

In questioning the representatives, it is more helpful to use language that encourages the person to stay with her physicality rather than propel her too much into her thinking. Questions such as "is this better or worse?" require a simple response that is totally experiential, and even the most physically alienated person is likely to be able to answer. The focus on 'difference from before' is the easiest distinction for people to make, so questions such as "is this better than before?" will likely bring forth a clear answer. Some facilitators work predominantly with this form of questioning, deeming that the resolved constellation is when everyone feels a sense of 'rightness' and comfort as to their place within the constellation. These positions in space that feel 'right' to the representative often, but not always, follow the physical representation of the systemic principles as described in Chapter 3.

In the individual session, the representative phenomenon is harder to replicate and may be harder for the client to trust. A client who witnesses people she essentially does not know enact those that she does know with accuracy and commitment quickly comes to trust what evolves. In the individual session the client is less likely to trust so quickly what she herself comes up with for representational purposes, and may well view sceptically what the therapist or facilitator comes up with. After all, the client is likely to view the facilitator as having an investment in a good outcome for her and may see his contribution as a representative as biased to that end. It is easier for a client to go with information that conflicts with her established and long-term view of a situation when it comes from a person she does not know, as a representative in her constellation, who is unlikely to have any investment in a particular outcome, than it is to go with what comes from herself or the facilitator, certainly in the beginning.

This is the skill of the individual constellations facilitator: to create a frame of reference where both the client and the facilitator can trust what they each come up with as representative information, to provide the necessary conditions for the client to side-step his 'story' and to trust himself and the integrity and honesty of the facilitator. Techniques and strategies for supporting this process will be explored further in Part 2.

The Representative Experience and Transference

There seem to be some differences between the representative experience that we see in constellations and what is generally understood in psychotherapy as 'transference'.

The term transference is applied to the process whereby a client unconsciously projects onto the therapist certain aspects of her concept and experience of a significant person in her life, usually her mother or father, and then behaves towards the therapist accordingly, often being incapable of seeing the difference. The therapist for his part may find himself behaving and feeling towards his client in ways that are not common for him, and may then consider that his experience is part of the transference process. At the same time, the therapist endeavours to separate off what may in fact be his own input into the situation from his personal world (counter-transference) of his experience and what is actually to do with the client.[43] The client in her projection and subsequent experience and behaviour draws the therapist into a certain relational structure. One of the purposes of some forms of therapy is to make these projective processes conscious, thereby diminishing the client's tendency to draw others into such transferential relationships, increasing her ability to see people as they actually are; another is for the therapist to be a willing and conscious participant in order for the client to work through her problematic issues with her parents through her relationship with the therapist. Much therapy may be a mix of both.

The representative experience in constellations is not a

---

[43] There seem to be two meanings of the term 'counter-transference' in the psychotherapy field: one is the experiences of the therapist in the current situation that arise from his own personal background issues; and the other is where the therapist's experiences reflect what is being unconsciously communicated by the client, but nevertheless actually belongs to the client. This latter is distinct from what the client projects as transference (essentially characteristics and experiences that belong to a significant other in the client's world), and can provide invaluable empathic information for the therapist of what the client may be unable to verbalise of his experience.

projective process as far as we can tell, but more a kind of deeply connected receptive empathy with someone from the client's system. Representatives do indeed often replicate behaviour and thought patterns of the represented person, but they also have a tendency to come up with other information that would generally be thought of as not within the transference frame, and which often is not what the client expects, or sometimes even recognises. In addition they are often called upon to take up the representation of people other than those we would tend to think of as significant (in the sense of a parent), such as an aunt, uncle, grandparent, great-grand-parent etc. In terms of the constellations workshop too, the representative is consciously invited to be a representative, whereas transference in the beginning is always an unconscious projective process, which takes the venture to a different starting place. However Sparrer (2007) discusses what she and Varga von Kibéd call 'accidental constellations', which they regard as potentially happening at any time:

> "In accidental constellations other people slip into a family system and become representatives of excluded family members, whereas in transference the main person sees family members in other people". (ibid)

She goes on to state: "the process of the accidental constellation occurs passively, while in transference the main person actively projects onto others". (ibid)

A further, perhaps exciting, possibility is that all transference processes (including counter-transference and projective identification) in some sense have always been representative experiences as we think of them in constellations, and if so this could potentially re-configure classic notions of the process of transference and how to work with it.[44]

---

[44] This may seem an ambitious proposal, but that doesn't mean it isn't worth considering. See Appendix 4 for a further discussion of the potential contributions of systemic constellations to psychotherapy.

Facts or . . .?

"Is using the Knowing Field in this way unreliable? Yes, it is unreliable when our sole motive is to look for facts, but if our motive is to find resolution for disharmony, then the Knowing Field can be trusted, tested and relied upon." (Payne, 2005)

My experience, and it seems of other facilitators, is that it is not possible, and even if it were, would not be good practice, to use this process as a divinatory tool; in other words to divine facts that have been hitherto unknown or uncertain, or which may pertain to the future. What is revealed in the constellation is best understood as symbolic rather than factual when it is without corroboration. For example, it would be wrong, I think, to assume that because a constellation shows a client's mother as confused as to who her father is, and the supposed father also confused as to his relationship with his daughter (the client's mother), that this necessarily means that the client's actual mother was not really the daughter of her assumed father. This takes the power of the constellation in helping us organise our lives better to an unhelpful extreme, even to the irresponsible. The most we can say in a situation such as this is that there is some confusion. Whether this confusion is about an actuality or something deeper in the psyche and soul of the family we cannot know. It could be that confusion of relationships is generally present in this system, or that the couple so strongly looked for others in each other that they never really saw the other as their husband or wife.

The constellations process is not the harbinger of factual truth. The constellation's truth is a metaphorical and experiential truth, a means to understanding the way from tension and discomfort to more balance and harmony. It is a responsibility of the facilitator to go only up to the line that is shown, as it is shown; to go further is speculation. It is only the client and his system that know - either consciously or unconsciously - and it is the client who constructs his own meaning as it is appropriate for him. The facilitator and representatives are in service to the client, and whatever we may think, the only meaning that counts is that of the client.

In the same way, it is not possible to divine factual answers about the future; we can only understand better what would be more useful in the present in order to move towards a future aspiration with a more harmonious and balanced way of being. This is the seeding in the present of something that may grow in a certain way in the future ... but it may not. This seeding is always best done on a wave of movement in a certain direction that is already there. Setting up a representative for a goal we aspire to may offer us useful information about the road to possibly achieving it, but only that. Along the way the actuality of the goal may change as more information and outside events affect our journey, and so, what we may then wish for. Another way of putting this, and one that from my experience I am happy to hold as valid, is that we can only know what is useful to us right now. Who or what makes this decision I do not know, but I presume it is some essential part of us that really does know what is right for us at present, that part of us that we might consider guides us in all things, if we allow it.

Representing the Dead

The dead are invisible, they are not absent. *Saint Augustine*

And as a response to the previous section: one of the remarkable things that we find in the constellations procedure is that representatives for those who are actually dead, whether recently or from many generations back, are often vibrant and lively, and have much to contribute. Sometimes representatives may even experience facts that can be corroborated: I have seen a constellation where a representative for a client's long dead great grandfather complained of feeling lop-sided and unbalanced, with numbness in one of his legs, as if he would fall over without support ... and the client informed us that her great grandfather had lost his leg in the first world war.

This is so consistent, and in the understanding of trauma and the impact of events across the generations, integral to the process, that it brings us again to question our conventional notions of being. The phenomenon of the representation of those who are dead may cause us to reconsider notions of life and death. How is it that a living person who has no knowledge or understanding of the nature of another whom he is invited to represent in a constellation, who may have been long dead, seems to be able to access the personal spirit and nature of that person in a way that resonates for the client? Indeed sometimes for the whole group. What does this tell us about death? Is the "knowing" or "in-formational" field so available that we can, under certain circumstances, connect with all life from all time? I don't have an answer to this, but when I think about it my conventional notions of dying and death are jolted and questioned.

Over my time of involvement with constellations I find it easier to align with Saint Augustine's view stated at the beginning of this section. My sister died in a car accident aged 34 while she was living in Australia, when I was 27. I had not seen her since I was 18 when she emigrated, nor had much other contact (in those days international phone calls were expensive and usually only made at Christmas and other special occasions), and due to the age gap between us (7 years) I hadn't had the opportunity to get to know her as an adult. Now, some 35 years later I have a relationship with her that has grown and matured over the years. On occasion I feel very aware of her, and very close to her, and find that a comfort. Whether the relationship I now have with her would have been the relationship we would have had had she lived, of course I cannot say. But I have more of a relationship with her now than I ever had before she died.

The Client's Representative

Increasingly when I have seen Bert Hellinger work he has put the actual client in the constellation to represent herself, but in

113

the earlier days he used to say that it was better to use a representative for the client since the client was likely to be too entangled to be able to allow anything fresh. Either way, using a representative for the client does have some other advantages that are worth mentioning.

The notion of service is something that arises spontaneously out of the constellations process, particularly in the group, where group members are in essence offering themselves in the service of the client's work. This action of service is no small thing, and for a person to have an experience of others representing himself and his family system with dedication and commitment is in itself an event of profound impact. In the particular representation of himself, this act of service can combine the relief of having someone else experience his burden for a change, with an opportunity to see himself from a distance. Sometimes the client's representative can say things that the client has only dimly allowed himself to think, can speak the unspeakable and express the inexpressible. It can be helpful for the client to have reflected back to him things about himself that he knows, as a kind of confirmation and affirmation of the truth of his experience and existence. Sometimes the representative for the client acts and speaks in ways that the client does not recognise as his own ... nevertheless, given the opportunity, usually the client sees something in this that resonates with him and can inform him of a useful next step in his life.

Sitting outside the constellation and observing what happens can give the client immediately a less entangled perspective, and perhaps also an experience that is less immediately traumatising. The service done by his representative in the expression of extreme feelings and situations can be immeasurable.

In the group setting, the question as to when, or if, to bring the client into the constellation is an important one. The judgement as to whether it is more helpful for this particular client to be able to be separate from the entanglement for this time, and observe the dynamics of the constellation from the safety of his seat, or whether it is important for him to have the embodied experience of the new situation that his representative now finds himself in, is one that really only comes with experience. In general, it would seem that the only possible usefulness of putting the client into the constellation is if you deem that the client is in an open enough state to be able to absorb this new experience helpfully. On the other hand, one could also say that dropping the client into the new situation may have the effect of startling the soul into a different perception.

In the individual session, generally speaking one does not have the luxury of choosing between these options. Setting up the constellation with markers does give the client some distance. However, the client must be in her constellation, often representing not just herself, and we will consider this further in Part 2.

Chapter 7

The Constellations Procedure

Begin at the beginning and go on till you come to the end:
then stop.
Lewis Carroll (Alice's Adventures in Wonderland)

In this section I am going to discuss in general the process of
the constellation as it takes place in the group, to help us move
to thinking about the individual session.

Dynamics of the 'Stuck' System

The process of a constellation, once it has been set up, usually
begins by showing the nature of the 'stuck' systemic dynamics
as relevant to the issue brought. For example, if we set up a
constellation of three people, 'A', 'B' and 'C', and instructed
the representatives to move as they felt drawn the following
might occur:

1. Representative A moves towards representative B;
2. B then moves further away from A.
3. C steps in between A and B.
4. A moves around C and again towards B;
5. B moves away from A.
6. C tries again to get between A and B, and so on.

The feeling is as if it would continue like that forever without
something else happening to move the process on. I have done
this many times: invited the client to set up the constellation
and then just waited to see what the representatives do.
Almost always a similarly repetitive pattern emerges. The
"something else" that happens may be in response to an inter-

vention by the facilitator, or a spontaneous action by one or more of the representatives, which produces a shift in the energetic forces of the constellation. The sense of stuckness may stimulate one of the representatives to try something different, or to give up his repetitive motion. It is as if, by setting the constellation up, we take the frozen, stuck image and give it the space to unfold and go to the end of what is possible under these particular circumstances. In this process the elements involved become increasingly aware of the futility of their collective endeavour. . hence eventually the trying of something different or the giving up. Either of these is an important novel systemic movement, which then gives the constellation space to find something new.

The facilitator's interventions assist the process of re-ordering in relation to the principles given in Chapter 2: including someone or something that has been overlooked, forgotten or is otherwise missing; inviting representatives to say statements that may relieve them of some entanglement, or re-positioning the representatives according to the systemic principles. (For more on these interventions see Chapter 11.) If a client has an issue it is because there is a situation that is fixed, frozen in the system, and this is because someone or something, some information, awareness or emotional expression is missing or misplaced. Albrecht Mahr has put it as follows: the healing potential of the constellation is increased by our ability to include that which has been excluded (missing)[45]. This concurs with his notion of "radical inclusion" discussed above (Chapter 6), by which he implies an attitude by the facilitator of ongoing and persistent inclusion of whatever arises during the constellation's process as having some potential relevance to the issue at hand.

The missing element could be a child who died young and, because the grief was too great to allow, was purposefully forgotten. It could be that someone did something that brought shame on the family and they were 'excluded' by never being

[45] Verbal communication.

mentioned. Additionally it could be that some event that happened to the family was so traumatic that those involved never really got over it, and it is as if the event sits in the system silently as an energetic force drawing everyone's energy, at the same time being ostensibly invisible, unmentioned and unmentionable.

Setting the Scene

Before elaborating on the constellations procedure I would just like to say something about setting the scene for a group. This is not so pertinent for the individual session, but is as well to have in mind. It is useful to agree as an explicit contract some clear boundaries for the functioning of the group, and briefly I would suggest stating something like the following:

- Participants respect information shared by others. The issue of confidentiality is a delicate one in that it is impractical to ask group participants to hold a rigid confidentiality boundary around the work. Our process of integration requires us to talk about our experiences with others outside of the group. Respecting information shared calls us to take care of each other, of what we do and say in the group and afterwards out in the world. A minimum stated requirement might be to restrict the mention of people's names and identifying information. In my experience any particular requirements in this area are best negotiated between group members.[46]
- Participants can decline the request to be a representative. It is important that people know that they have choice over this, and that they are encouraged to attend to their energy levels and emotional constitution when invited to be a representative.

[46] In the beginnings of constellations in the early '90's Hellinger's demonstration events drew hundreds of people, and consequently issues of confidentiality were impractical and didn't arise.

- Violence, aggression and sexual feelings are likely to be part of the constellations process and need to be given space and included. However, representatives must refrain from endangering each other by giving these feelings physical expression. The simplest thing is to ask representatives to just state the impulse, as in: "I feel furious with rage and I want to hit this person", or: "I feel strongly sexual when I look at her".

- In terms of the work we do, we can only ever do what the client has resources for. This sets a tone of respect for the client and allows the process to be what it is without pressure on the client, representatives and facilitator.

The Initial Interview – Clarifying the Issue

The primary purpose of this phase is to determine the issue and the starting point of the constellation. The question of where and how to start is important and sets the tone for the whole process. As Hellinger has put it:

> "So there is always the question about how to begin; you have to be very precise and you can't think it up. You have to get in tune with the whole family and then you suddenly know how ... " *(2008)*

This phase is often the first contact between the facilitator and the client. Different facilitators vary considerably in their approach to this phase. Some facilitators require very little information from the client and may stop her from saying too much. Other facilitators may feel that until the client has shared a certain amount about herself, emptied herself so to speak, she is not grounded and connected enough to be available for the process. And there are many degrees of facilitators' preferences between these two.

The question as to what actual information a facilitator requires again varies from person to person. Some facilitators assiduously enquire into who is in the system: siblings, parents, grandparents, important uncles and aunts and so on. Some facilitators focus on important events that happened in the system and to whom. Some facilitators prefer to sit with the client and see where the client goes, only asking questions that they feel strongly prompted to ask. My preference is more for the latter, in that I do not see the point of asking a whole lot of questions, the answers to which may have little to do with the client's issue. In addition, I do not expect the client initially to have a clear, conscious understanding of what the issue is, and expect there to be a process of a deepening understanding if I sit with her in respectful quiet and wait. Questioning a person invites her into her thinking function, which is less useful than if, by sitting quietly with her she feels more able to connect with herself at a deeper, embodied level. My belief is that, in order for there to be space for new ideas and insight to emerge the facilitator needs to quieten his own mind, and in the quiet of the facilitator, the client can also quieten. Of course, some clients find this hard in the beginning and may talk rapidly for a while. However, I find if I persist with my quietness, I can promote this quieter way of being in her; this can be strengthened by gently, on occasion, bringing her back to herself by asking questions like:

- So what should we do?
- Now what do you think the issue is? – this alerts the person to the fact that her issue might be changing as we deepen our enquiry
- What do you want from this?
- If we set up a constellation, what would be a good outcome for you?
- So what is it that you want?[47]

If I really cannot get a good starting point I will tell the client so and see what that brings forward. I may also ask the client what she thinks we should set up. There are many roads to Rome!

[47] For more on questioning and use of language see Chapter 20.

The "getting in tune with the whole family" that Hellinger mentions (above) is a particular feature of the constellations facilitator. A conventional psychotherapist may attempt to get in tune with the client (attunement), but will rarely think in terms of getting in tune with the whole system. This is an approach where we, as the facilitator, are in service not just to the client, but to the whole system.

> "... our way of seeing our clients and their problems becomes more inclusive and respectful of all system members, regardless of what they have done. We develop a less judgemental, more understanding attitude, in some ways finding ourselves both at a distance and yet also present to the system as a whole, with a motive towards finding possible resolution that is good for the *system* as much as for the client." *Broughton (2004)*

Often this tuning in to the client and the larger system takes us to a moment where we cannot *not* set up a constellation; the irrevocable movement towards setting up the constellation is in the client and the facilitator.

Setting up the Constellation

Generally speaking the constellation is set up by the client, who chooses people from the group in a group situation or objects in the individual setting, and places them according to her inner sense of the situation. This is an intuitive process and it is helpful to invite the client to tune into her embodied experience of the issue rather than any thought processes she may have about it. The client who sets up the constellation quickly and sharply is unlikely to have tuned into her inner space sufficiently and the facilitator may ask her to slow down, centre herself more and re-position the representatives. However, it is also true in my experience that once chosen the representatives (people) can easily place themselves, and even if the client does the placing, the first phase of the constellation may well involve the representatives re-positioning themselves according to the experiential information that they have. I have seen clients try to place a representative who became part of the constellation instantly when chosen, and who knows where he must be. It is best in this instance to allow the representative to go where he would even though it is not where the client would put him. In the individual session, where the initial impulses of the representatives are not available, the initial constellations picture that the client sets up offers much useful information as a picture of the client's version of how things are. I will go into this further in Part 2.

The Initial Phase of the Constellation

After the setting up of the constellation, which is usually done by the client himself, although at times Hellinger and other facilitators may do the choosing and setting up themselves, the constellation proceeds. Depending on the style of the facilitator this may take the form of questioning the representatives as to their experience, which may contribute further to understanding the initial dynamics of the constellation, or the facilitator may leave the constellation for a while to see what movements or strong needs emerge. During this phase the non-helpful or 'stuck' dynamics of the system are likely to become apparent. In the individual session, this phase is particularly important in offering the opportunity for the client and facilitator to share their observations. It is helpful not to rush this phase, and the ability of the facilitator to be patient and trust the process is crucial here:

"The reward of patience is patience." *Saint Augustine* in *Blum (2004)*

The Experimental Phase: 'Including that which has been Excluded'

The initially set up constellation is primarily an exploration to understand better what the issue is. In this sense, because there *is* an issue, the ability of the system to find its own way towards harmony and better balance must be compromised, and so the

dynamics as they unfold usually become repetitive and obviously incapable of finding a resolution. Since the constellations
process is always to do with reinstating that which has been
excluded or missed - whether a person, event or something else
hidden or unexpressed - it is unlikely that all the necessary
elements for a resolution will be set up in the initial constellations
image. It is usually through observing the initial process that it
becomes clearer what or who may be missing. This phase
includes bringing in that which has been missed, whether a
person or an abstract (such as 'the secret' or 'the person who is
looked for'). Again I would stress the experimental nature of the
constellations process. It is not about being right when one introduces a new element to the constellations picture. It is about
understanding more what helps and what does not. To include an
element that seems to makes no difference to the constellation is
not a mistake, it just tells us more about the situation, and if the
representative does not feel herself to be an appropriate part of
the constellation she can just sit down again. Of course it is true
that facilitators who are very experienced in the work are more
likely to include elements that have an important effect than facilitators who are more at the beginning of their learning.
Nevertheless the constellations process is always best engaged
with as an ongoing experiment, whose outcome is not a foregone
conclusion.

The Contact Phase

I call this the 'contact phase' because once that which has been
missing is included there is a process where contact and
connection with this missing element occurs, and the previously absent representative is seen by the other representatives
and the client. This 'seeing' is a validation that often occurs
spontaneously and can be supported by ritual statements such
as "I see you", "I include you" or "you have been missed by
us and now we include you". The quality of the contact made
is directly indicative of the power of its contribution towards
a possible resolution. Sometimes this contact happens between

representatives within the constellation with the client as a witness, sometimes the client is brought in to experience the contact moment himself. Whichever procedure applies, the depth to which the client himself can experience this moment of contact is probably indicative of the possibility of integration and change for the client in his life. The contact that occurs between people has an impact on everyone present; it is an experience that moves us and empowers us. It may change everything in that moment. It engages primary emotions (see Chapter 10) in the protagonists and the witnesses. During the process of the constellation there may be a number of contact moments, each one releasing energy within the constellation, which then leads to the next movement. At this stage the process may oscillate between the experiment and contact as it moves towards an ending.

The Resolution Phase

This is the phase during which the original tension in the constellation has changed and there is a more peaceful and relaxed feeling in the representatives, client and probably the holding circle (those who are not representatives). In this phase the issue is seen clearly, the client feels relief, perhaps some rituals and statements are made that confirm the new situation.

The following characterise this phase:

- All members of the constellation (representatives) feel in a good place and relieved of their original uncomfortable experience. The original tension is now relaxed and more harmony and balance are in place.
- The client has seen or experienced something that changes his inner sense image of the situation.
- The client understands better how to move forward in his life.

At times the resolution phase has a feeling of completion, as if there really is nothing else to do, and at others it can have a more open-ended feel to it, as if you could continue. I think it is a mistake to try and take a constellation to a place of total completion if it does not naturally do so. It can result in an 'over-worked' constellation, where everyone loses energy and patience. This is not helpful to anyone. There are times when the constellation seems unable to find a satisfactory conclusion. There is insufficient information available and the limits of what is possible at this time have been reached. It must in this case be enough to know that some step has been taken and that in time this will present a clearer picture for the client. An unfinished situation is not a disaster, it can often be very creative and the best thing for the client at that time: an open field leaves the system free to find its own way forward into the future. To end a constellation too sweetly, with all things neatly tied, leaves little space for the client's process to unfold. In some instances I think "Who am I to say what is the right ending for this constellation. . perhaps it is best left to itself for now."

The Ending Phase

This is where the constellation is brought to a close and the representatives are cleared of their roles. Opinions vary as to how this should be handled, and as to how difficult or easy it is for the representatives to disengage themselves from their roles. Generally, the more experienced one is at being a representative, and the more aware one is about one's own issues, the easier it is to step into and out of representations. It is frequently the case that people are chosen to represent those in situations with similar issues to their own, and in such a case it may be that the process also provides insight and relief to the representative in relation to her own issue. But it may instead be the case that her issues are stimulated to an extent by the role she has, and she feels less able to let it go. A short ritual may be required to clear this unresolved residue for the representative. An example is to stand her opposite the client

125

and invite her to say to the client something like 'I have carried this role for you and it is also in some ways close to my own situation. Now I leave with you what is yours and I keep what is mine.' Another situation where it may be more difficult for the representatives to step out of the roles is if the constellation has been a particularly painful and difficult one, and has not found a satisfactory conclusion. In this more complex and unresolved constellation, it is more likely that a representative may continue to be entangled in the systemic representation. In such a situation it may be up to the facilitator to help the group to find a good way of moving on using perhaps the ritual outlined above.

Chapter 8

Phenomenology, Embodiment and Meaning-making

"As for me, all I know is that I know nothing." *Socrates*

According to Socrates, the secret of the wise person is the ability to prevent the mind from forming hardened patterns of knowledge, that are then difficult to change, and so keeping the process of knowing in a receptive and open state of creative chaos, out of which new insights can emerge. This is the ground for a phenomenological approach.

"Phenomenology ... means subjecting myself to larger contexts and connections, without needing to understand them. I accept them without any intention of helping or proving anything. I submit without fear of what might arise ... I face everything exactly the way it is." *Hellinger in ten Hovel, (1999)*

The constellations process is an applied phenomenological bodywork. Our interest therefore is focused mainly on the embodied experience of the representatives, on the phenomena of experience as opposed to the interpretation of these phenomena. The less-interpreted truth is that which we find in the experiences in our bodies. It is by attending to the experience in our bodies that we can reach the understanding that we are, for example, grieving. The experience of loss is a deeply physical and emotional experience, a collection of embodied phenomena that our mind terms as 'grief'. Attending to the actual description of phenomena keeps one closer to the actual reality rather than one's perhaps biased interpretation (hardened patterns) of that reality.

So in a phenomenological approach description is valued

over interpretation, and all phenomena are regarded as having equal potential value in the beginning; ideally it is the process that shows what is and what is not important. To attribute value too quickly is interpretative.

> "Our phenomenological approach relies on moment-by-moment observation, a non-judgemental approach to all phenomena as having potentially equal relevance, and a high tolerance of uncertainty. It places a strong value on the emergence of a truth that we may not have any previous knowledge of. This asks a lot of us as practitioners. It is constantly a delicate balancing act between trusting the constellation and the process, and listening to ourselves, an intimate negotiation between hypotheses and energetic possibility, between what we may think should be and what actually is." *Broughton (2008)*

As facilitators therefore we are required to cultivate:

- interpretative restraint,
- a high tolerance of uncertainty and the unknown,
- a lack of intent,
- a willingness to be guided by the process of the constellation,
- an openness to new information,
- the ability to be unattached to any hypotheses, and
- a diminished need to be right

> "What is necessary is for the therapist, the client, and the representatives to be completely free of intent and fear, and to allow the essential reality to emerge. They have to agree to this reality as it is, without resorting to previously held theories, biases, or experiences. This is a psychotherapeutic application of a phenomenological stance." *Hellinger (2003)*

In the representative experience, it is usually of more value to begin with the embodied experience of the representative rather than interpretations of that experience. Embodied experience is best expressed in terms of change, for example as in 'what changed in you since that happened?' or: "does this feel better or worse?" Most people answer this sort of question readily and it gives them a clear indication of how to answer. Questions such as "what is happening now?" or "what happens when you do that?" can also be useful but are less clearly oriented to the body. Questions such as "What is important?" or "what do you think?" orient one more towards thinking and interpretation and are likely to take the representative away from their embodied experience. Ideally a facilitator helps the representatives stay with their embodied experience by minimizing questions, focusing on the physical and experiential and keeping it simple.

In the individual session particular care is needed in the process of helping a client become available as a representative in their own constellation (see Chapter 25), as in the absence of the fertile responses of the representatives there is a strong pull to be more interpretative.

Meaning Making

We are all compulsive and fast meaning-makers. In our more perilous past (as hunters and gatherers) speedy meaning-making saved lives. However, we often make meaning as if we were still in a dangerous situation. Our impulse to premature meaning-making (completing partly completed pictures where insufficient information is available) is usually motivated by fear of the unknown, insecurity about uncertainty and a cultural need to be right. But of course this 'filling in of the gaps' sometimes gets us to the wrong place; two and two become five rather than four. In the beginnings of our facilitation experience it may seem a frightening situation to be in, and may stimulate for us other frightening and even traumatic situations in our lives, where knowing what was what seemed crucial to our survival. Or it may re-stimulate a primitive need to know the answer, to be right.

There are two difficulties with the facilitator making interpretations from his own meaning-making. One is that as social beings we are drawn to consensus and agreement, and in the vulnerable atmosphere of the constellations process it may be easy (or easier than to resist) for the client to agree to my meaning. Secondly if I make interpretations, they may conflict with the other's interpretation and then how do we decide on which to follow? Again, the client's vulnerability may bias him to agree with me. As a facilitator I can offer my view on something, but the meaning that a person makes of his own life is and should be his own. My own position is that I am never cleverer at this than the client . . . after an hour or two of working with the client how can I possibly know more about him than he does, whether his knowing is conscious, semi-conscious or unconscious. In my view, as a facilitator Socrates' stance is more helpful to me, and to the client.

Section III

Working with the Constellation

Chapter 9

Constellations Types and Levels

The work of constellations is applicable to such a broad range of issues and operates at such a variety of levels of disclosure, that it is hard to categorise different constellations. However, there is a reasonably clear distinction between constellations at the more personal end of the spectrum and constellations within the larger systems at the more organisational end. If we think in terms of breadth - meaning the range of domains in which we can apply the process - and disclosure level - by which we mean the expected level of personal disclosure (this would include the level of overt emotional experience and expression, and perhaps the existential nature of the issue) - we can see a pattern. In the diagram below I have taken the original diagram from the Introduction and added a 'disclosure level' indicator to show where, in terms of a personal threshold, one is likely to be working. For example, a business coaching contract, while having as its primary purpose helping the client deal with work and social issues perhaps from a more behavioural standpoint, may from time to time dip below this threshold. This will be understood and acceptable within the explicit contract. Whereas the contract between an organisational development consultant and a manager with whom he is working on issues to do with a team in the manager's department, is unlikely to dip below this threshold, although momentarily it is possible that an individual may inadvertently touch on more personal issues. Contracts further along the spectrum to do with large organisational issues such as mergers and take-overs, or political constellations are more and more unlikely to venture below this threshold.

One can define various different types of constellations in a rough way. These are not to be taken as rigid categories, but rather as signposts pointing to areas of emphasis.

- Personal constellations: usually focused on the client's family of origin or their current family or both, but may at times move to larger societal, racial or national issues, for instance if the family at some time was forced to migrate or was subject to collective persecution, or now lives in a country other than their original country.
- Intra-psychic constellations
- Enquiry constellations: where there is nothing particular to be solved, but there is an interest to understand a situation better.

Figure 8 Diagram showing the breadth and disclosure level to which constellations can apply.

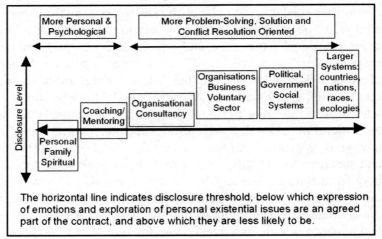

The horizontal line indicates disclosure threshold, below which expression of emotions and exploration of personal existential issues are an agreed part of the contract, and above which they are less likely to be.

- Structured constellations: these are constellations that are set up to a particular structure, using pre-ordained elements; or they take place within a particular structure (Sparrer, 2007). See Chapter 26.
- Autopoietic[48] or leaderless constellations: usually used for large collective-interest issues without a facilitator as such, but does include someone who asks representatives to say their experience. No formal interventions are made.

Having already described the personal constellation above, I will describe briefly some other types of constellation.

Constellations of the intra-psychic

In this type of constellation the emphasis is on setting up the inner aspects of the client, the split off parts or more fixed psychological functions. This is often an important starting point in a constellation where, in the initial interview, the client connects with some deep feeling that is beyond her normal range. I may then suggest she choose a person or a marker to represent this aspect of herself. For example, the feeling of grief or despair that she is experiencing. Then one can work with the constellation in the usual way, introducing other aspects, sometimes including system members who are identified as important.

Physical constellations

Also known as constellations of body components or functions, these constellations focus on a particular illness or physical

---

[48] There is some dispute about the use of the term 'autopoietic' in this way, since, in general systems theory, "an autopoietic system is autonomous and operationally closed" (Wikipedia), whereas in constellations we are always working with permeable boundaries, emergent phenomena and an oscillation between the macrocosm and the microcosm. However the term autopoiesis is from the Greek, literally meaning 'self-creation', which does not exclude relationship and exchange as part of the self-creation, and has been used in the constellations field for this kind of leaderless constellation.

dysfunction of the client. Insa Sparrer has developed what she calls the Body Constellation (2007) where individual body components: (organs, systems and functions) thought to be relevant are set up, along with, if required, representatives for outside intervention (medicines, medical treatment such as operations, chemo-therapy, and other interventions such as dietary change, homeopathy etc) as well as relevant family members. The notion here is to assist better communication between internal components, resulting in insight for the client. Another perspective on the physical or illness constellation is the notion that systemic family entanglements are replicated in the physical disability or illness of the client. One can think of illness as a systemic symptom in the same way as one can with psychological disturbance and problematic behaviour.

Problem-solving/solutions-focused constellations

These are similar but approached from different viewpoints. The problem-solving situation assumes that the problem can be solved or fixed, whereas the solutions-focused view states that the solution will have little or nothing to do with the named problem. The problem-solving view is therefore more backward (past) oriented while the solutions-focused view makes a solution the focus and is more forward (future) oriented.[49]

Enquiry constellations

These are often used in working with environmental, ecological, social and political dimensions where a resolution per se is unlikely, but increasing our understanding of the underlying dynamics is helpful and informative.

---

[49] The work of Sparrer (2007) and Varga von Kibéd has provided a primarily solutions-focused view and methodology to the constellation resulting in what they call the 'solution-focused systemic structural constellation' (SyST). Their work brings together their own structurally based method of working with constellations with the solutions-focused brief therapy work of Steve de Shazer, Insoo Kim Berg and the Brief Family Therapy Center in Milwaukee.

Structural constellations

I will go into this particular kind of constellation in a little detail because it will give you a sense of the variety of work being done within the domains of "systemic constellations". If you are not interested you can of course skip this section.

The structural constellation is in particular the work developed by Sparrer (2007) and Varga von Kibéd. It provides a structure of generic elements with which to set the constellation. Sparrer and Varga von Kibéd tend to decide in the initial interview (which is performed along solutions-focused principles) on the particular type of constellation to be done to meet the requirements of the client. Much of their work takes place in organisations[50] and the structured nature of the constellation provides a clearly understandable process that concurs with organisational needs. An example is what Sparrer calls the Problem Constellation, which requires the following elements:

The Focus: this is the term used for the client's representative. The word "focus" incorporates only that aspect of the client that is involved in the issue, there being other aspects of the client that are less so (for example, the role of the client as a husband is not considered relevant for an issue connected with his role as a team-leader)

The Goal: "with every problem, we must assume that there is a desired goal that cannot yet be achieved." (ibid)

Obstacles: of which there may be a number. If there were no obstacles one must assume that there would be no problem, nothing standing in the way of achieving the goal.

Resources: again, there may be one or several representatives. "In Systemic Structural Constellations, as with Solutions Focused Therapy, we start from the assumption that the client already possesses all the resources needed to solve the problem." (ibid)

Benefit: "the benefit is what is useful about the problem not yet having been solved." (ibid) What in the psychotherapy field we might call 'secondary gain'.

---

[50] This is by no means the only work Sparrer does since she has a psychological therapeutic background.

> **Future Task:** "After the goal has been achieved, there is normally a new task that needs to be performed." (ibid) Sometimes it is this future task that inhibits the person from taking the necessary step towards their goal.

Structural constellations work as well in the individual context as all other types of constellation. As such the solutions-focused constellations facilitator may resist or diminish the representatives' (and the client's) impulse to look back into the past.[51]

Autopoietic constellation

The autopoietic constellation was developed in Germany, I believe by Siegfried Essen[52], and is a free-form constellation with no outside intervention. Usually it is around a stated issue that everyone has some interest in. Relevant elements are brainstormed and then individuals take up the representation of whatever element they feel drawn to. The facilitator makes no interventions and may merely go from representative to representative (often with a microphone) to have them state their current experience. There is no specified goal/outcome/ resolution focus as such, exploration being the main purpose. The process continues for a specified time or until there is a sense of resolution, completion or nothing more can be done at this stage. Information that emerges is used to understand better the dynamics involved, each individual often finding something personally valuable in connection with the issue.

---

[51] There is a view here that a solutions-focused approach is a good approach for working with trauma as it persists in encouraging the client to focus on resources and what goes well, rather than slipping back into the trauma and potential re-traumatisation. However this entails the facilitator restricting any impulse on the part of client and/or representatives to move to the origins of entanglements in the system other than acknowledgement of its existence. This becomes part of the dispute referred to earlier (Footnote 26) as to whether the traumatised person does indeed need to re-visit and express the emotions of the trauma or not. It would seem in the solutions-focused approach that the view is not.

[52] Essen has nothing published in English on the subject, only in German.

Chapter 10

Movements of Being and Emotional Expression

There are two basic movements of being in life: towards engagement or away from engagement. In the work known as the 'interrupted reaching out movement' we are looking at the interruption of our natural inclination to move into engagement and relationship, to reach for the other, that initially occurs in the child's primary reach for the mother in the bonding process. Dependent on the success or disruption of this initial movement will be our ability to engage with ourselves, life and others generally. In her very intimate and subtle work, Ursula Franke observes very carefully the body language of the client as she asks in the interview about his mother or father. A slight movement back indicates a move of disengagement thereby the potential for disruption in that particular relationship. From this basic understanding of movement into or away from relationship we find two categories of emotional expression:

Primary Emotional Expression:

Primary emotional expressions are clearly expressed and not confused, they are means of engagement rather than avoidance. There is no ambiguity. Grief is clearly grief, fear is clearly fear, rage is clearly rage and love is clearly love. The person is fully in contact with herself and her need for expression; her emotional energy is in tune with this need and there is no effort involved. In addition she is able to make clear eye contact with another in a movement towards engagement, life and vibrant expression.

This kind of emotional expression is a healthy, natural part

137

of human existence. In many tribal cultures the necessary expression of emotion may be given formal recognition and space by ritual, as in collective keening which supports the grief-stricken person to allow their grief full and clear expression in the company of others. It is usual in these communal rituals for everyone to experience and express whatever residue of grief they are holding and share this together. This expression takes us with the person into the realm of their deep feelings. We, as the witnesses, are moved and understand in an embodied way what is being expressed as if it were our own; it is beyond words, it is pure, primal experience; in some cases there is a oneness of my experience of the other in this expression.

The properties of primary emotional expressions are:

- It enables the person to move on and allows for change.
- It is accompanied by a sutble inner movement forwards, towards engagement, which may be observable.
- The expression is strong, clear and is over quite quickly, rarely more than a few minutes.
- It flows freely, is voiced clearly and there is no sense of interruption.
- It is sometimes quite subtle as in a particularly deep breath or sigh and relaxation in the body.
- Expression arises from the belly rather than higher up in the body.
- The expression involves the whole body; the body becomes in the moment an integrated whole.
- It can be clearly defined as grief, anger, fear etc.
- The emotion expressed and the intensity of expression is situation-appropriate.
- Evokes resonance in witnesses; they may feel it as their own.
- Once expressed it is past and, while it may occur again, as for instance in the process of grieving, it is always different, satisfying and complete in each instance.
- It can not be forced or invoked.

- The person needs the right time, place and experience of support (both personal and environmental).

Secondary Emotional Expression

Secondary emotional expression avoids true contact with what is needed, and is usually a substitute for the primary expression. The feelings shown are ambiguous. Feelings such as frustration (instead of anger), depression (instead of grief), irritation or aggression (instead of rage), anxiety and panic (instead of terror); love is expressed as need, enthrallment or slavish loyalty; misery, petulance, self-pity, melancholy and endlessly welling tears are all typical secondary expressions of feelings. The experience is as if the feelings never resolve, never go anywhere and remain hopelessly entrenched and persistent. The person does not feel sufficiently supported to allow himself to feel the primary level of expression, it is too frightening or threatening. It is likely that the suppression of the primary expression is due to the full expression not having been allowed in the person's past; suppression has become a habit of the person, or of the system as a whole; or the experience of primary feelings takes him too close to his unconscious trauma, and is defended against vigorously. The person is not fully engaged with his feelings, avoids contact with himself and others. He will avoid real eye contact because in the moment of eye contact he would be unable to stay in the realm of the secondary emotions. The needed intensity of feeling is never reached. As witnesses we are usually untouched, often feeling distant, uninvolved and even impatient. Secondary emotional expression maintains the illusion that we can change the unchangeable. Anger is a specific example of this. Many years ago one of my early psychotherapy teachers said that anger was frequently an "instead-of emotion"; that we will often feel and express anger as a protection against feeling the primary feeling underneath. Anger is a high energy emotion and its true function is boundary setting and making change, but it also can foster the illusion that we can change things that in fact we cannot. This unconscious avoidance and delusion then becomes a systemic habit.

Case example 4

Some years ago I worked with a man who complained that his persistent anger and violent outbursts were threatening his relationship with his wife and his three daughters. He had a history of ending up alone as he rarely found anyone who would tolerate being with him for very long. He told me that he had done many years of therapy, anger management workshops and so on, and was rather sceptical that anything could help. As we talked more he said that his father had been a very angry and violent man himself and that his own childhood had been miserable and that he had never been able to connect with his father in any way other than through their arguments, rows and sometime physical violence. Presently he was having no contact with his father and only had contact with his mother sporadically and without his father's knowledge. At one point he said "I wish I could change my father". The next piece of information that emerged was that his father had been one of seven children and that *his* father had died suddenly when he was 6 years old. The children had been separated and had gone to live with different aunts, two of them remaining with their mother, neither of which had been my client. When we set up a constellation using markers, and I turned the marker for his father towards the marker for the grandfather, leaving a good distance between the markers to start with, my client sat for a very long time in silence. Eventually when I asked him what was happening he quietly said, struggling for the right words, "there's a kind of ... connection feeling." As he looked at the markers, and as I encouraged him to imagine what might happen should this miracle opportunity be possible, he sat still, obviously struggling with complex and unfamiliar feelings and emotions. It was clear in this constellation that anger in his father and in himself had become a systemic currency for the men for maintaining the illusion that the tragic situation of the loss of the grandfather could be avoided, and even magically changed. The mode of anger then becomes a habit of relationship in order to avoid the unresolved feelings of grief and loss.[53]

Properties of secondary emotional expression:

- Purpose is to defend person from feeling the deeper, primary feelings.
- Inhibits change and maintains stuckness.
- Is observable by a subtle movement away or of deflection, perhaps a slumped posture.
- Indicates unwillingness to experience deeper feelings.
- Expression never peaks and seems never-ending.
- Is not definable as a clear emotion such as grief, anger, fear, but is always a mix.
- Appears to originate high up in the body, often in throat, which may feel constricted.
- Does not seem congruent with the situation.
- Does not evoke resonance in witness; on the contrary evokes impatience and frustration.
- Is never quite finished, does not reach a satisfactory completion.
- Recurs, and feels and seems repetitive and endless.

[53] It is interesting to note here that, when working in an individual context with someone who perhaps is older and has already a lifetime of avoiding the unbearably painful feelings (a process that is of course unconscious), it may be a distraction to attempt to get them to take up a position on a marker and be a representative. Simply to sit with him while observing an unfamiliar configuration and invite him to imagine what would happen in this situation is enough. The reason is that the older one is the longer one has lived with the habitual perspective and experience, and often the less one can envisage any change. Such an individual might find it extremely hard to separate himself from his perspective enough to take up a valid representation.

As facilitators it is not helpful to fall into a trap of trying to force a person into a primary emotional expression. Instead, it is more helpful to understand that the full expression of the needed feeling is just too frightening for the person, and that they are not yet sufficiently supported to be able to do this. This must be accepted by the facilitator who can then focus on what support might be needed. Given sufficient support and the right circumstances usually the person will then be able to fully express what is needed. (For more on support see Box 5 below)

> **Box 5:** On Support
>
> **On support (1):** I have witnessed Ursula Franke work in a very graphic way with the issue of support for a client (she usually works with the actual client as opposed to the representative). She may stand right next to the client having established a distance from the issue (which might be a representative for the mother or father) that is comfortable for the client. This 'comfortableness' is experienced as being able to breathe easily, a sense of relaxation in the body, lowered heart rate and so on. She will then, standing next to and slightly behind the client, move forward with him, sensing each moment whether the client continues to feel free (ie supported enough) to move forward. The moment that the client contracts, stops breathing, tenses in his body she will stop with him, and work with what has arisen in the client until the client feels supported enough to make the next step. She continues supporting the client to make each step as it is within his capacity, until the full primary expression is possible.
>
> **On support (2):** Another way of working with support in the constellation is the use of abstracts, including a representative for 'loving support' or 'a loving ancestor who is not connected with this issue', or 'the help that is needed right now'. It is important to keep these abstract values clearly undefined as in the last example, since one cannot necessarily know what or who is actually going to be useful. To put in a client's mother or grandmother as 'support' may possibly lead the

constellation into greater confusion and more entanglement, whereas to introduce 'someone from this system who is not entangled in this issue and is able to love and support this client' allows the constellation the freedom to choose who from the system this might be. It is not unusual in this case for the representative or the client to know in the end who this represented person could be.

In workshops with Franz Ruppert I have experienced as a representative for 'love' in this way of working how, in the field of a severely traumatised and secretive system, I could only become the 'love that is possible within this system'. I experienced myself as dispirited, depressed, useless and unseen. At the time (2006) Ruppert was working with introducing abstract supports until such time as the system could feel strong enough to make the necessary move to expression. This was most common in constellations representing trauma of the whole bonding system (see Chapter 5) where the tension between expression and suppression was tremendous.

Daan van Kampenhout, the shamanist constellations practitioner, does a kind of structural constellation where he sets up representations for the present, representations for the time when the trauma happened and representations for the 'ancestors before the trauma' who, having not experienced the actual trauma, are always able to be supportive and loving to those who are suffering later.

A primary principle of solutions focused therapy and the work of Insa Sparrer and Matthias Varga von Kibéd is looking to what resources the client has and what is going well in her life. The focus of their work being that solutions do not necessarily have any relationship to the problem, and are more likely to appear when the client is in touch with her resources.

In the constellations process there is also the unique situation where a representative can experience and express primary feelings for a client who may not at that stage feel able to do so. My belief is that our interconnectedness and ability to empathise may allow the representative for the client and the client to enter a mutually resonant state. The representative may resonate with unexpressed physical and emotional aspects of the client, and the client experiences physical and emotional activity in resonance with the representative. This may be sufficient to move the client towards a fuller ability to express in the future. The service that the representative does for the client in this instance deeply connects the two in that moment. The ability for a client to have a representative express what she feels unable to express is one of the unique and invaluable aspects of the constellations process: to be able to witness another 'self' express what in the moment one cannot.

In the individual session in such a situation, I have found myself engaged in a primary emotional expression on behalf of the client while standing on a floor marker. This is not something that would happen very often, but it seems possible at times when the client and I have a particularly strong collaborative resonance with the work being done. It is not something I would prepare or plan, but something that I agree to in the moment.

Case example 5:

A client came because of persistent pervasive depression in her life. When she set up the constellation using floor markers, she piled them all on top of her marker, so that it was not visible. This graphically showed her experience of being in her family. The other markers we used were her mother and father, and one living, younger sister and one older, dead sister and her mother's mother. The marker that was immediately on top of hers was the older sister who had died aged 3 when the client was just four weeks in her mother's womb. The next one up was her grandmother, her mother's mother, who had died when the client's mother was only three years old, then her mother, her sister and her father:

144

Figure 9

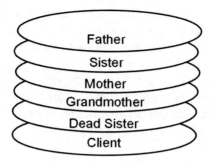

We discussed this initial image, which, she said, showed the rather controlling, tyrannical nature of her father. This image indicates that real contact between system members is unlikely, since contact needs people to have enough space between them to be able to see each other. This lack of contact represents one of the ways in which unresolved trauma is held in place: to look at anyone properly would involve real feelings, the trauma feelings, which are avoided at all cost.

So having seen this initial image and talked about it we could then spread the markers out so that they were separate, as if people as representatives could stand on them, thereby making contact more possible. I invited her to stand on her marker and see what that was like, and as she did so, I briefly stood on the other markers to give her a sense of there being an actual person there. As we moved on with the constellation there came a moment when I stood on her marker as she stood on that of her dead sister, both facing each other for the first time. In that moment I felt an enormous rush of emotion, so much so that I could not stop the tears that came and the deep intake of breath as I looked into the client's eyes as the long dead sister. She also, as her sister, could see and feel the experience. I then suggested she stand on her own marker and feel what, in effect, she had never been able to feel, which she did, while I stood as the sister. She said many things as herself to her

145

dead sister, her feelings of guilt and resentment for as long as she could remember, and her intense feelings of loss and unexpressed grief. I as the sister felt an overwhelming love and pleasure in seeing her, which I told her.

Conversely, the representative, freed of his or her own inhibitions and systemic prohibitions, can find a fluidity and pleasure in the expression of another's primary feelings that can be profound for him or her too.

Case example 6:

I ran a group very early on in my time as a facilitator and there was a man who was chosen frequently to be a representative since, as is often the case, there were not as many men as women in the group. He did not do a constellation and seemed very happy to participate as part of the holding circle and as a representative. Some weeks after the group, he wrote to me saying that he had found the experience profound. He had always experienced himself as cut off and unemotional, seeing other people's emotional expression as somewhat mysterious. He had been quite startled at his ability as a representative to feel strong emotions, had enjoyed these new experiences, and had since found that he was feeling and expressing more emotionally in his everyday life. This is a lovely example of the collaborative healing potential of the constellation, not just for the so-called issue-holder, but for everyone present.

In the individual session with a client who cannot breach his defences against true feelings and expression, I invite him to set up a marker for the part of him that holds all the unexpressed emotions, or the part of him that has to hold back from expression. The process of choosing a marker for this other part and placing it in the room often puts him more in contact with the actual feelings, sometimes even being enough to move him to a fuller expression.

146

There are two further modes of expression that need some elaboration.

Systemic Feelings

This is when a person experiences feelings that are rather more taken on from the system than actually their own. For example, if a woman's mother lost her brother very young and was not able to express the natural grief involved, and the woman was affected by this grief in bonding with her mother as an infant, she may all her life experience everything as tinged with grief. She may not express it herself as in a primary expression, but it is always there. In Case example 5 above, the client held within herself at the very least her own unexpressed grief at the loss of her unknown sister but also possibly the unexpressed grief of her mother at losing her own mother and her daughter. It is not uncommon, in my experience with people who frequently feel suicidal, that they are suffering from systemic feelings that have not had expression, sometimes two, three or even four generations back. Systemic feelings may also be expressed as primary or secondary emotions as described above.

Transcendental or Higher Consciousness Expression

We all have moments of transcendental, meta or higher consciousness feelings. These are the essential expressions of undiscriminating love, transcendent courage, unwavering trust, awe, reverence and wisdom. These feelings arise out of moments of deep interconnectedness with all things. For most of us they are fleeting, coming at moments of great insight, heart opening and absence of fear. If there is fear, there cannot be transcendent experience. "They are feelings without emotion." (Hellinger, 1997), "a sort of compassionate dispassion." (Francis, 2008) And: "Their function is to serve life selflessly." (ibid)

Chapter 11

Processes and Techniques: The Constellation as Experiment

As facilitators, we will have our own preferences as to how we see the constellations process, how we understand the dynamics of systems and therefore how we work with the constellation. This may depend on the nature of the context in which we are working (whether a personal issues workshop or in a coaching session with an organisational manager for example), and the nature of the issue at hand. Our approach and the context in which we work will guide us as to our facilitation style whether in a group or individual context: Are we more or less directive? Do we move the representatives or allow them to move themselves? Do we ask the representatives for information, or do we instruct the representatives not to speak? Do we intervene at all, or do we stay right outside the constellation? Are we, as facilitators, managers of the constellation (as one might be in a more organisational context where often confidentiality and sensitivity are more predominant, and concrete outcomes and tasks are required), or are we holders of the space where all things that need to are permitted to emerge? (See Chapter 12 for more on facilitator style.) All of this will influence how we use the following processes.

Working with the constellation can generally be divided into three different categories. (Sparrer, 2007)

- **Positional work** or "bringing order by re-arranging representatives" (Stam, 2006)
- **Testing hypotheses:** experiments and proposals
- **Process work** such as clarifying identifications, suggesting sentences and statements, rituals and so forth

In practice these three all often overlap, so that positional work may become a test, and a test, if successful, may become part of the process work. Any intervention made in the constellations process can be seen as an experiment, whether re-ordering the representatives, testing hypotheses or suggesting sentences and rituals: these interventions continually provides us with information that moves us to the next step.

Positional Work

In positional work the facilitator moves the representatives, and so takes a more directive approach. This is often used in less personally oriented work such as coaching, organisational and problem-solving/solutions-focused work. However, this more directive approach is applied by some facilitators in personal constellations and may at times be an essential component in individual contexts in the absence of people as resources for representation.

The primary purposes of moving the representatives are:

- To experiment with a new position which may support shifts in the dynamics of the constellation;
- To open the possibility of better contact between representatives;
- To re-order the elements according to a certain view of an image for a more healthy system (see diagram at the end of this chapter);

The idea that a constellation is always about reinstating that which has been missing, excluded or forgotten implies that the dynamics of the system have been to look away from that which it does not want to see, what or who it wishes to exclude or avoid. This then is the issue: what is it that no one wants to look at? Or one could say: what no one can bear to look at because it is too painful.

Therefore, with positional work the facilitator can keep this in mind and:

- invite the representative to look at what he avoids by turning him towards another representative or by bringing in another representative to be what or who is avoided;
- test to see what it is that people don't want to see by including an abstract marker for 'that which everyone wants to avoid';
- see what happens if two representatives are turned to face each other;
- see if moving a representative helps her, or anyone else in the constellation feel better;
- clarify an identification/entanglement (see below).

One definition of a resolution in the constellation is that point at which all representatives feel a sense of being in a good or 'right' place, usually accompanied with experiences of being able to breathe more easily, or by a deep exhalation. Re-ordering the representatives is one way of doing this. However, it is important to remember that re-ordering the representatives without the required testing and process work may jump over crucial steps which, if missed, may in the end undermine the possibility of the constellation having a lasting effect. On the other hand one can also say that what the client needs to do or experience that is missed this time, they may come back to at some point at a later date.

Even so, in some cases, for example in a problem-solving situation or if the client for some reason is emotionally constrained, and process work is not possible or easy, it can be useful to move directly to a possible resolution image by re-ordering the constellation's elements. This certainly can give a client a glimpse of a possible way forward, some different picture of what his life could be.

Testing Hypotheses and Experimentation

The constellation is a container for experimentation. The facilitator will have insights and hunches along the way that can be tested in the constellations process. The facilitator does not have to be 'right': the purpose of the test is to determine in what way the intervention was effective, all interventions having *some* effect, if only to tell you that you are on the wrong track. The facilitator can test their hypotheses by:

- Bringing in a person or element;
- Suggesting a representative say something to another representative;
- Moving a representative to a new position;

The effect can be assessed by checking if things feel better or worse for the representative(s).

Process Work

Process work helps the constellation move from tension towards release (resolution) and takes the form of suggesting sentences and/or rituals. "The aim is to initiate an inner movement in the representative [by] saying .. words to another representative, who hears ... " (Stam, 2005). This can also serve the purpose of testing a hypotheses (see above).

Ritual

The function of ritual is to embody an archetypal movement that reaches beyond our habitual frame of reference. Any ritual cannot truly be performed without the origins of the movement already being present. There has been a tradition within the constellations field since the early days of Hellinger's work, of introducing the ritual of bowing. In my view at times it has become a tyranny whereby a person is required to bow, however reluctantly, before another, without any sensitive understanding of the basis of their reluctance.

Resistance as such is not something to be pushed against and overcome. It is a signpost of some truth that needs to be recognised and heard by the facilitator; an indication to the facilitator that you are not asking the right questions or not making the right proposals in the right way. It makes no sense to suggest that someone bow before another unless the person's body is already forming the movement however subtly and unconsciously, and even then why suggest it? Why not let the client find their own gesture for themselves? If the person is not already at that point, the movement is hollow and meaningless and best not suggested.[54] Another profound ritual that I have witnessed in a constellation (again as a spontaneous need on the part of the person involved rather than anything directed or choreographed) is a movement to prostration. This can be a deeply spiritual movement of surrender to something greater, but is only that if it originates in the person, and I have indeed witnessed people do this.

Simple rituals come in the form of suggested sentences that powerfully state the *isness* of the actually situation. Some of these might be:

- 'Yes' – signifies agreement to what is now seen as the truth
- 'Please' – signifies a request for contact and connection
- 'Thank you' – signifies gratitude
- 'I agree' – signifies agreement to what is

The function of other ritual sentences is to:

- **Promote clarity:** example: You are my mother, I am your child.
- **Face a truth:** example: You are the only mother for me, I can have no other

[54] For those interested there is a debate in *The Knowing Field, (Issue 5, December 2004)* between Hunter Beaumont, Eva Madelung, Wilfried de Philipp and Jakob Schneider on the subject of bowing in the constellations work, where they confront their differences and explore in depth the purpose, efficacy and ethics of proposing this movement.

- **Confirm boundaries of fate:** example: that is your fate ... not mine
- **Confirm temporal order:** example: You came first, I came later.
- **Agree to things as they are:** example: this is how it is, I will make something good of my life even so in honour of me (or in honour of you, whichever is appropriate)
- **To change a previously unconscious, unhelpful movement into a new consciously chosen, more helpful movement:** example: now I will remember you in a conscious way by giving you a place in my heart

Ritual sentences are in one sense only as good as their result. They are usually short, clear and to the point, stating as simply as possible what is true. The way to know if a resolving sentence supports movement is by observing the effect on the saying and receiving representatives, and the constellation as a whole. If you are not sure you can ask both. If a sentence is clearly not effective you can ask the representative what would be true for her to say and take it from there.

Some sentences may turn into tests. For example, if you ask a representative to say something and he says it but without conviction, you can experiment with the following:

- Ask him what would be right for him to say right now – this will give you information
- Ask him to say the opposite – this will always clearly define what is important here.

Never think that because a sentence you have suggested has not had the desired effect that it was not useful ... often the representative will only know what is really true for him by being offered something to say that clearly isn't; this gives him a bench-mark by which he can know with more certainty what is right.

'Resistance': support & challenge in the constellation process

What is called 'resistance' is an attempt by the person to protect the safety and status quo of his position in the face of a challenge/risk that may seem too much for him, or in relation to a line of enquiry that instinctively he knows is wrong. In the first instance the client attempts to conserve a protective mechanism, which may have been a useful adjustment to a difficult past situation that perhaps he perceives in the present. In the second instance the subtle agreement or contract between the client and the facilitator is momentarily lost, and it is the facilitator's job to understand why this is. A client will always move towards what is growthful and creative, towards the integration of what has been split off or excluded, if she experiences sufficient support for her to make that movement. Support in either case requires something from the facilitator. If you are working with the client herself in a constellation and you suggest that she say something, and you meet with *strong* resistance you can understand one thing clearly: you are on the right track, so don't give up! If she tells you it does not feel quite right you can ask her what would feel right. But if she says forcefully "I can't say that" it must be interesting to explore this. Change the wording slightly or enquire about her reluctance. It is only a proposal after all. Why would she be so strongly reluctant if it did not have some relevance to her? Such enquiry will re-establish the facilitator/client good contract.

Support

In respect of the issues of support vs challenge, there is a simple equation:

$$\text{Stress} = \text{challenge with insufficient support}$$
$$\text{And}$$
$$\text{Challenge} = \text{stress with sufficient support}$$

In other words, in order to help someone to move on from an adaptation which may no longer be relevant, one has to look to increasing support. Once a person experiences sufficient support then the stress becomes a challenge to which she can feel equal. Essentially our experience of our family and ancestry should be of support to face the challenges of our life . . . our urge to disentangle ourselves from the entangled issues of our family is so that we can experience the support that we know should be possible from our roots and ancestry. As a facilitator you can always add support in the form of abstract markers or ancestors who "freely love and support this person".

Confrontation

One option, which *is* a strong confrontation, is to suggest the client say the opposite. For example:

> *Facilitator*: say to your mother "You are my mother, you're the only mother for me. I give up on my anger and my wish that you had been different." (This confronts the illusion that the client can have a different mother or that her mother will change, or could have been changed in the past.)
> *Client*: I can't say that . . . I won't say that . . . she failed me . . . I am angry with her."
> *Facilitator*: waits a while
> *Client*: I can't say that . . . she never loved me. . (and so on)
> *Facilitator*: okay, say to your mother: "I'll stay angry with you all my life, until I die, whatever the consequences for me and my life, my children and their children."

This will either produce a deep insight in the client, or strong reaction against you! Or both. Either way it will have initiated some understanding that cannot be put back in the box so to speak. It may take time, and fury with you is a means for the client to give herself the time and space to allow it to settle. This "settling" of something that obviously is so challenging may well take months, sometimes years. Best used judiciously and with experience!

'Rebellion'

> "The manifestly rebellious or delinquent child may actually
> be the most loyal member of a family."
> *Boszormenyi Nagy & Spark (1984)*

Jan Jacob Stam said in a workshop I attended that the rebellious person does something extraordinarily courageous and loving for the system: he risks being excluded for saying that which no one wants to hear, and he does this for the system. It is too simplistic to dismiss rebellion and rebellious action as a nuisance and "just making trouble". Far more useful and elegant to assume that something of what he is trying to say is essential, and to try to find a way to include it rather than, as the facilitator, be the instrument of exclusion. This follows Mahr's notion of 'radical inclusion', pursuing an insistence on continually including that which has been or is likely to have been excluded. Better to see it as symptomatic . . . a signpost to attend to.

Other 'Inclusions'

Representatives from the holding circle
The constellations process, if allowed to, has ways of making sure that all necessary elements are present for a resolution to be possible. One instance of this is where someone in the surrounding circle (not chosen as a representative) begins to have strong experiences that are different from how she was feeling prior to the start of the constellation. In my view it is helpful to include this person as somehow being relevant to the constellation. It will become clear in time just how important this representation is, and usually the process settles when the person is able to include whatever this experience is.

Role confusion
This is a situation where a representative seems to cover two roles, presumably because both are important and only one is currently represented. A representative for a person or

abstract quality has experiences and behaves in ways that are contradictory to the actual person or quality represented. This is most commonly seen with abstract representation, where for example a person represents a value such as 'unconditional love' and yet behaves in a contradictory manner: feels weak, sad and tearful for example. In this instance it is likely that the representative is covering two roles, the second one being someone or something that is missing in the constellation but may need to be included. The simplest thing to do is to bring in another representative or marker for the second role and state clearly that this second marker represents this other role. Stand these two next to each other and usually the situation will become clearer.

Identification
In the work of constellations we talk of a person being identified or aligned with another as way of thinking about entanglements that cause disturbance. For example, a representative seems to have a particularly close alignment with the representative for someone two generations earlier who suffered some trauma, or committed some crime, or experienced some other significant event. This is called an 'identification'. Very often the later representative will seem to be held in a kind of fixed trance of connection with the earlier representative, and the reported experience often confirms this: "he is the only person I can see or am interested in".

One way of working with this is to bring the later representative closer to the earlier, so that they can really see each other. The idea of this movement is that when they really see each other it will startle the later transfixed representative out of the trance. Suggesting statements of truth is helpful (eg "your fate is different from mine" or "I have held a strong but unconscious connection with you, now I remember you consciously"), or letting the two representatives say whatever they feel a need to say to each other, watching carefully to see if the transfixed representative seems to become more present.

Another way of working with this is to take the later representative right up to the earlier representative and then quickly turn her around to face where she has come from. This movement has the effect of startling the representative out of the trance[55]:

Figure 10

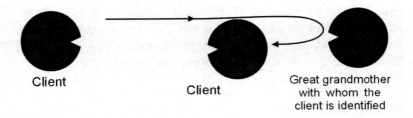

Client

Client

Great grandmother
with whom the
client is identified

In both of these methods it is possible to use the client herself if the later representative is the client's representative.

[55] I believe this technique was originated by Insa Sparrer and Matthias Varga von Kibéd.

Figure 11:   Diagram of Hypothetically Ordered Constellation

Below is a diagram that gives a general image of the order in families as oriented through time.

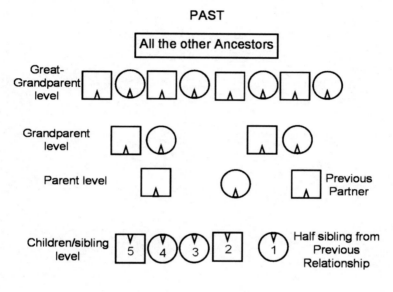

This shows the basic temporal ordering from past to future and from right to left.

While this seems to be generally how things are, it is always important to test it with the constellation as quite often they are not. This can only be used as a generalised framework that often has exceptions.

Section IV

Further Considerations of Practice

Chapter 12

Facilitation: Style and Intention

> "I don't go further than my inner guidance allows me ... On that basis of deep mutual respect and love, something can flow between the client and the therapist. There is no actual difference between them. They are on the very same level all the time." *Hellinger (2001)*

The first thing to say about the facilitation of constellations is that the business of becoming a facilitator is an ongoing and open-ended process, a journey that is never finished, and the best facilitators are acutely aware of their possible limitations and continuing capacity for learning something new. One very experienced facilitator I know, when asked recently by a student "How long does it take to become good at this work?" answered: "Ten years". In some ways this seems a fairly arbitrary answer; excellent work will happen along the way, as well as perplexing and disappointing work, and even the most experienced practitioner will miss things at times, feel more connected or less connected at times, and will always be learning. Although 'ten' is an arbitrary number, 'ten years' is a good answer in that it clearly emphasises the need to persist and not expect to be able to be confident and eloquent in a short time. It expresses the fact that, as with anything really worth doing, true expertise and accumulated experience only come with time. That 'ten years' can be an extraordinary journey of personal discovery and growth, a persistent immersion in the river of learning. Very effective constellations will take place during that time and within the learning facilitator's limits. Like many things, the first constellations an aspiring practitioner facilitates will often work very well indeed, which is encouraging! It is worth the novice remembering that in general, the representatives in a group really want to help the facilitator find a good resolution, and they will work very hard to do so, so listen to them very carefully.

Over the years of witnessing the work of Bert Hellinger it has been possible to see him move from a more interventionist, directorial approach. Increasingly, having set up the constellation, he waits for the movement to emerge, intervening only when he feels in tune with the deeper motives of the constellation. This is a shift from a stance of the facilitator being in charge, more or less directing the process of the constellation to a conclusion, to a stance where the facilitator intervenes as little as possible, and the constellation itself seems to be in charge, for the most part finding its own way to its conclusion.[56]

The extremes of on the one hand a strongly directing style and on the other a less or non-directing style are, of course, rarely taken up as absolutes by anyone. Rather a facilitator will have a preferred overall position on this continuum, but will be flexible in relation to what is possible in the moment: the context and the possibility. A facilitator's style, therefore, is mediated by two things: the temperament and overall philosophical preference of the facilitator, and the here-and-now circumstances the facilitator faces.

---

[56] I am reminded as I write this of a quote attributed to the gestalt therapist Laura Perls, the wording of which may not be quite right but goes something like this: *Give [the client] as much support as necessary and as little as possible.* This is a beautiful piece of guidance on the balancing of therapist intervention so it doesn't become interference.

For the purposes of understanding these styles I am going to explore the more extreme ends of the spectrum, and would invite you to reflect on your own movements, preferences and choices.

A More Directive Mode

A more directive, intervening approach tends to maintain control over what happens in the constellation, thereby it seems requiring the facilitator to trust her own hypotheses rather more than the impulses of the constellation. If she 'holds' her role too tightly, the representative information begins to become more mediated by what the facilitator permits; in some cases representatives are only 'allowed' to speak when the facilitator asks them for information; they quickly 'learn' when to speak and what to speak. The more directive facilitator often moves the representatives herself in tune with her view of what is necessary. Any attempts to make a contribution by someone from the holding circle may be seen as coming from that person's own material and may be rejected by the facilitator as having nothing to do with the constellation or as likely to confuse the issue.

In an individual setting this kind of facilitation may involve the facilitator moving the representative pieces, saying all the statements that in the opinion of the facilitator need to be said, and may at its most extreme, result in the facilitator presenting the client with the 'resolution' as deemed by the facilitator.

In terms of the language of radio technology, this approach views the constellation as having a high static (interference) to signal (pure sound) ratio. What then is clear is that someone (usually the facilitator) has to be in charge of deciding what is interference and what is signal. This stance is at risk of conveying an attitude on the part of the facilitator that is less trusting of the process, and a desire to reduce confusion and uncertainty. It allows her to stay in charge and control of what happens.

There may be advantages to this at times, but as a general stance I do not believe that this honours the full potential of the constellations process. An advantage could be said to be that the facilitator is likely to be able to ensure a 'good outcome' for the client. In general I personally would prefer not to be the one to decide on what a 'good outcome' is for another. However, it is also true that in certain very complex and difficult cases, this may seem necessary.

In the individual setting our resources in terms of representative experience are somewhat restricted and time is usually limited.[57] If the client is unable to be open to the representative process for whatever reason (and this does indeed happen) then as a professional facilitator in that instance one may feel that one has a responsibility to help the client find something useful, and we can do this by taking a more directive approach.

One way is simply by re-ordering all the elements in the constellation into a meaningful configuration. This might be where, in a group, for example, all representatives have some feeling of improvement. In the individual session it is possible to invite the client to re-order the markers into a configuration that feels right to him. From this he may understand better some of the movements and processes that might be necessary in time. Or the facilitator might re-order the markers according to some suitable ordering (such as in the diagram at the end of the previous chapter), inviting the client to consider the effect of seeing this new image in himself. This movement to what we might call a possible solution picture can be very helpful to a client, giving him an idea of what he can, in time, move towards.

The problem, I think, with a more interventionist approach is that the more the facilitator controls the process, the more she needs to be the person who knows what to do and has the answers; and the more she puts that kind of pressure on herself, the more she needs to control the process. There is a danger here of a potential spiral of tyranny (to facilitator and

---

[57] One has, after all, to keep to appointments in a busy day!

client, and, in the group, to the representatives). It can invite unpleasant things such as representative rebellion, where the representatives do not feel properly valued and heard by the facilitator. This may result in the representatives discon-necting from the process, and the facilitator then having to take even more control. The energy in the constellation in this kind of situation can end up feeling lifeless and pointless. In the individual session this may result in the client resigning himself to the facilitator's processing of his issue, which is not likely in the end to be helpful to the client.

Advantages:
- Allows the facilitator to maintain control over the process of the constellation which may in certain circum-stances be useful;
- Can be helpful in some difficult and intractable circum-stances especially when the constellations process doesn't seem able to find its own way;
- Can be helpful to find a 'good solution' that will help the client, or give him an idea of what he might be moving towards.

Possible Disadvantages:
- Relies more on the facilitator's own concepts and hypotheses rather than allowing for what the facilitator may not consciously know;
- May result in the representatives 'learning' what is and what is not acceptable to the facilitator as information they provide;
- May result in the client's motive and issue being lost or superseded by the facilitator's hypothesis;
- The facilitator is likely to become the 'author' (and thereby the 'authority') of the constellation;
- May miss the creative and collaborative possibilities of the constellations process.

A Less Directive Mode

The less directive mode is more challenging for the facilitator. While it gives the facilitator the space not to know the answers, it also requires a high degree of trust in the process and a willingness and ability to be extremely patient, tolerating uncertainty, confusion, not-knowing and risking seeming incompetent. It involves surrendering authority to the client, the representatives and the constellations process, at the same time holding the space for this to unfold.

In this mode, to return to the radio analogy above, the facilitator assumes a high signal to static ratio ... in other words whatever happens in the constellation is signal and to be noticed, valued and included. It requires us to remain open to the possibility that there is little that happens that is not relevant. To restate Mahr: "The healing potential of the constellation is increased by our ability to include that which has been excluded."[58] (See Chapter 4) This mode assumes intelligence beyond our own, a more collective and collaborative intelligence, and can support the more powerful and autonomous movements in the constellation.

To quote Ruppert:

> "A principle of systemic therapy says that the system is its own best descriptor and holds the potential for its own self-preservation as well as any appropriate adjustment to environmental conditions. A constellation in this sense can be seen as its own focused systemic description of a client. Constellations can thus find solutions in the most complicated emotional entanglements, *which even a very experienced therapist would not be able to suggest to his client. However, it requires a great deal of patience on the part of the facilitator not to follow his own ideas immediately, but to give the constellation the time it needs to get to the heart of the problem and then to find a way out.*" (my italics) *(2008)*

---

[58] Verbal teaching.

This approach allows the constellation to unfold with minimal intervention by the facilitator, assuming that "constellations can ... find solutions in the most complicated emotional entanglements ..." (ibid). But in essence the facilitator stays mostly in the background, venturing only into the foreground if the constellation cannot resolve its own 'stuckness'. To quote Ruppert again:

> "The intervention of the therapist, who is outside the system, is necessary to expand the system by including those elements that need to be seen to provide the total context within which the problem first arose. He also has to intervene when he sees that the system has caught itself up in a paradox that it cannot resolve by itself." (ibid)

The representatives move and interact spontaneously, the client observes, and the facilitator intervenes if the energy in the constellation runs into the sand. At such points an intervention might be to ask the client for comments or more information, or to invite the representatives to experiment with different placings, or to suggest simple condensed phrases capturing the situation as it is in that moment.

The facilitator – with all senses alert - may stay physically outside the constellation for most of the time, even sitting down throughout. When the vital connection point for the client is reached, the facilitator may help to recap and brighten the awareness of what the constellation has shown, at the same time allowing for the movement of emotional energies to sink in for the client.

In this style, the facilitator holds the space in such a way that the constellation itself is treated as an external, coherent intelligence, using the facilitator and the group as it needs. The facilitator and the group work as one together in the service of the constellation, and the locus of responsibility for the outcome lies more within the constellation than within the facilitator.

Advantages:

- Allows for responses, experiences and possibilities that lie outside the consciousness of the facilitator. For example the constellation can tell the facilitator what support is needed in a particular situation via the representatives' information;
- Good chance that all representatives will say what needs to be said on behalf of the person they represent, and at the end of the constellation, will feel complete;
- Good possibility of including all significant aspects of the client's field (radical inclusion);
- Easier for representatives to trust what comes up within themselves, to be spontaneous and take the initiative;
- The creativity and collective intuition and wisdom of the group is more supported and so more available;
- Abstract qualities that are represented are free to change into a more accurate version of what fits in the constellation, for example, becoming an important missing person of the system;
- 'Resistance' can be more easily seen and respected as a creative adaptation to an impossible situation as it was.

Possible Disadvantages:

- Constellation process may take more time;
- Over-dramatic representatives may dominate and obscure the core issues. However, if one works with Mahr's notion of radical inclusion one may assume intuitive coherence of the choice of representative ... i.e. they represent someone who also was dramatic;
- High degree of trust and tolerance of uncertainty required by the facilitator which does need experience and courage;
- Possibly a constellation that seems rather chaotic, and which may involve more entanglements emerging, particularly with an inexperienced facilitator;
- Representatives may feel freer to act out what they feel physically, which may threaten boundaries and safety of

participants (See Chapter 7 for explicit contracts for boundaries in the group);

- Participants without prior experience of being a representative in a constellation may initially find the process confusing;
- Greater risk of missing dissociative behaviour and re-traumatisation of a representative, particularly if facilitator is less experienced.

The really creative possibility of this less directive approach is that the constellations process can fulfil the rich potential of becoming a collaborative, co-created process where everyone, client, representatives, holding circle and facilitator are involved and changed by what happens, and where the whole can draw on the emergence of a collective wisdom.

In the individual context it is surprising how much one can do the same. You might think that, with only oneself and the client present, it would be much harder to find these autonomous nuances of systemic integrity and intelligence in the field of the emerging constellation. However, in my experience it is all there and available to the client and the facilitator. Of course one has to be patient, and willing to trust oneself and the client, and the powers that urge for movement, emergence and change. If you can be truly collaborative with the client, rather than authoritative over the client, you will both find the way.

At the end of this book (Appendix 3) is a chart listing the qualities, requirements, dangers and difficulties of these two polarities. It is important to remember that they are polarities, and that no facilitators are fixed in any position.

A Complex Web of Relationships

It might be instructive, if perhaps a bit daunting, to look at the multiplicity of relationships in which a facilitator is involved, as seen from the facilitator's perspective. I include this to remind us of the extreme complexity of the field in which we are working. In the moment with the client, all of this is in the ground.

Figure 12   Diagram Showing the Complex Web of Relationships
in which a Facilitator is Engaged

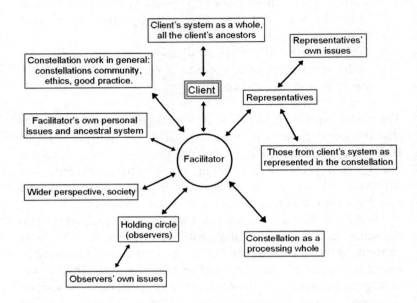

Summary of what constitutes the requirements of a good facilitator:

- An increasing and constantly evolving understanding of the principles involved
- A phenomenological attitude, focusing on what is actually there more than hypothesis
- A persistently inclusive approach
- An approach of judgemental restraint
- An attitude of interpretative restraint
- A willingness for and tolerance of uncertainty, not-knowing and confusion
- An attitude of intelligent innocence
- An approach that supports collaboration and co-operation
- A diminished need to be right

- A continuing aspiration for humility and the capacity to remain reflexive through ongoing personal and professional learning and development

This takes us to the next chapter which is based on Hellinger's orders of helping, his views on what it takes to be a facilitative helper.

Chapter 13

The Orders of Helping

*"Actually I am not a therapist ... I am ... a philosopher,
and therapy and helping is for me 'applied philosophy' – not
any kind of philosophy of course, but philosophy in service
of life." Hellinger (2003)*

As an extension to his development of the basic orders or principles of systems and the orders of love, Hellinger developed what
he called the orders of helping. This is a collection of principles
addressing the stance of those who put themselves forward as a
'helper' to others, such as psychotherapists, counsellors,
coaches, social workers and constellations facilitators. What
follows are the basic orders of helping with some excerpts from
Hellinger's paper (2003) to help with understanding.

Helping

It is natural and healthy for us to want to help; it is part of our
interdependence with each other and all life. The experience
of empathy and the move to help is innate. However, helping
is also a process of giving and receiving that requires
balancing out. If I help you, you are likely to feel in debt to
me and I may for a while feel superior to you. You may feel
guilty at your inability to redress the balance and may end up
hating me. I, in turn, may continue to feel superior to you and
in order to protect my sense of innocence and superiority I
may prevent you from helping me, and I may hate you for
that. It is in the end better for our relationship if you are able
to do something for me that in some way balances out the

transaction. And I must welcome the opportunity to take from
you, then we can remain friends.

In certain instances this possibility is limited, such as
between parents and children, between those who care for
those who are in some way unable to care for themselves, and
between professional or charitable helpers and those they help.
In these instances the helping impetus can for the most part
only be in one direction. What our parents give us is too great
for us to return and it denigrates the gift if we try. A child
then can do two things in this relationship: he can receive
what is given as it is with gratitude, and he can pass the gift
on to his children. In addition the child may give to the parent
when they are elderly, which again is not reciprocated in kind
by the parent. In the other instances this also holds: those in
receipt can only receive with gratitude and thanks, and pass it
on in whatever way they can, for instance in the case of charitable work by making the best possible use of the gift and
passing the benefit on to others.

giving
↓
receiving

So we can see that there are two levels to giving and
receiving: one is reciprocal and one is not. In some ways the
second is the greater while at the same time requiring a great
deal of both the giver and the receiver. The receiver has to
consent to receiving with gratitude and give up on their need
to repay and reciprocate. The need to repay and reciprocate,
if not relinquished, can lead to bitterness, resentment and
hatred. The giver has to see her giving as part of something
much larger than herself, and then she can stay steady, with
her feet on the ground, and not succumb to grandiosity, self-
importance and a patronising attitude.

These Orders of Helping are directed particularly towards
those in the helping professions.

1. We can only give what we have and can only expect what we need.

We cannot give anyone more than we are, which is all that we
have. To try to do so is not respecting ourselves and those we

173

are trying to help. Knowing one's limits in terms of the following helps with knowing what we can give:

- My own self-understanding and self-awareness, what and who I am;
- My place within the systems of which I am a member (both family and professional);
- Clearly understanding and seeing what is possible in each situation and respecting that.

To try and do more results in the following:

- The helper becoming entangled with the client thereby prolonging the process;
- Helper burn-out and exhaustion which exacerbates the entanglement as the boundaries between helper and client become blurred;
- The client being infantilised and further enmeshed in their difficulties.

2. Helping can only go as far as circumstances permit.
A realistic sense of the systemic and personal possibilities of the client, together with the wider contextual and historical realities, indicate what is permitted in any given situation. To try to go further is a waste of time and energy and arises from grandiosity on the part of the helper and a disrespect of the client.

3. Helpers must confront their adult clients as adults and refrain from becoming substitute (better) parents.
It is seductive for helpers to think that they can do a better job than the parents, immediately entangling the helper in an infantilising attitude to the client. Many clients will look to their helper to supply what they long for from their parents and it is up to the helper to avoid this temptation.

"Many helpers remain caught in the transference and counter-transference of the child and parent relationship and create a situation where it is more difficult for the client to leave his parents and also difficult to leave his helper." *Hellinger (2003)*

What is required here is a stance of creative impartiality, where the helper stays in a place of creativity and interested indifference, with an insistence on seeing the person as an adult even if she behaves with the helper as a child. The facilitator internally agrees to the parents and the family system as it is with respect and humility regardless of what the client tells her about them.

4.   The Helper's empathy must be systemic not personal.
The helper consistently holds an empathic relationship with the system-as-a-whole and is therefore never divisive and always inclusive. The helper's seeing of the client includes all that is of the client-system and never the client in isolation from this.

5.   Loving each person as he or she is, no matter how different he or she may be from me.
This is a stance of restraint of judgement, which allows the person to be as he is within the limits of his system. It is probably impossible for anyone to be completely non-judging. We are after all making assessments and appraisals all the time, so it is more helpful to be aware of this process in ourselves and practise restraint.

Ways of Seeing

Hellinger also talks about the maintenance of these orders requiring a certain kind of 'seeing'. This 'seeing' is applicable in all our work as facilitators:

Observation

This mode of seeing is the faculty used in science and technology. It engages the intellect and our qualifying and quantifying faculties.

> "Observation is sharp and exact and focused on details. Because it is so exact, it is also restricted. It misses the surrounding picture, both up close and more distant." *(ibid)*

Perception

Perception is softer and less concerned with detail but sees detail within its context. It is a mode of apprehending by means of the senses of the mind. It is less of the intellect but not without it. Perception is about understanding and comprehension.

> "Perception keeps its distance. It demands space. Much is perceived at the same time because there is an overview and an overall impression can be gained." *(ibid)*

Insight

Insight grows from observation and perception. It is more of the body than the mind, being understood as more of a gut understanding.

> "Without observation and perception there could be no insight ... insight without observation and perception remains without any reference point." *(ibid)*

Intuition

Intuition is the direct perception of truth, independent of any reasoning process. It transcends rational scrutiny, is born out of a connection with the whole, with something larger.

> "[intuition] is related to insight, resembles it but is not the same. Intuition is a flash of insight into the next step. Insight is often shared and understands the context as a whole ... Intuition recognises the next step and thus is more precise." *(ibid)*

176

Accordance

This is a resonance with what is, and an agreement to things as they are.

"Accordance is perception from within and is all embracing ... it is focused on action, primarily .. helping action. It demands that I resonate with the [other] that I am on the same wavelength, and understand him or her in this way." *(ibid)*

"Because I am in accordance with [the client] I leave my own intentions behind me, my judgements and my super ego, what it desires and what it thinks. ." *(ibid)*

"I become in accordance with me [sic] and with others. And others can come into accordance with me without losing a sense of themselves or needing to be afraid of me. I too remain in myself. I don't surrender myself to him [sic]. I keep my distance and space while being in deep accord with him [sic]. Because of this I am aware of exactly what I am able to do and what is appropriate to do in order to help." *(ibid)*

"So accordance is fleeting. It lasts only as long as helping action lasts. Afterwards each of us can again move to their [sic] own tune, in their [sic] own particular way. So with accordance there is no transference or counter-transference, no so-called therapeutic relationship, no taking over of responsibility for another. Everyone remains free." *(ibid)*

Chapter 14

Keeping Safe: Understanding Trauma Processes in Your Work

Whether one works directly with trauma as the underlying issue of systemic entanglement or not, it is as well for a facilitator to have an understanding of trauma processes, post traumatic stress disorder symptomatology and the signs and symptoms of potential re-traumatisation.

It is just as possible for a representative to suffer a re-triggering of their own trauma as it is for a client to be re-triggered, and it helps if the facilitator is aware of what to look for and strategies for management in the group or individual session. Even in organisational work, there is the potential for people to be close to their own trauma experiences; and it is in the nature of the trauma process that the person is unlikely to be aware of this possibility. They will just be aware of an extreme discomfort, which, naturally, they will engage all their resources to suppress, keep hidden and defend against.

It needs to be understood that our trauma is traumatising ... just as our fear is frightening and our terror terrifying, and we are all more likely than not to steer well clear of our own internalised actual trauma experience or that which we have inherited. This has led to what Ruppert, in his book on working with trauma and constellations has called a cultural 'trauma blindness' (2008, p. 105, quoting Riedesser, 2004). This is where, due to the psychotherapist's, facilitator's or social worker's own unconscious sense of their internalised trauma, and their resultant reluctance to go near it, they in turn are blinded to the trauma in their patient, client or client-family. In my view this is why, as workers with the emotional and psychological processes of human beings, it has taken us so long to embrace an understanding of trauma processes in a really constructive and helpful way. In spite of, for example, the massive collective and individual trauma experience in the first world war, a war that shook the world in its terribleness, it is really only in the last twenty years or so that we have developed the beginnings of good trauma theory.

Pat Barker's Regeneration Trilogy (1990-1995) records in a work that is generally a fiction the real work of Dr W H R Rivers, neurologist and psychiatrist, with "neurasthenia" (shell-shock) victims during the First World War[59]. However it was only in the 1970's that the term "post-traumatic stress" came to be formally recognised, and was included in the DSM II (Diagnostic and Statistical Manual Version II). For many people who have lived with what we now would call PTSD (Post Traumatic Stress Disorder) for many years without diagnosis and helpful treatment it has been a long time coming.[60]

War trauma is a particular subject on its own, involving perpetrators, victims and bystanders, carers, whole communities and nations. The return to civilian life presents countless potential incidents for re-traumatisation, along with the reali-

[59] The two English 'war poets', Siegfried Sassoon and Wilfred Owen, were both patients of Rivers. Sassoon was referred to Craiglockhart Hydropathic Hospital where Rivers was working, by the authorities who judged him unfit for service. He was treated for neurasthenia. Sassoon's deepening depression at the horror and misery he saw in active service completely influenced his later poetry. Owen was also sent to Craiglockhart for shell shock having been trapped in a shell hole for three days in the battlefields. He met Sassoon at the hospital who had a profound influence on him and his work. He was killed in battle one week before the end of the First World War. (Wikipedia)

[60] As evidenced by a programme aired on Australian Radio in 2004 "All In The Mind", when Vietnam war veteran Ted Fish states that he had not heard of post traumatic stress disorder until 2000 when he realised he had suffered from it for over 30 years. For a very moving transcript of this programme go to http://www.abc.net.au/rn/allinthemind/stories/2004/1214098.htm.

sation that what has equipped one for action and survival in war in no way equips one for civilian life. Indeed the continuing hyper-vigilance, emotional control and habitual preparation for ambush, horror and death translates ordinary events into terrifying re-visitations.[61]

There are two books that I would recommend that deal with post traumatic symptomatology and processes, and propose useful ways of working: Waking the Tiger by Peter Levine (1997) and The Body Remembers by Babette Rothschild (2000). In Appendix 2 I have offered some brief notes extracted from Rothschild's book on working with PTSD. (Work that takes place with the originally traumatised person is generally known as post traumatic work, and the condition is formally referred to as Post Traumatic Stress Disorder (PTSD) (DSM IV 2004). For more information on PTSD see Appendix 1)

As a facilitator, whether in a group or in an individual setting, it is as well to have some knowledge of what to look out for and what to do in a situation where someone is re-triggered into their trauma. Many organisations suffer from collective trauma due to events within the organisation such as redundancies, badly handled hirings, firings, promotions and demotions ... and larger organisational events that have big personal impacts such as mergers, bankruptcies, closures etc. In addition many top managers and CEO's carry inherited and/or personal trauma, which may strongly influence their leadership style and effectiveness. It would, I imagine, be useful for people who work with organisations at the very least to have some understanding and ability to recognise trauma symptomatology. Perhaps at times an organisational consultant's business is lost or confused because of a lack of understanding of trauma in the people he works with.

---

[61] For more understanding of the insidious effects of war trauma on those who survive and those around them I would recommend Jonathan Shay's book *Odysseus in America: Combat Trauma and the Trials of Homecoming (2002)*

Following is a kind of First Aid memoir that in my opinion is the minimum that you need to have in your kitbag.

How to Recognise Trauma Reactions

Both Levine (1997) and Rothschild (2000) emphasise the importance of trauma state recognition. In their work, a major strategy is to help the client become more aware of the symptomatic experiences that she has, not just interpreted as "panic" or "extreme anxiety" but with a good understanding of the phenomena involved, for example heart rate, breathing etc. The intention is that she will be more able to manage the symptoms of arousal if she knows what they are and can recognise them in her experience before a major hyper-aroused state is reached. They focus on the following main symptoms, which broadly come under the term hyper-arousal:

- Rapid breathing
- Increased heart rate (rapid beat or pounding heart)
- Increased blood pressure
- More dilated pupils
- Pale skin colour
- Increased sweating
- Cold skin – possibly clammy
- Decreased ability to digest food

Some of these you may observe, and others, such as increased blood pressure and decreased ability to digest food, you will not.

I have translated these into symptoms that you might easily see:

- Person has a glazed, unfocused look
- A degree of dissociation from the present circumstances, they don't answer questions or responses are delayed
- You may have a sense of not being able to connect with the person

- The person may be either hyperventilating (exaggerated breathing) or holding their breath and seeming not to be breathing at all (frozen response)
- The person looks frozen and is unresponsive or
- The person may be agitated and obviously anxious

And those you may not be able to see, but may be able to ascertain by asking the person:

- Dizziness
- Pounding heart (you can of course feel the person's pulse)
- Nausea
- Fearfulness
- Anxiety or panic

Do not be afraid of stopping the constellation for a few minutes while you check the above. This will reassure you and the group (if working in a group) and the person involved. The constellation process is always robust enough to tolerate such an interruption.

In extreme (dangerous) hyper-arousal Rothschild cites the following differing pictures which are combinations of very high activation of the SNS (Sympathetic Nervous System) and the PNS (Parasympathetic Nervous System):

- pale skin or reduced colour, cold sweat, slow heartbeat;
- widely dilated pupils with flushed colour;
- slow heartbeat with rapid breathing;
- very slow respiration with fast heartbeat.

These are what we might call "red flag" situations. Action is needed and quickly, and the facilitator may have to be quite strong in his insistence on the person staying in contact and in the present. This is because the re-traumatisation process projects the person back into the original situation (if a personally experienced trauma) quite dramatically and to quite a high degree. Very often in a re-traumatised state the person will close her eyes, which makes her projection back to the trauma very strong as it increases her dissociation with the present reality. The important thing therefore is to keep her in the present as much as you can, and demand that she keep her eyes open. Check with her what she can see and if she can hear you.

How to Proceed

If the person is a representative:

Pause the process, stand in front of him and speak to him directly using his name. Ask him if he is okay. If the effect you are noticing is to do with the person represented the person will come out of his role straight away and be able to answer you and reassure you. It is sometimes useful in particularly difficult representations to ask the person if he can hold the experience, or even say that you have seen the distress and he does not need to express it any further, in which case he will just act normally. If you feel worried about the situation or the person, if you don't feel reassured by him, just take him right out of the constellation, tell everyone else in the group to sit down and that you will come back to the work as soon as you are certain everything is okay. When you are satisfied that the person is alright you might choose to continue the constellation with another person in his place. As we know, it is very often the case that representatives are chosen to represent people with whom they have some resonance in their own system, and so it is not unusual for the trauma of the person represented to also resonate with the representative's trauma. However usually this is quite manageable by the above procedures.

If the person is the client:

Stop the constellation, ask everyone to sit down and pay complete attention to the client. Help her stay present with you, keeping her eyes open, and encourage her to feel her feet on the ground, and the weight of her body in the chair.

Try and engage her in conversation, inviting her to tell you what is happening. Speak in an every-day voice and keep checking that she stays present and connected with you. After she has recovered it may be important in a group to just stay aware of her for a while and check on how she is doing. It might be necessary to discontinue her constellation at this time.

The potential for re-triggering of trauma of the client himself, whether in a group or individual setting, is a particular case in the sense that the trauma experience, whether his own or inherited, needs in some way to be revisited to become integrated. This revisiting may incur strong emotional experiences, which, in the group, may be expressed by the representative, but in the individual session will be for the client to experience, and he needs to feel psychologically held and contained in this by the facilitator. This would be by helping him to stay in contact and present in the here-and-now rather than getting lost in the original experience. The danger with re-triggered personal trauma (as distinct from an inherited trauma) is that the person re-experiences the event as if he is still in it. The way out is to experience the feelings while at the same time knowing that he is not back in the event, a kind of more dissociated experience. This needs to be done slowly and carefully, continually maintaining contact with the present situation. This is an instance when the facilitator's style might move quickly down to the more directive end of the spectrum in order to keep the client safe (see Chapter 12).

Chapter 15

Trust & Truth

"Question always and doubt deeply, especially your own
motives." *Krishnamurti*

"My freedom to take risks is a function of my trust in the
other, and it brings us both great rewards."
Hellinger (1998)

'Trust': to allow without fear[62]

Trust is the facilitator's greatest resource and her greatest
challenge: to allow something without fear or need of control.

Trust as a way of being and working, only comes with
experience, and fluctuates according to our ability to be
present, collected and internally quiet. Trust is of oneself and
of the other, and of the process, and is well illustrated by an
exercise that Jan Jacob Stam did at the end of a 3-day workshop I attended: everyone in the room moved around and met
up with someone. They stood in front of each other and each
one said to the other:

"I honour you ... and I honour me ...
I honour what guides you ... and I honour what guides me."

Hellinger writes:

"This kind of love is the basis for respect. I respect a person when
I tell her, 'I love you – and that which guides me and you. I love
you exactly as you are, because I see what guides you and me.'
And for self-respect, it is the same. I look at myself exactly as I
am and say, 'Yes, I love myself - and that which guides me.'"
(2001)

Trust of myself must go hand in hand with trust of the other.

---

[62] Dictionary definition: WordNet® 3.0. Princeton University

The two must meet and affect each other. My trust in myself must be tempered by my trust in the other. It helps no one when I trust myself more than the other. That route can lead to grandiosity and control. I must trust the other even when it seems that everything the other does appears to resist resolution; even when *she* does not trust herself. I must trust even *that* as being important and true, a statement of truth about her, something that can guide both of us. Even when what she says and does goes against what I would trust in myself, I must ask myself how, perhaps, can both be true? What must I listen to in what she says that may resonate with what I trust in myself? It need not be a case of either/or, but of both/and. In a situation where I feel untrusting of the client I might need to ask questions such as: what is it that the client is saying about what we are doing? Are we going too fast? Is this too much for her right now? What am I not seeing? Am I too attached to my hypothesis? What if I let go of my hypothesis and just stay with what we have?

I take it as a most telling signal if I start putting too much energy into finding a good solution; then I know I am going wrong. I have lost trust, in the client, in the process and in myself. And it is likely that the client has lost trust in me. I have realised that this usually means I am falling into something that is not clear, I am too attached to a certain hypothesis, I may not be listening to the client well enough . . . I am trying to persuade her of something instead of seeing her unwillingness to be persuaded as an important signal that I can trust.

Case example 7:

I was working with a woman in an individual session and everything was going well until I began to realise that I was working too hard, I was moving around trying to find something that worked, some way of bringing the client to life, to a good and warm resolution. . I was jumping to conclusions, trying very hard to get it right for her. Eventually we brought it to an unsatisfactory conclusion and sat down. As we were getting ready to go she looked at me and said that she felt bad; that she always got things wrong and that she had got this wrong (which of course was exactly what I was feeling!).

Sadly I didn't engage her further in the conversation, but after she had left I remembered that right at the beginning she had talked about her fear of offending her mother and how paralysing she found it. I realised that, blinded by an exciting hypothesis I had formed about what needed to happen, I had inadvertently fallen into the role of her mother and, instead of trusting her enough to support her to find her own way with the constellation, I had become directive and controlling, in a way that she couldn't resist and yet also evoked her silent stubbornness as her only way of managing.

Trust frees me up just to be there, to be present, to *not* know, to be empty of hypotheses and ideas. At the same time, trust is not blind and thoughtless. It requires integrity, questioning and intelligence, and then it can put me in connection with that greater energy and resource that can hold me and the client in the process as it takes us irrevocably towards resolution, relaxation and peace.

Trust reformulates every instance of what we might call 'resistance' into a signpost to the truth, something to be gathered up and valued; to be heard for the secrets it has to offer. Trust redesigns the obstacle into a resource; trust says that everything, but *everything* is important and that there are no coincidences, only truths that must be heard. Trust is not a place where I only trust myself and tell myself that the other must be wrong if they do not agree. My hunches and intuitions may be right, but only so right ... there is a rightness that when seen from another angle is a different thing. Trusting the other whatever they may be saying or doing is that deep respect that we all have a right to; if we are not trusting of the other then there is something about the other that we do not understand or are not in touch with.

Of course in our every day lives we may not feel trusting of another, in a financial transaction or some other daily event. But in our work this trust comes from a compassionate dispassion, an agreement to the possibility that all of us are being who we are as best we can within the context of many transgenerational events, dynamics and mysteries. Trust is a surrendering to something greater than I, from which I can only learn something new, all the time. If I am not learning from my client and my work I must ask myself: why not? Am I complacent in my trust in myself? Even trusting myself I must question that trust within the context of the other.

> ... what was heretofore known as 'truth' dissolves into
> shadows: the shadows interweave, interlace, intertwist, and
> from the fuzzy symplectic ball they build emerges the New.
> *Vladimir Dimitrov and Judith Bihl Dimitrov*

Part 2

The Individual Context

Every object, every being, is a jar full of delight.

Mevlana Jelaluddin Rumi

Section I

Introduction

"Who is my enemy? It is the person whose story I have not heard." *Henry Wadsworth Longfellow*

The facilitator in the individual session, at least in the beginning, is likely to be the only one with a conscious sense of the 'presence of many'. Over the years since my initial contact with Systemic Constellations in 1996, as a psychotherapist in private practice, I have, in parallel to my interest in running constellations groups, always had an eye towards one to one work. In the early days of my connection with constellations work, it was generally thought that it was not really possible in the individual context; that it was too difficult for the client to disentangle herself enough from her issues and systemic ties to be able to act as a reliable representative in her own constellation. In the absence of other people to be representatives, it was also thought that the client could not take up this role in any useful way. Indeed, in those days even in groups, the client rarely entered into the constellation until the problematic dynamics were revealed and the issue was clear, the stated theory being that the client needed a representative to be able to see beyond her fixed view. (Currently, in groups, some facilitators have the client in the constellation right from the beginning.) The idea of trying to do a constellation without the group resource, with just the client and the therapist, to some seemed preposterous and likely doomed to failure. Individual context work was generally considered the poor cousin of the group session.

Even so, since most of my practice at that time was one-to-one, I persisted in my interest. I was helped in 2003 by the publication in English of Ursula Franke's book 'In My Mind's Eye: Family Constellations in Individual Therapy and Counselling' (2003), and then in 2004 by a further contribution by Eva Madelung and Barbara Innecken: 'Entering Inner Images: A Creative use of Constellations in Individual Therapy, Counselling, Groups and Self-Help' (2004). I realised then that I was not alone in my quest for discovering and refining the use of constellations in this setting. However, as is often the way, while both of these books helped tremendously in my thinking, neither of them addressed sufficiently for me some of the issues that I was interested in. At the time of their publication I wrote a review and a comparison of the two books for the Systemic Solutions Bulletin (2004)[63] – which helped me to put some of my own thinking in place.

Further, as I progressed as a facilitator and began teaching constellations to others, I always included a focus on working in one-to-one sessions, which proved very popular with the students. Now my opinion is that very valuable work can be done in the individual context. The private consultation provides an opportunity that some people will feel more able to take up, finding it less threatening than attending a group. I learned that there are ways of helping a client become an adequate and useful representative in her own constellation, and that the facilitator, too, can make a useful contribution as a representative, without overloading the meaning and emphasis of the constellation in favour of his hypothesis of the situation.

What follows builds on everything that has gone before in Part 1, and hopefully provides some useful practical information specifically on working in the one-to-one context.

---

[63] Now called *The Knowing Field International Constellations Journal*

Chapter 16

Basic Stance and Assumptions for the Individual Context

I see the work of constellations as having two basic components: broadly the **philosophy** and the **practice**. To state these more clearly:

1. **Philosophy:** An approach that understands the role of belonging, the power of loyalty, the different consciences, the principles that apply to relationships, and the effect of trauma and systemic entanglement over multiple generations;

2. **Practice:** The process of the constellations method, including the relevance of spatial relationships and the phenomenon of the representatives' experiences.[64]

A practitioner working in an individual context who works with a profound understanding of this philosophical approach may not set up formal constellations, but her view of her client will include a context of many generations and a broad societal perspective. She may see her client as embedded in a potentially ordered constellation. She will understand the power and ubiquitous likelihood of the representative experience - even if no actual constellation is set up, both client and facilitator may, at times, spontaneously take up some form of representation, the awareness of which is crucial and useful. If she is a psychotherapist or counsellor, she will also understand

---

[64] These two components are exactly what differentiate the work of constellations from conventional psychotherapy and counselling (see Appendix 4 for a fuller discussion).

the representative experience in the light of transference theory. All of this will affect her way of working (her practice), whether or not she sets up full constellations. She may merely invite the client to imagine his mother standing somewhere in the room, and suggest that he say certain things; or she may ask him to close his eyes and imagine his parents standing in an open field together and work from there. A practitioner who sets up configurations of a client's family without this philosophical understanding will not be working with constellations. He will be setting something up, which may be very useful, but without this broader perspective the results, in the end, are likely to be limited.

With these two aspects clearly understood, we can then be very flexible as to the practice of constellations with respect to the individual context. Whether I am working within a conventional psychotherapy practice or seeing people on an ad hoc basis; whether I am working with personal, coaching or organisational issues, at a deeply spiritual level or at a problem solving/exploration level; whether I am sitting in a consulting room, or in an office, a cafe or on the beach: all of this can come within the framework of constellations work. To say that for work to be judged as truly constellations work it has to be done in groups, to involve the formal setting up of a constellation using people as representatives, it has to work at a deep 'soul' level, it has to focus on the family/personal, it has to find an 'ordered' resolution: these constitute a constricting definition. The constellations facilitator has a certain approach, a certain perspective and a certain attitude that defines her.

So in looking specifically at the work in individual settings I am going to assume a wide and flexible view of the practice of constellations, along with a sound embodied understanding of the philosophy and general principles of the work as in Part 1, and focus mainly on ideas for the method and practice of working individually.

Chapter 17

Differences & Similarities Between Group and Individual

The move from the larger group experiences of this work to the more intimate and confined setting of the individual context has benefits and challenges for both facilitator and client.

The Facilitator

The group constellation is a collaborative venture where the facilitator can work with the representatives and the observing circle, even getting direct help from either or both. There is much support available to the facilitator in the group. In the individual setting there is only the facilitator and the client to decide what to do next. Some facilitators and therapists feel intimidated by the notion of having to manage a group (although my experience of constellations work in groups is that the group manages itself very well if I am willing to trust that it will), and feel more comfortable in the individual setting. On the other hand, in the individual setting a facilitator may feel even more acutely his helplessness in the face of not knowing what to do next without the resource of the group, and consequently may find himself becoming more managing and directive of the process than he would like.

The facilitator may choose to help the client by occupying a marker in the constellation, and if she does, at times she may experience the feelings of that person as if they were her own, much as she might as a representative in a group. Along with her role as facilitator of the session and the constellation, she does this in service of the client, with a willingness to be whatever that is for the moment. This makes for an increased complexity of responsibilities for the facilitator in the individual session. Some facilitators may choose not to do this. Indeed, I would say that to agree to do this does require a good degree of clarity and discrimination on the part of the facilitator, enabling her to move from facilitator to representative, and back to facilitator in a clear and disciplined manner that keeps the process free of confusion for the client.

The Client

For the client there are some significant differences. For some people groups are intimidating, and their preference is for the privacy afforded in the individual session. The individual session may be a starting point, and he or she may go to a group later, or it may be preferable to ever going into a group. Some people feel ashamed and sensitive about their issues, their confusion and their lack of ability to sort things out for themselves, and the privacy of the individual session may make this a preferred option. Couples also may prefer privacy rather than the potential embarrassment of having their relationship opened up in 'public', particularly if one partner feels that he or she is likely to be classified by the other as the "problem".

In a group the client may have another person stand in for her as her representative, whereas in the private session she does not have this service and may have to assume this function herself, as well as standing in for many of the other marker-representatives that are set up. The client's representative in the group may take on expressing some of the unexpressed feelings on behalf of the client, and while the client usually resonates with the feelings expressed from her seat outside the constellation, there still may be some relief in having another do this for her. In the individual session there is only the client, and at times the facilitator, to feel and express whatever feelings arise from any of the markers set out, not just the client's own marker. Put simply, the client in the individual session must play a more active role in her constellation than is often the case in the group, and may experience strong feelings that arise from markers other than her own. Thus a client, standing on the marker for her grandmother whose older brother was killed in battle, may experience deeply the grieving feelings that we attribute to her grandmother, but that in a sense are systemic and therefore hers to express on behalf of herself and her grandmother. She may also choose to stand on the marker for the dead brother and experience as well his own feelings of grief, perhaps also terror and trauma. While the client in the group will resonate with these feelings as experienced by the representatives, she does so from a more removed place than she is likely to do in the individual session.

The client comes to the individual session in a different frame of mind than if she were going to a group, which can be helpful. In the individual session she knows she will do some work, she knows that the time is hers and that there will be no interruptions, and she will not have to make room for others' needs. In the one-off consultation contract such as I now generally do, the client usually arrives focused and clearly ready to do some work, expecting that we will have the time and resources to permit a good outcome. Within an ongoing therapy contract, she knows her therapist and the level of support available from him and the trust she can have in him in their continuing relationship.

Process Differences

1. Observing the initially set up constellation:

In the group this is less crucial because the representatives will tell you or show you what the initial picture reveals. Additionally, things may happen quite quickly in the group constellation that may restrict the time for observation of the initial picture. In the individual session this initial observation becomes a very important part of the process for two reasons:

- It is the starting point of understanding the spatially expressed relational dynamics within the system, and these can be very revealing in the absence of the shared experiences of the representatives, and a good point of departure for client and facilitator as they discuss what they see and the possible implications.
- Very often we are working with a client who may be completely new to constellations, or if not he is likely to be new to the process in the individual context, and a major part of our work then is to help him become a useful representative in his own constellation. The stage of sharing observations provides a helpful gap between the issue clarification and his moving to being a representative.

It is startling how revealing this initial picture can be. I have even found at times that we do not move from the initial picture; that enough insight and understanding emerge from it for the client to feel satisfied.

2. Use of media instead of people:
In the individual session we use floor markers, table-top markers or visualisation in order to facilitate the constellation.

3. The Client as his own Representative:
As his own representative the client will be involved in all experimental statements, rituals and processes either from his own marker or from that of other elements in his constellation. See Chapter 23 for more on this.

4. The Facilitator as a Representative:
The facilitator, in addition to holding the space and facilitating the process, may make herself available in the experiment and dialogue processes, taking up another marker than the one the client occupies, thus providing a focus for the client to connect with. For more on this see Chapter 23.

Chapter 18

Work Setting and Contract

Apart from the distinction of whether one works at the psychotherapeutic end of the spectrum, or within the coaching or organisational domain, there is the simple difference of whether one works with constellations as one of a number of skills and tools of practice, or whether the constellations method is completely central to one's practice.

1. The constellation as an aspect of one's overall practice. Here we consider the case of the psychotherapist or counsellor who works with clients on a regular, usually weekly, basis in what one might describe as a conventional psychotherapy format; or the coach or organisational consultant who uses constellations as part of his or her overall professional resources in an on-going client relationship. In this instance, the word 'constellation' may or may not be used, but the process and thinking become part of the contract when useful.

For those therapists for whom experimentation is central to their work (such as gestalt therapists, psychosynthesis therapists, play therapists and drama therapists) the transition to actually setting up a constellation may be easier since their clients probably expect something of this nature to be part of the work. This transition may be harder for the therapist or counsellor who relies on the therapeutic relationship as the crucible for healing or finds the move from the therapist and client chairs unfamiliar, as in the more analytic, psychodynamic and person-centred traditions. To introduce a process like the constellation in this setting might well be disconcerting for the client if they do not expect it, and in the beginning for the therapist.

A good way forward for the therapist wishing to make the constellations process more a part of his practice might be to include this in the initial contracting session as part of how you work, and even a way in which you gain information about the client. It is possible to invite the client to set up something with floor-markers, table-top markers or a genogram (see chapter 25) in her first or second session, as a way of showing both of you the nature of the family relationship structure, without necessarily doing anything more with it. For a while when I still saw clients on a week by week basis, I did this in all my initial sessions. It helped me to persist with making the methodology of constellations a part of my work, and was always illuminating for the client and me.

Another useful strategy is to introduce the constellation in a very small way, perhaps by simply marking places for the client and another part of himself as in a traditional two-chair experiment, and then expanding on this.

2. The constellation as the central aspect of your work.

When I began to include the constellations process overtly in my work with on-going clients, it sometimes happened that the constellation surfaced many things that were new for the client, and in our subsequent weekly meetings we would find little to do other than reflect on what had happened in the constellation. I felt uncomfortable with this, because such discussion and analysis is not always an appropriate way to assist the integration of the effects of the constellation, and yet I didn't know what else to do. Eventually, because my primary interest was in constellations, I took the step of winding down my traditional psychotherapy practice and instead offering sessions on a potentially one-off basis specifically working with constellations. This step does not preclude the need for some people to have the regular holding of a conventional psychotherapeutic or counselling contract, but I took my practice in a different direction. Now from time to time I get referrals of one of their clients from other therapists for one session, after which the client returns to their ongoing therapy. Some therapists find this a helpful adjunct to their work with some clients.

My current preferred style:

I offer this as an example. It works for me at the moment, but might not for you. Perhaps it will give you some ideas of how you might organise your practice.

Currently I offer an initial one-off session, which may have follow-on sessions depending on the needs and requirements of the client. Since the session is essentially in the beginning a one-off session, and often I have not met the person before, I send her a clear letter (usually as an email) before the session confirming the date and time, and giving detailed instructions as to how to find my workplace. I also require people to pay for the session in full, well prior to the appointment. Since we have no formal contract other than our verbal agreement, I am unwilling to put two hours of time aside as a definite proposition without payment. I have not yet come across anyone who does not understand the need for this. As this is my beginning structure I tend to hold to this for any follow-up sessions that are booked.

I see people for between one and a half and two hours during which we clarify the issue, and set up and work with a constellation. At the end of the session I suggest that if he needs to contact me afterwards by phone or email to clarify something, if he is concerned about anything, or indeed if he wants to share something that has happened as a result or some insight that came later, to feel free to do so. I am clear that I do not discuss anything else with him so that the boundary is in connection with the work that we have done together, or in connection with the next step that he may wish to take, and the contact does not turn into phone therapy. I also suggest that he allow sufficient time for the emergent information and embodied experience to unfold and settle within him, and when he feels ready to take the next step, if he wants to do that with me, he contact me. I also make it clear that he may well choose to do the next step of his journey with someone else or in some other way, and that he should follow his own sense of this.

If I have not met the person before, I allow an amount of time for us to meet and find a way of forming a kind of readiness contract so that we can proceed. The time needed for this varies from person to person, but usually I find that ten minutes are enough. Then we can move to exploring the issue. This can take anything up to twenty minutes, but usually between ten and fifteen is enough. I don't like to rush this process in the individual session because I think that it is only when the person has told me everything that he wants to, when he has emptied himself enough so to speak, that he is in a good state to move to becoming a representative in his own constellation. If he is still mulling over in his mind the many strands to the issue then he is less available.

Many people who come to see me for this initial session do come back at varying intervals of time later, and may eventually attend a workshop. For the person who is anxious about attending a workshop, the opportunity to build a relationship with me in the private session is helpful.

Chapter 19

Methods and Markers

In place of people as representatives for the set up constellation we can use either floor markers or table-top markers. A third method of working in the individual session is with visualisation, which can be with eyes open or closed. A fourth for a simple two-element constellation is using the hands or the two sides of the body. Each of these has different benefits and challenges and it is useful to familiarise yourself with all approaches. At times in my work I may combine two methods or more for different reasons.

Floor Markers

For example:

- Pieces of paper
- Shoes
- Cushions
- Cut-out pieces of felt

It is important that the direction in which the representative is facing is clear. With pieces of paper you can draw an arrow. With cushions you can make clear which corner is the facing direction. Pieces of felt can be cut into the symbols shown in Example 1 below where the circle represents a female and the square a male. The notch indicates which way they are facing.

Figure 13

The pieces of felt that I use are all different colours, one male and one female of each colour. The colours are not important to me; I have found though that it makes it easier to remember who is who than if all the pieces of felt are the same colour. On the other hand, the colour is often very important to the client, in the same way that the choice of person in a group to represent a particular family member is often also very important to the client. On occasion a client will choose the male and female of the same colour to represent a couple.

Madelung and Innecken in their book, *Entering Inner Images* (2004) include an aspect of art therapy in their work by inviting their clients to do a drawing on a piece of paper for each person represented. They suggest that the client creates the drawings with their non-dominant hand in order to by-pass the more rational left-brain, and connect with their more intuitive side. Additionally this helps the client with any self-consciousness she may have about her artistic ability. As any therapist who has worked with art in this way knows, this often results in profound insights that can greatly enhance the constellations work. These drawings can then be used as floor markers in the constellation.

Benefits of using floor markers:

- It is revealing to look at the patterning of the constella-tion from above. In this way a client can see just how isolated her mother is in the constellation, for example, which then allows her more understanding of how her mother had been with her as a child.
- The physical movement of laying out the markers in the

room connects the client more to her body and helps separate her from her habitual mode of being and thinking about the issue, awakening her to some extent from the trance of the problem. You can suggest that she leave the issue and all her thinking behind in the chair as she gets up; this spatial distancing helps. A client of mine, as soon as she stepped onto her own floor marker, immediately told me that she was feeling and thinking things that she hadn't been feeling and thinking before when she was sitting down.

- In the processing of the constellation, the transition from one marker to the next (and so from one representative experience to another) is assisted by the physical movement, which increasingly may take her into new possibilities. Sometimes I will suggest that when coming off a marker she take a short walk away from the constellation before returning and standing on another marker.
- Different things can be done with floor markers, that are not possible with people: they can be piled on top of each other, for example, which graphically shows the client's experience of her family.

Case example 8:

I had a client who put her marker underneath that of her older brother who had died when my client was 3 years old. This then developed into an increasing realisation of how much she had felt over-shadowed by her brother's death. When we separated the two markers and faced them towards each other my client was able to express her own grief at her brother's death and, when standing on her brother's marker, as her brother she experienced a great love for herself as the younger child. Her sense of guilt at having in some way been responsible for her brother's death evaporated, leaving her with a simple experience of her brother's love for her.

Possible disadvantages:

- Requires space and so might not be possible in a small consulting room.
- For clients who are very close to their trauma feelings, it can be too much, whereas working with the table-top figures may give her some distance from the feelings that may be overwhelming. See Case example 9:

Case example 9:

One client I was working with, when standing on the marker for her mother's brother who had been gassed during the second world war, was in that moment tipped into an extremely strong trauma reaction where she almost passed out. I immediately sat her down and, having taken care of the immediate trauma reaction by grounding her and keeping her present with me until she was able to proceed, brought out a table and set up the constellation using figures, whereupon she was able to complete the constellation in a good way while staying present and leaving the trauma reaction with the figure representing her mother's brother on the table. At the end of the constellation she asked if she could have the figure of her mother's brother to take with her, which I readily agreed to. I saw her some while later when she gave me the figure back saying that she no longer needed it, that the trauma was now fully with her mother's brother and was clearly not hers.

Suggested procedure using floor markers:

- Invite client to choose all representatives first and lay them in front of her.
- Suggest that she stand up and hold each piece in turn and find a place for that person in the room. I suggest that she tune into who the person is and then allow her feet to

guide her to the right place. If she has difficulty with this I may suggest she use me as the representative, placing me in the right position, and then we will put the marker down where she has placed me.

- After looking at the constellation and having some discussion, invite the person to stand on each of the markers to experience what she feels there.
- The facilitator can stand on other markers briefly one after the other to give the client a sense of the markers representing actual people.

Table-Top Figures

For example:

- Playmobil people or other kind of toy people
- Abstract objects such as stones which have a clear directional indication
- Pieces of card or paper with arrows to indicate direction

Benefits of table-top markers:

- Useful if space is limited
- Particularly helpful if the client is close to her trauma feelings, giving her more distance from the trauma by the contracted perspective of working on a table. She can also lean right back in her chair when she needs more distance, and lean forward when she can engage more.
- The Playmobil people (or other models of people) invite the client into her right-brain, playful self which can help her disconnect from her habitual view of the situation, while at the same time protecting her to an extent from difficult powerful feelings
- Can have a lot of people represented in a contained and manageable way

207

Possible disadvantages:

- For some clients who are disconnected from their feelings, or who are accustomed to managing their lives from their thinking faculty, this may be less fruitful than the more embodied work with floor markers.

Suggested procedure using table-top markers:

- Invite the client to choose figures or markers for all those needed and place each one on the table in the way that has meaning for her.
- When inviting the client to connect with the representatives it is helpful for her to touch the marker lightly with a finger, and it may help her to close her eyes.
- The facilitator can also touch and connect with the figures.

Case example 10:

I once saw a mother and her 14-year old son for a session. The mother was very worried about her son because he was self-harming, aggressive and withdrawn, not going to school and clearly unhappy. In the session the son sat sulkily in his chair and was generally uncooperative, refusing to talk or take any interest in discussing the issue. Eventually I suggested to the mother that I work with her on the issue of what made her feel helpless in her life. We set up a constellation on the table with the Playmobil people and worked with it. All the while I could sense the son was getting interested, but I continued to address the mother and work with her. Eventually when the mother had finished the constellation the son could hardly wait to get his hands on the little figures and we moved on to do a successful constellation with him.

Visualisations

In this approach the client processes the constellation in his mind's eye with the assistance of the facilitator. I have not yet met anyone who cannot visualise to some extent, and the creative possibilities are great. There are two types of visualisation:

- With eyes open: this is a simple technique where you might simply bring a certain person into the space by asking the client to imagine where in the room the person might be.
- With eyes closed: allowing the images to unfold as though watching a movie.

Benefits of visualisation:

- Needs little space and no objects, just chairs for the client and the facilitator
- Taps into the client's unconscious easily and privately
- May allow the client to feel less self-conscious
- Allows for imagined physical contact with those in the constellation: for example hugging, holding, embracing, or hitting.
- Can include many people
- Can allow for client to see facial expressions on others in their image, which is often important.

Possible disadvantages:

- For some clients who have a tendency to do so, a visualisation may send them into a dissociated state, which is not useful. If the client seems to go very dreamy and disconnected, or the process as she relates it seems to become rather strange and fanciful it is better to bring her out of it and resort to a table-top or floor-marker constellation. The constellations thinking and process are definitely not about fantasy and illusion (which are common dissociative means) being more focused on confronting reality and dispelling illusionary ideas.

- Likewise some people who have experienced creative visualisations that are largely symbolic before may think that this is the same process. This is not helpful for the constellations procedure, which is much more focused. At the same time I have found that some people's symbolic images are extremely appropriate. Experience will help you be clearer about this.
- Visualisations may slip into reified images of how a person is seen. A client I worked with found it impossible not to see her mother in an apron in the kitchen being angry and cut-off. We worked better with the floor-markers, particularly when I stood in the mother's place so she had to see something other than her image of her mother. After this there was more space for her to stand on her mother's marker and be open to a new, and as it turned out, unimagined possibility.

Suggested procedure for open eyes visualisation:

- Ask where in the room a certain person might be standing, for example a mother or grandmother. Often you will already know, because during the prior conversation about the person the client has consistently tended to glance in a certain direction.
- Ask her to imagine the person standing there and proceed as you might in any other constellation by suggesting statements, asking the client to imagine others behind or to the side etc.

Suggested procedure for closed eyes visualisation:

- Invite the client to make herself comfortable, close her eyes and imagine herself standing in a large open space outside, perhaps a place that is familiar to her.
- Then suggest that she "allow to arrive" in her image whoever is the focus of the constellation, perhaps the client's mother or father. I use the term "allow to arrive"

because it encourages the client to be passive rather than feel she has to be doing anything much. I also suggest that she let the person arrive however he or she comes. This is to stay away from defining anything too much. The person can be any age, in any state, and I trust that however he or she comes is saying something about the issue needing to be worked with. See Case example 11.

Case example 11:

"Allowing to arrive". A woman came to see me who complained of relationship problems. Over the years she said that she found she was persistently attracted to men who, she felt, were unable to appreciate her. She thought she ended up looking after them and giving up on what she wanted in her life. Currently she was in the process of trying to negotiate something different with her husband, but felt bleak as she thought she was repeating all the same patterns from before.

Her own father seemed to have been rather absent, and at the same time she said that he treated her mother like a child.

We began with a visualisation in which I suggested that she allow her mother and father to arrive however they came. After a few moments as I watched her I noticed a slight change of expression. I waited a few more moments and then asked her what was happening. She said that she saw her father standing in front of her and her mother as a very small child in his arms. I asked her how she felt as she watched this. She replied that it made sense and that she and her father had always somehow had to look after her mother . . . and then she started to weep. She said she understood why she had always felt so lonely in her life, and she was confused as to whether she wept for herself or her mother. She said her mother looked apprehensive and unhappy. I suggested she see if her mother's mother could be there. After a few minutes she told me that her grandmother also looked rather young, not as young as her mother, but still not much more than a child. Then she told me that her grandmother's mother had lost her first child when he was three years old and her grandmother was two. We invited into the visualisation the great-grandmother and the grandmother's brother. My client breathed deeply and then began to sob as she saw spontaneously in the visualisation her great-grandmother take the boy in her arms smiling. After a while I asked how the grandmother was doing, and she said that she was now with her mother and her brother, and seemed to have grown up.

We moved on and gradually found a way for the mother and her mother to connect and then have her mother stand with her father, with her grandmother, great-grandmother and great uncle all standing looking at her. I suggested she say to her mother "you are my mother and I am your child. I see how much you needed your mother and when I look at you or think about you I will include in my view and my thoughts your mother, my grandmother. . and now I entrust you to her care." I then checked with her how everyone was doing, and she smiled and said that everyone was just fine. . and her father looked happy and less anxious.

Simple two-element constellation with hands or body

This is useful for an intra-psychic dialogue (between two parts of the self) or other two-element constellation. The client can put one element in one hand and one in the other, or designate a side of her body as one, and the other side as the other. Then proceed as in a normal constellation, perhaps in the former case suggesting she put the hand that she is connecting with forward and leave the other resting, and in the latter case suggesting she lean into the side of the body that she was wanting to connect with.

Section II

Procedures and Processes

Chapter 20

The Basic Procedure

Contracting

Contracting in this sense is the subtle process by which the facilitator and the client agree to what is proposed at a certain moment. This process also occurs in groups.

A first contract is made by the client initiating the session. After that the facilitator remains mindful throughout as to whether she and the client are working in a collaborative way (which would be 'with contract') or in a conflicted way (which would be 'without contract'). From this perspective 'what is known as 'resistance' never happens. What we might call 'resistance' is a sign that we are 'without contract': as yet we do not have the support together to proceed with what is proposed. For example, let's say I am sitting with a client who is telling me about some aspect of her life. I suggest we set up a constellation and she ignores what I have said and continues talking. At this point I know that I do not have a contract yet to make that step to set up a constellation. Either there is something important that the client needs to tell me that she has not told me yet, or she has told me something important but I have not really heard it and she needs me to do so, or she does not feel safe enough with me yet to take that step. The question at this point is: what do I need to do to enable a contract here? Do I need to let her talk some more, listen more acutely to what she is saying, or see what else might be needed for her to feel safe enough to proceed?

Another example: I suggest an experiment in the constellations process and the client responds with a lack of energy and a sense of not being present for the experiment. I have 'lost' her in a sense, and am on my own with this particular move. We are 'without contract' at this moment. Perhaps I have moved too fast, or I have moved into a particularly sensitive area that as yet she cannot consider pursuing (insufficient support for the perceived challenge). Either way it is the time to pause and see what is necessary for us to regain our contract, our collaborative nature.

This does not mean that I cannot challenge, but it does mean that even the challenge can be part of a collaborative contract. It is not that the client does not want to be challenged where necessary, but she does want to feel that she is challenged by a friendly and generally supportive person, that the overall nature of our relationship is friendly. A strong overall contract of collaboration can withstand momentary disruption. It can be that I feel in the moment that I have a contract to challenge.

Those times of feeling like we don't have a contract are not a mark of failure, they are just information for the facilitator. It may be a point where I discuss it openly with the client, perhaps saying that I feel I have lost a certain connection with her, and for a moment I feel I have lost my way or am going in the wrong direction. It is the same as in a group: checking with the client that the constellation is on the right track, that we are, so to speak, in the right scenario.

This process is again an indication of where one considers the overall locus of authority in the work to be. If I attend to these subtle moment-by-moment nuances of my relationship with the client, taking the client's behaviour and state of being as an indication of how we are doing, then I am continually agreeing that the main locus of authority for what we do and how we proceed is in the client, both consciously and unconsciously. If I do not attend to this, then it is likely that more and more the overall locus of authority for what we do is with me, and necessarily this will take me into a more directive approach.

Clarifying the issue (the initial interview)

In a sense this is the most important part of the constellations procedure. In my experience in individual sessions and groups, more constellations go awry because I have not spent enough time on, or listened carefully enough during the clarifying process, and subsequently have set up a constellation that does not have sufficient energy or focus.

> "So there is always the question about how to begin; you have to be very precise and you can't think it up." *Hellinger (2008)*

"You can't think it up". That says an awful lot! And I believe it is so. The point at which we can set up a constellation is that point at which there is energy in both the client and myself to do so. Of course, sometimes this is more tangible than at others. Nevertheless, it does not hurt to wait a little longer if you are not clear. Do not expect the client to be clear about what they want; they are likely to be clear up to a point, but only up to a point. On the other hand very often the client will say something crucial in the first sentence or two, so listen carefully. The process of clarification takes time and patience and requires the facilitator to be centred and fully present.

In terms of how you might conduct the clarifying process, I would suggest the following as helpful.

1. Adopting the same use of language as the client. By doing this the facilitator supports the client's exploration rather than, by using language that does not resonate for the client, jolting him out of his flow.[65]

---

[65] For more on the use of 'clean language' I would recommend *Resolving Traumatic Memories: Metaphors and Symbols in Psychotherapy*. Grove and Panzer (1991).

2. Adopting a method of questioning that is open and unspecific allows for emergent information.

First questions: open up the space for the clarification enquiry. The questions should be undefined so that the facilitator clearly indicates having no agenda as to what the issue is. Questions such as:

- What is it that you want?
- What would be helpful?
- What do you need to happen?
- What brings you here today?
- What would you like to happen here?

Follow-up questions: these stay "open" and undefined, but in the process of moving towards doing a constellation, keep bringing the client back to the defining of the issue.

- What shall we do?
- So where are you up to in terms of what your issue is?
- So what is your issue now?
- So what is it that you want now? (indicating that this is likely to have changed, clarified, deepened etc.)
- Perhaps if I ask you again: what is it that you want? You may be clearer about that now.

During the enquiry process the answer to the general question "what is the issue" will change as the client and facilitator journey towards clarifying the start of the constellation. I may ask this question (in different forms) three or four times during the enquiry, each time expecting that either the answer will be the same but in a different, clearer form, or that the answer will be different but closer to the deeper issues. I see this enquiry process as allowing a gradual deepening for both of us in our awareness and understanding of the less obvious subtleties of the issue.

Do not think that because Hellinger and some others seem

to be able to see the issue in all its clarity immediately, that they are always right, or that you should be able to do that too. In truth the constellations process is always an experiment. Better to be a bit more modest in your aspirations, and assume that you really don't know until such time as you absolutely do! To quote Hellinger: "Sometimes I have the impulse to intervene but I don't do anything until I'm shown the next step ... we have to wait." (Hellinger, 2006) This indicates his own very experimental and phenomenological approach.

Case example 12:

A woman came to me who I had never met before. She talked quickly and intensely about many things. Her voice was quite harsh and strained. She had much she wanted to say. After a while I understood that the talking had helped her to maintain a sense of control in her very troubled and unhappy life. She talked to survive. She talked to keep away from the trauma. She talked to spell-bind me into submission and inactivity. She talked to keep still, and avoid change as much as she talked to try to prompt change. It was perhaps all she knew how to do and she clung to the talking for dear life. Gently I suggested we do a small experiment. I suggested she choose two markers: one for the part of her that talked and one for the part of her that was wordless. Instantly she understood, and chose the two markers. Looking at the constellation, she began to talk (in much softer, more tentative, and even tender, tones) about the brittle, thin and fragile nature of the part that talked. Then, connecting with the wordless part she said that that part of herself "holds all the feelings that I can't express." I suggested she go and stand on the wordless marker as a further part of herself that could, perhaps, speak on behalf of the wordless part. (After all I must respect the wordless part as being truly wordless. Invoking a part that can 'speak on behalf of' allows for the wordless part to maintain its integrity of wordlessness.) On the wordless part, speaking for it, she said that that part represented spontaneity and that it wanted to play . . . and later to the talkative part of herself: "you can trust me, you can trust this part that holds the unexpressed feelings." For her this represented an extremely important understanding . . . that she didn't have to be so scared of this wordless part, that perhaps she could even listen to its softness in a more trusting way.

Setting up the constellation

When we have clarified the issue as far as we can, we will move to setting up the constellation. In Chapter 23, I go into some detail as to how to help the client become a good representative in their own constellation, which includes taking this process of setting up the constellation quite slowly and carefully, allowing her time to adjust.

It is usually easiest to invite the client to choose all the representatives first, and then when setting them up to instruct her to:

- Take one marker at a time
- Connect with the person the marker represents
- Allow your body to decide where this representative should be
- Take your time and (with floor markers) follow your feet until you find the place
- Place the marker and then wait a moment to see if that is right
- Do the same with each of the remaining representations

Of course, some people in the individual session will, even so, find it hard to do this in a collected and grounded way and in this case you will work at the level that the person is able to connect with the work. Some facilitators in groups, I know, may refuse to work with a client if they think the person not ready to work at the level they consider necessary. Perhaps they do the same in the individual context. I think it a more inclusive attitude to agree that some people simply cannot function in a collected and grounded way at this time. However, I believe that even so, this client has chosen to come to me and I do not see it as my place to decline to work with her. I take the stance that individuals' life journeys are often very complex and mysterious, and I do not know enough. Better in my view, to do what we can and trust that she will take from what we do what she needs, and I prefer to leave it at that.

The initial phase – sharing observations

This phase is much more important in the individual context than the group for three reasons:

- Lacking the experience of representatives, we need to focus on what is revealed in the initial picture, which is usually a considerable amount.
- It allows the facilitator and client to move into a more collaborative relationship of sharing observations and thoughts. (A collaborative relationship relieves the facilitator of any pressure of having to know the answers.)
- It provides a transitionary stage in the introduction of the client to the representative process (see Chapter 23).

I suggest you do not rush this stage, allowing time to sit together, even without conversation, to see what might arise in both of you as you look. First observations are useful, and emergent later observations are often quite startling. Looking at their family system in this way will often draw forth unexpected insight and understandings in the client.

Case example 13:

Having set up his constellation, as we sat together looking at what he had done, Ethan slowly started to cry. I waited, not understanding what was happening for him. Eventually he started to talk about his brother who had died at birth when Ethan was just 3 years old. At this point he had not mentioned this brother and yet, in setting up the constellation it struck him forcefully who was missing and evoked in him feelings he had never allowed himself to feel before. Many facilitators will check in the initial clarification process who is in the family, asking about other 'lost' children. Sometimes I do this and sometimes I don't. On this occasion for some reason I hadn't. Ethan continued to talk about his enduring sense of guilt that it might have been his fault. We then moved on to include this brother and engage in some very touching process work.

Case example 14:

Sarah was startled, having set up her constellation with a Playmobil set on the table, to see that her mother was nearly off the table and her father was right beside Sarah, on the other side of the table, looking towards her mother's back. She said: "This is just how it is, but somehow I hadn't really realised just how far away she seems . . . when I was a child I always went to my dad, my mother seemed so distant, but I thought it was to do with me. I now see that it is to do with her, not me." She went on to say that she had also always felt a bit uncomfortable with her closeness to her father. She said that there was nothing wrong, but somehow it was too close, that she tried to look after him a lot. When I asked her who her mother might be looking for she said: "her mother . . . her mother left home when she was 2 years old and she never saw her again." I suggested we include Sarah's grandmother, her mother's mother. She put in a marker for the grandmother with tears in her eyes, and we moved on from there.

Introducing the client to the representative process

This phase is very important in that there is a dual process going on: at the same time we are beginning the process of the constellation *and* introducing the client to being a representative. I go into more detail about this in Chapter 23.

The experimental phase

This is the phase of introducing what seems to have been missing, moving markers to create conditions for better contact, suggesting statements to clarify the actuality of the situation, experimenting with the client according to what information has arisen from the process so far. For the client new to constellations this is a continuation of her coming to understand the representative process, and the possibilities for new information to arise from the markers and patternings.

The contact phase

This phase is the turning point, supporting the enactment of the needed contact between those who have been missed or excluded, and those who need to connect with them. In this phase both the client and I will probably stand on markers, moving from marker to marker, changing places so that each can experience a place, say important words and phrases to each other, and so on. It is the time when the client may have a strong emotional reaction, perhaps connecting with the trauma as it is held within her.

The resolution phase

This is the phase when what has emerged is clearly seen, movement seems possible, insight occurs with an increasingly fluid ripple effect, insight upon insight as the new images and understandings flow into each other. We may sit down for a bit during this time, re-connect with each other and discuss what we have seen. It may also become clear that some further statements need to be made to finalise and secure the understanding, in which case we can re-enter the constellation and do so. We may re-organise the constellation into a new configuration that seems right to the client now.

The ending phase

In this phase there is a certain satisfaction for both of us. I tend not to clear the final constellation away too quickly ...

we may sit and look at it for a while. Some clients bring a camera and like to photograph this final image. I tend at this stage not to engage in too much further conversation and when the time feels right I will invite the client to collect up the pieces, give them a shake (floor-markers) or put them back in the bag (Playmobil people, toys or markers) and we will then finish.

Because of how I now do my sessions (on a one at a time basis) I will tell the client that it is best to just live with whatever change and evolving process has been started here, and that should she have any questions or concerns she is welcome to contact me. Additionally I say that she is welcome to come back if she wants to at some time, when perhaps she feels that there is a further step to be taken. I don't assume that I will see her again, and say quite clearly that it may be her choice to go to someone else for whatever the next step may be. I tend to stay out of requiring feedback or follow-up situations. The work is done as best as I can, and to me that is enough. I will have a certain view of what we have done and it may differ from hers. Indeed I have found on the occasions when I do see someone again, that often this is so. I trust her in what she will take and use and feel is important. I do not know in the end.

Post Session

If the client contacts me after the session with some concern or question I will spend time on the phone or by email to answer as best I can, but I will not move into future work. I will only address what we have done. This seems to me a useful boundary to hold, and for the most part my experience is that people understand this very well.

Whatever your practice you will of course need to adapt what I have written appropriately. I offer this as part of my own continuing process of discovering good ways of working with people. You will devise your own and what I have written may offer you some ideas to develop.

Chapter 21

Understanding Relationship Pictures

In the individual session using floor markers or table-top objects can make it much easier to get a graphic picture of the constellation than in a group. The ability to look down from above gives a different perspective and makes the initial picture particularly helpful. When working in groups with people as representatives it is easy for the facilitator to miss out this crucial step, since we are captured by the spontaneous movements and expressed experiences of the representatives. However in the absence of representatives, this forms a potent part of the process, offering the facilitator an emerging sense of the dynamics of the system based on the physical representations of the systemic principle of 'place'. On occasion, this stage can offer so much for the client that moving to a fuller constellation is superfluous.

It takes a bit of practice to understand what you are seeing, and I try to make it a collaborative process with the client by asking him what strikes him about what he has set up first, and then offering whatever I see simply as an observation, initially without interpretation. This is my style and may not be yours, but my preference is that all interpretative information ideally comes from the client.

Here are some examples of some typical configurations and what they may suggest, and questions they might lead to. (Square images represent males and round images represent females. The notch indicates which way they are facing.)

Figure 14: Example 1

Observations:
The round is facing the square directly whereas the square looks past or away from the round. The markers are quite close. This 'past' or 'away' is important in that the energetic impulses of the two are very different. Looking 'past' may mean that the person looks towards someone or something else. Looking 'away' may mean that the person cannot bear to look at the other, and so avoids doing so. In the first instance the presence of the round marker may be immaterial, or even invisible, to the square marker. In the second the presence of the round marker is integral to the avoidant positioning of the square marker. If I ask the client if the square looks past or avoids she may well have a sense of which it is.

Possible Interpretations:

- Round seeks connection. Square deflects connection.
- Square looks for someone else (faces towards another as yet unplaced representative). This might indicate someone missing.
- The square marker perhaps wishes to leave the situation.
- The round is stopping the square from leaving.

Questions you might ask the client:

- Does the square image turn away from the round to avoid her, or is he looking into the space as if he seeks someone else?
- Does the square want to move further in that direction?

- What might the round be saying to the square?
- What happens to the square when the round says that?

Sentences that might be suggested:

- Round to Square: "I'm looking at you", or perhaps: "I want you to see me", or: "I don't want you to go".
- Square to Round: "I can't look at you", or: "I am looking elsewhere", or: "I don't want to see you".

These suggested sentences are primarily of a phenomenological nature in that they make no more interpretation than staying absolutely at the edge of what is seen. The client, of course, is likely to be more interpretative than this. I am using these statements here as an example of how the facilitator, within his own thinking, can stay at this more clearly phenomenological edge. This is important because the client is always more likely than the facilitator to be coming from an established view of the situation. The more the facilitator can hold this more open 'clean' phenomenological stance, the less likely he is to get entangled in the client's narrative.

Now, I am going to add one marker, putting it in a different place in each of the following two examples. As an exercise, look at each of the examples one at a time, and for each of them write down your observations, hypothetical interpretations and some questions that you might ask, before you look at mine.

Figure 15: Example 2

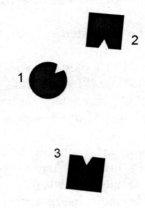

And then go on to the next example and do the same:

Figure 16: Example 3

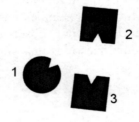

Both of the above examples have a different feel, and affect how we would consider these relationships. In the third of these examples there is a feeling of No. 1 being excluded and pushed outside, whereas in the second example there is more possibility for No 1 to be involved. A sentence you might come up with in the second example for No. 1 to say to No. 2 could be "Can I get your attention?" or "Do you see me?"

At this level of simply looking at the graphics of relational dynamics we can get a sense of something of the nature of the relationships between these three.

If, however, we now decide that one is a mother, one a father and one a child it changes again. Try changing them around so that you feel the effect when, say, 3 is the child, and 1 and 2 are the parents, or when 2 is the child and 1 and 3 are the parents

From this perspective, setting up a constellation will always reveal something, just on the level of taking this inner, sometimes vague, sense of how things are and externalising it into a physical form.

In order to exercise your understanding further I am giving some more examples below.

Figure 17: Example 4, a more complex picture

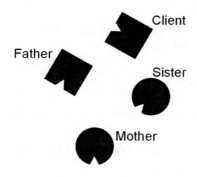

Observations:

- The only person looking at anyone is the sister who looks at the mother.
- The mother is the only one who can't actually see anyone (if you think of them as actual people standing there, everyone else could at least see someone out of the corner of their eye).
- The mother is facing away from the constellation.
- The father and the client are also looking away from the constellation but not so completely away as the mother.
- In a way the whole constellation seems to orient itself around the mother.
- The father and mother look in the same general area, but not exactly the same direction.

Possible Interpretations:

- The mother is leaving.
- The mother is looking for a missing person
- The sister is following her mother or is concerned about her mother.
- The father also looks for someone who is missing, as does perhaps the client.

Possibly useful questions:

- Would the mother move further away from the constellation?
- Is the mother moving towards someone or something else or away from the group?
- Who might the mother be looking for?
- What might the sister be saying to her mother?
- Is the father aware of the mother?

And so on. Questions such as 'who might the mother be looking for?' sometimes prompt a spontaneous intuitive response from the client. If the client answers immediately or says something like 'the first thought that came was. . .' It is likely to be truer than if they think for more than 5 seconds, or seem to be digging around for an answer. My suggestion is that you encourage and trust "first thoughts", those instantaneous "pop into the head" ideas, as usually having something important to offer the situation. With most people, the "thought-through" thought is more likely to come from the old well-established view.

Figure 18: Example 5

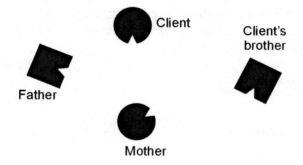

Observations:

- Everyone is to a certain extent looking towards the constellation
- The brother is further away and is the one most looking away and is separated from the rest of the constellation
- The mother looks directly at the brother
- The client looks directly towards the mother
- The father looks at the mother

Possible Interpretations:

- The brother looks towards someone who is missing, or for some reason he cannot stay in the system
- The brother for some reason is outside or on the periphery of the system (perhaps excluded or rebellious)
- The client tries to stop the father from going to the mother
- The client tries to get the attention of the mother
- So does the father

Possible Questions:

- Who or what is the brother looking for?
- Is the brother wanting to move in that direction?
- What is the mother saying to the brother (her son)
- What is the client feeling?

And so on.

Figure 19: Example 6

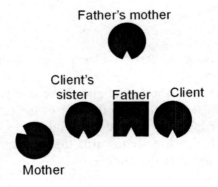

230

Observations:

- Everyone is looking in the same direction except the mother who looks back and away.
- The client's sister stands next to her father as if she were his wife (in the conventional wife's place. See Figure 11 at the end of Chapter 11)
- The client also stands next to her father.

Possible Interpretations:

- The mother looks for someone missing, perhaps her dead mother? (if this has been revealed in the initial clarifying of the issue, or if not this might surface it).
- The sister takes up the place of the mother next to her father, the mother being psychologically and emotionally absent.
- The client also tries to support her father.

Possible Questions:

- Who does your mother look for? And: What perhaps happened to her mother?
- What is it like for the sister next to her father?
- How is it for the father?
- What is the mother feeling?

And so on. The next section will expand on ways of exploring these early possibilities and of coming to a fuller sense of the dynamics of the system.

Chapter 22

More on Methods and Markers

In this section I will look further at the specifics of working with floor markers, tabletop markers and visualisations. This is a kind of pot pourri of suggestions, techniques and helpful hints, all of which are things I have learnt or experimented with over the years and found useful.

General pointers to remember as a facilitator with floor and tabletop work:

Maintain a collected inner state. The more you can do this the more you will communicate this to the client, helping her to find a collected inner state.

Slow down the process and the client.

Be clear with your instructions to the client. Speak slowly and clearly, especially in the beginning. Remember you are the one who understands the procedure, and it is up to you to maintain clarity and simplicity throughout.

Pay attention to detail (e.g. in looking at the positioning in the constellation)

Stay in contact with the client, at times checking to see how she feels with what is happening.

Floor markers

Where to stand as the facilitator

Always be clear about where you are standing and why. The most common problem for the facilitator is inadvertently becoming part of the constellation, in which case you will lose your detachment and clarity. As a general rule there are two places that I think are pretty safe. One is to stand right outside of the constellations space, and the other is to stand just behind and to the left of the client. The advantage of this position is that you are just out of the client's view if she is looking straight ahead, so you are unlikely to distract her from whatever she is focusing on (her embodied experience or seeing the other markers etc), and yet by a slight turn of the head she knows you are there. Most clients seem to experience this as a supportive and helpful place for the facilitator to be. Here you are also within a good distance to touch the client lightly on her shoulder when inviting her to get in touch with her embodied experience, a physical anchoring that supports this physical awareness.

Example 1: where the outlined markers are the actual client and facilitator, and the filled-in markers are the floor markers.

Figure 20

Client's marker   Client

Facilitator

It helps maintain clarity for the client if you only stand in front of her when you are on a marker, and so clearly part of the constellation, being in relationship with her as a representative. Otherwise, stay out of the direct view-line of the client while moving around the constellation. The 'alongside' position is by its nature a collaborative, co-journeying position as opposed to, for example, the almost directly opposite positioning of client and psychotherapist in the conventional therapy contract, which is predominantly about the relationship between therapist and client. In the constellations process

233

the relationship between facilitator and client is important, but in the background. It is not the central focus.

Movement

Notice any kind of body movement that the client displays when on a marker (or even when sitting down at a table-top constellation). Over time your powers of observation of small shifts and movements in your client's body and facial expressions will improve. If you see a movement you may draw her attention to it and invite her to follow that movement as it is in her body. Where would the movement end up? Much as we see in the group constellation, clients are often taken by a movement while being a representative on a particular marker. However, many people will not consciously notice this, and may unconsciously compensate thereby missing something potentially important. It will be for the facilitator to notice and encourage such movement into consciousness.

Contact

At the point of the needed contact between the client and whomever they need to connect with, it may be more lively for the client if the facilitator stands on the other marker to 'receive' whatever the client may need to say, and even to respond. In this instance the facilitator can state clearly before stepping onto the marker that, while on the marker she will share whatever she experiences and speak whatever feels right. This helps the facilitator feel free to become a representative in the constellation.

It may also be useful to invite the client to stand on the 'receiving' marker and for the facilitator to stand on the client's marker and repeat what the client has just said. This will help the client understand the effect of what she is saying on the other person. For example, if the client is facing a dead ancestor with whom she has felt connected in her life experiences of depression, I might invite her to say to the ancestor:

"You are an ancestor of mine, and I have held a memory of you all my life. Now I consciously see you and I will remember you and keep you always in my heart." To say this may be moving for the client, and, if I am on the ancestor's marker it may be moving for me. I may, as the ancestor, have some response, which I may offer. However, it may also be useful for the client to experience being on the ancestor marker herself, and you can suggest changing places, and, as the client, repeat the sentences. She will then have her own experience of being that ancestor. If, for example, while on the ancestor marker you have a particularly strong experience, perhaps one that challenges the client's perspective of that person, you can offer it or not, depending on the circumstances. In either case I think it is important that if possible the client take up that position and experience what may be there herself, because it is the new experiences that support change, and in the end it is better for the client to have this new experience.

Case example 15:

A client held a perception of her mother as cruel, vindictive, mean and persecutory. She described her mother's behaviour as crazy and said that she had never felt that her mother had any interest in her.

During the constellations process she had seen that there was much suffering in the background system of her mother, some of it going back several generations. This information came from inviting her to include whatever events or people had been involved in similar suffering to her mother's in previous generations, a suggestion that had made sense to the client, and so she had included many male markers piled up on top of female markers.

We had done some intense processing which involved creating enough space between the client and her mother's marker for her to feel freer, breathe easier and look in the direction of her mother's marker, which she had not been able to do before, so I invited her to tell her mother that she wished not to follow her mother by behaving and being like her, but that she now decided to honour the suffering of her ancestors by living well and happily. The client then connected with her deep sense of loyalty, as this sentence immediately stimulated feelings of guilt and of having betrayed her mother and the other women in the system. This confronted the whole modus operandi of her life, and her first response was to think that her mother and other female ancestors would castigate her for her disloyalty. I was standing on the mother's marker as she said this, and I told her my experience: "As I stand here my experience is that, while in most of me I feel crazy and I can hardly make sense of what you are saying, there is a very small part of me that agrees with what you say, with what you wish to do."

At this point it seemed important that the client had her own experience of her mother's marker (rather than rely on my statements) and so I suggested she come and stand on the marker. . I went to her marker and repeated the sentence for her to receive as the mother. Then I moved off the client's marker and went to stand next to her as she stood on her mother's marker, and asked her what her experience was. After a few moments she said that as her mother, she felt absolutely fine about what she, as the client had said; that it was good for her as the mother that her daughter should live well, and that it made no sense for her daughter to relive the experiences that she as the mother had had.

As I stood next to the client on her mother's marker I felt such a strong feeling of respect and understanding of how much the mother had tried to deal with these terrible sufferings and how, in fact, all of her behaviour and actions had in some way been an effort to compensate and remain sane for her children. I told the client these thoughts as she stood on the mother's marker and she was very moved. When we sat down together outside of the constellation we talked little more before ending the session.

This example also shows how the facilitator can offer what-ever experiences he has to support the process of the client.

Case example 16:

I had an instance once where the client mentioned in the course of the work that her father's father (her grandfather) had brought shame on the family by committing fraud in the family business, causing the business to go bankrupt, which affected the whole family at the time. This grandfather had been branded a bad person and was never talked about in terms other than to do with the fraud and his criminality. When we included a marker for this grandfather and I eventually suggested she go and stand on it with an open mind and an open heart she did so. After some little time she drew herself up and as the grandfather spontaneously said: "yes I did wrong, but I was also a good father to my children. A criminal is not all that I am."

Moving the markers

It is useful to maintain clarity with the markers, and this may involve moving them as the client moves when on a marker and as the constellation evolves. For example, if the client stands on a marker for her father and senses that he turns and takes some steps in a certain direction, when she has completed the movement you can move the marker to where she now is as the father. Place the marker either just in front of her if she needs to stay in the new position for a while, or place it where she has been standing if she now needs to step off the marker and do something else.

Other means of representing

Another way of holding a representation on a marker is for the facilitator to stand to the side of the marker and hold her hand up where the face of a representative would be, i.e. at head height, palm facing the client. This provides the client with a focus that is at the appropriate level. Using the hand as a reference point instead of standing on the marker herself allows the facilitator to keep her facilitation role separate from a representative role. This is useful if you do not feel that the client is yet able to tolerate the facilitator becoming a representative; perhaps she needs the facilitator to remain clearly in the facilitation role for a while.

Table-top markers

Working with tabletop markers is similar to working with floor markers in many respects. The client and facilitator can connect with the markers by touching them lightly. It is less likely that the facilitator will take up a representation as with the floor markers, but not impossible. I find I do so less with the table work.

Some clients can connect quite easily with the markers, even without touching once they get into the flow of it. I think it helps with the general clarity of the constellation if the client only talks as the representative when in contact with the marker, and we keep it quite clear when she is discussing something with me as herself.

If the client seems to have difficulty connecting with a marker you can always set up a section of the constellation with floor markers to help her have a more embodied experience. This combining of two methods works very well in helping to sharpen the process.

It is not unusual for the client to change in his body and demeanour when he connects with a tabletop representative, even though he is sitting down. Again the facilitator's observation of these slight movements and shifts grows with time and experience and can tip the process quite dramatically.

Case example 17:

I was working with a man whose life had been persistently blighted by chronic depression. When he connected with his great grandfather in a table constellation I noticed a very slight slumping in his body and that a subtle sigh escaped him. When I drew his attention to this and the fact that it happened when he connected with his great grandfather, he looked startled and then told me that his great grandfather had supposedly committed suicide when he was the same age as my client now was. As we stayed with this he talked about his own suicidal thoughts. At this point I suggested he sit back and close his eyes, and see his great grandfather before him. When he did this I suggested he tell his great grandfather about his life, and particularly how his life was linked with his great grandfather's. He did this with increasing emotion. Eventually I suggested that he find a way of remembering his great grandfather consciously in his life and see how this would be for his great grandfather.

When working with tabletop markers, I quite often shift to visualisation when some specific contact is needed, as this provides a very vibrant and lively form of contact.

Visualisations

Visualisations have always held a place in psychotherapy either overtly or covertly. To start a sentence to a client "what do you imagine would happen if ..." immediately invokes imagery in the other's mind, and any therapist or counsellor who allows himself to put such a question is brushing up against a visualisation process. The withdrawing of our perception, by whatever means, from an external view to a more internal view moves us into the imaginary world of visu-alisations. In addition guided visualisations have been an overt part of many therapists' resources for many years, used to invoke support, to connect a person with a possibly wiser more resourced part of himself, to explore illness and healing possibilities and so on.

Whether an entire constellation is carried out within the imagination of the client or the visualisation is used momentarily to enhance a tabletop constellation, it is a useful adjunct to the facilitator's resources.

The visualisation process induces a trance state. In my experience with constellations and visualisations I have observed two types of trance that a person may go into:

- One is a trance state where the person is available for new things to emerge, where he is relaxed and at ease and at the same time can stay focused and in contact with the facilitator. There is liveliness to this trance and no sense of the client losing connection with where he actually is. A client will be able to enter this state, and leave it easily. He will not get lost.
- Another situation is the sort of trance where the person slips back into the trance of the trauma. This state seems mesmerising for the client, and makes the facilitator feel mesmerised as well, and not in good contact with the client. This state is unlikely to be helpful to the client because he will be unable to allow anything new and is liable to dissociation and potential re-traumatisation. For us to get anywhere helpful we have to create space for the possibility of something new and ensure that contact with the present actual situation is maintained.

In working with visualised constellations it is important to bear these two contrasting states in mind. In the latter you may have to stop the visualisation and move to a more concrete and present-centred way of working such as with floor-markers or tabletop markers for a useful constellation to proceed.

Tips for working with visualised constellations:

- It is helpful to start small with no more than the client in the image and one other, or the client watching two other people, for example her parents. One client of mine who was adopted and had, now aged 45, found both of her parents, was troubled by the thought that because they had not stayed together they had not loved each other. In fact she also knew from her mother that she had got pregnant with her while a teenager and her mother's parents had forbidden her to see the father again. She started her visualisation with herself and her two parents. She sat next to me with tears trickling down her face. I asked her what was happening and she said that they had both come very young, probably about the age that they had met, and they were currently looking at each other in a very loving and touching way. As she watched they held each other and kissed. Then spontaneously they turned towards her in her image and invited her to come to them, which, after a little time, she was able to do.
- There are differences as to whether the client sees what is happening through her own eyes, or whether she watches herself in the visualization. In the former she is more engaged in the constellation, as if she were in the constellation herself. In the latter she watches from a more distanced place, as if she watches a representative for herself in the constellation. I generally enquire early on in the visualisation whether she is watching herself or looking through her own eyes in the constellation. This is useful information.
- The visualised constellation is a very intimate process. As the facilitator I may at times not know what is going on. You can always ask simply: "What is happening now?" In addition to inviting the client to keep you informed this also implies that the visualisation has a life and momentum of its own.
- If you have initiated something in the constellation, for

example suggested the inclusion of someone who was not there before, or suggested the client say something to someone, you need to know what the effect is in some way. You may be able to see by changes in the client's face and demeanour, or you may need to ask.

- Don't forget to ask the client how other people in the constellation are responding to whatever intervention you make.
- Be prepared even for unintended people to arrive. In one visualised constellation the client had three generations of women in place behind her mother, and she was facing her mother, when I was just about to suggest that she allow to arrive many more generations of women, and men, all her ancestors ... just as I started to speak she told me that all her ancestors had come into the picture.
- If the constellation seems to get stuck do the same as you might in any other way of working with constellations ... ask the client what needs to happen next.

Chapter 23

The Client and The Facilitator

Treat everything tenderly and with care at the beginning, so
that the return may lead to a flowering.
I Ching (1971)[66]

The Client

In an individual setting with a client who is new to the work,
the beginning of the actual constellation involves a two-
layered process. Obviously, you are working with the
constellation, but at the same time you are teaching the client
how to become a representative in his own constellation. This
requires a slowing down of the process and, for the facilitator,
meticulous attention in the beginning to the procedure of
setting up the constellation and guiding the client through the
initial steps. I cannot stress this too much: taking the beginning stages of inviting the client into this work of being a
representative with care and time will result in a more productive process in the end.

The more that one can help the client disconnect from his
own version of the story, the easier it is for him to take up a
useful representative role. I think of this as a question of
degrees: to what degree at *this* time can *this* client make the
shift into being a representative? It is a delicate matter. We
can help the client to some extent to move away from his
story, and this extent will fluctuate with the process of the
work. For example, if the issue is traumatic for the client,
which it often is, then the closer we get to the "turning point"

[66] Hexagram 24: The Return

or contact point of the constellation, the more the client is likely to recede back into the old story. This is simply to do with what Ruppert calls the "surviving self"[67], the function of which is to hold the boundary between consciousness and the buried trauma, keeping the trauma out of consciousness.

Ways of enabling the client to disconnect enough from his story include:

1. Allowing him to tell you the story he needs to, which may involve waiting until he comes to a stop, or attending to when he begins telling you the same story but in a different way. *Unless the client is relatively empty of his need to tell you about his difficulties, he will not have the space to do much else.* Of course, this does not mean letting him talk for hours . . . this is not practical or useful. In my experience, people have always told me enough after about twenty minutes maximum in the individual session . . . from there on it is usually repetition, or giving me more and more examples of the issue in different ways. Some clients are, to be sure, so enmeshed with their story that they cannot reach a place of relative emptiness, in which case you may need to bring it to a stop. (See section on "clarifying the issue", Chapter 20.)

2. Making a clearly defined separation between the telling of his story and the proposal to set up the constellation. If we have not come to a place where it is clear what we need to do, I might say to the client:

   a. "Well you have told me quite a lot now about your issue, do you think you are ready to set up a constellation?" or:

   b. "Perhaps we can stay with what you have said so far, set up something and see where we go . . . ", or

   c. "You seem to feel rather overwhelmed by all of this, let's just sit for a moment and see what we should do next".

---

[67] Verbal teaching

It does not help the client make a separation if I do not clearly stop the telling process. I might need to say very clearly that it is enough for now, and stop any further going back to the story.

3. Taking time to introduce the client to what we are going to do next: talk about the media we may use, prepare the room (bringing in a table if we are going to use table-top markers, clearing the furniture a bit if we are going to use floor markers). This may seem like an unnecessary formalising of the process, but it takes a few moments and those few moments of separation will help shift him out of the trance of immersion in his story – he can only make a movement into the new from outside of this trance-state.

4. Give him the media to hold and feel, either the pieces of felt or paper, or the tabletop markers. Take time over indicating any distinguishing features (notches in pieces of felt to indicate direction that the marker faces, male and female if your markers define this).

5. Invite him to choose, one by one, the markers for those to be represented, but suggesting that he does not place them yet.

6. Then invite him to take one marker, make contact within himself as to whom it represents, and place it on the table or in the room where he feels is right. If I am using floor markers I will invite him to stand, holding the marker, and follow his feet or his body to the place that feels right. Sometimes with floor markers, if I am not sure about his clarity in placing it, I will stand on the marker and ask him to check, as if he were placing me as a person to be a representative, that he has placed it in the right place. Then we continue with each marker in turn.

Of course, some clients will, in spite of all efforts on the part of the facilitator, set up the constellation speedily, and so usually representing their conscious idea of the family ... they have not been able to disconnect from the story. That is just how it is, and you cannot force it. It is best to accept this and go with the client at the level at which they can engage with the process.

7. Ask the client to stand on his own marker first. I have found it to be helpful in guiding him into the process to have the client stand on the markers in a certain order - from the seemingly easiest to the seemingly most challenging. Standing on his own marker is usually a confirmation of what he knows. It may heighten it for him, but often does not produce anything particularly new. This does not matter; it is the first step and introduces him to the business of standing on a marker and attending to his experience. I encourage him to be aware of his body, directing his attention to his physical experience first. I will use terms such as:
   a. "How do you stand when on this marker?"
   b. "How is your breathing?"
   c. "What do you notice in your body?"
   d. "Just attend to your bodily experience here."

8. To help him get a sense of being surrounded by people I may stand briefly on other markers around the one he is on, and then come back to him to see what, if anything, changes when he has this sense of others.

9. This process can be repeated for each of the markers. You will be able to tell as you go along how the client is doing at taking on this process, and of course it will speed up as you continue.

10. In situations where you do not think that the client is able to disconnect from his idea of things enough to get a good representation you can try the following:
    a. Ask the client as he stands up from his seat to leave all of his issue and concerns in the chair, and to consciously step away from it as he moves towards setting up the constellation. If you are working with tabletop markers, ask him to sit differently, to shift his position with awareness, so as to let the issues and concerns go. You could

    suggest he take a cushion and put all of his story and concerns into it and then place it somewhere in the room, at a good distance from where the two of you are sitting with the table.

b. You can set up a marker (either floor or table-top) to represent a neutral or meta place, or wise person place from which he can make comments on the constellation. He connects with his observing self. Sometimes in the middle of a constellation that has become complicated, I will suggest we both go to this place and connect with each other and comment together on what has happened so far.

c. Ask him if there is a part of him that knows what it is like not to have these issues (or a moment in his life when he felt free of the issues) and set up a marker for this.

d. Another possibility is to purposefully include in the constellation a marker for an abstract value such as: "unconditional love", "wisdom", "dignity", or something more specific such as: "what is as yet unknown in this constellation" or "that which has yet to be included", or "the person in this system with whom this situation originated". These more abstract markers can be very helpful because, while the client may have a very strong and fixed idea about how the known people in his story might be - to the point of not being able to disconnect enough to discover anything new - he is unlikely to be able to do this with an abstract or unknown element. Additionally, these abstract or unknown elements will often transmute into that which has not yet been included but is necessary for the constellation.

Most people become familiar with the process quite quickly, and you will be able to move on to working directly with the constellation, while using your client and yourself as good representatives. If at any time you have the sense that you have lost your connection with the person, or the constellation seems to have got stuck, you can always take both of you out of the constellation, see what is going on for the client, ask him to go to a more neutral place and so on. He may have gone back into his story too much; or it is often the case that he has been re-stimulated by something, and it is useful to take a bit of time out to see what happened.

As the client becomes more used to the process it will be easier for him to know how to move from marker to marker, and he will become freer with his contributions as a representative. As this happens the facilitator can also be more active as a representative herself, while the client can include the facilitator's contributions with more confidence.

The Facilitator

In the individual session the additional functions that the facilitator may take on during the constellation include serving as a representative, offering information from the representative position, providing a focus for the client to speak to and offering her experience of receiving what is said and so on.

The later movements in the individual constellation, when the client is more at home with the process, and I am able to freely use my skills and experience, may become rather like a sensitively choreographed piece, both of us moving with fluidity and surety, each checking with the other, using each other in a satisfyingly co-created venture. At this level, the client may have the confidence to ask me to stand on a particular marker so she can say important things to me, and I have the ability to shift in and out of roles freely as required, from marker to facilitator, and back to marker. I can share with confidence my experience at any place in the constellation because the client has come to trust my honesty and exploratory approach, my uncertainty and my certainty. She knows by now that I approach a marker from a place of curiosity and openness, that I will not use it as a means of imposing my hypotheses. She trusts her own experiences more now, and if she needs to, she knows she can follow me onto a marker to check the experience for herself. I feel able to immerse myself in the moment to an experience, even to the point of expressing an emotion that arises spontaneously and urgently.

As a client's long dead sister I have felt the most overwhelming love for the client and shown it with my eyes and my face; I have experienced the spine-tingling effect of standing in amongst a mass of markers representing the people exploited by a client's family; I have experienced the panic and dread of a long lost great grandfather who had been incarcerated in a concentration camp; I have felt the enduring grief of a mother who lost her mother when she was just a child.

Chapter 24

Abstract Elements, Values and Barometers

Abstract markers

The inclusion of abstract markers extends the possibilities of the constellation dramatically. We can include many people in one marker (such as all the ancestors before the traumatic event in this system happened); elements that might prove supportive to the client (such as an ancestor who can love this client, useful if it is hard to find anyone in the current system who can); and undefined elements that can then become whatever might be needed in the constellation, and have been missing such as "another as yet unthought-of option". If we think about the constellations process as the revealing of that which has been missing, then including such a 'missing' element in an abstract way empowers the constellation to define it in whatever way seems useful, and use it.

For example, in a constellation where you do not know what might lie at the root of the issue, you can include a marker for "that which underlies this issue". This assumes that there is something that is missing, and sometimes stimulates the client's unconscious to surface some important information that has not yet been included. It may also prompt useful responses from the representatives. On many occasions, when working with a constellation that seems to be struggling with insufficient known information I have included a marker for 'that which is still unknown in this system', or 'the trauma in this system that continues to affect this person'. Very often, without ever knowing exactly what this marker represents, the response from the representatives, sometimes quite dramatic and at others less so, allows the constellation to move towards a conclusion. In fact I would say: if you get stuck and don't know what to do, consider including an abstract marker ... for example 'that which knows what is needed here', or 'what is needed right now'. Ask the client to stand on the marker and trust whatever immediate thoughts come.

Values Markers

These are markers representing values and universal qualities, which can provide a less entangled overview of the situation. In the individual session providing a marker for such a value invites the client, when standing on it, to connect with a place within herself beyond her own conscious understanding of the issue, with often surprising results. Some examples that you might use include:

- Universal or unconditional love
- Courage
- Beauty
- Truth
- Respect
- Knowledge
- Dignity
- Integrity
- Deepest values of the client
- Wisdom

Barometer markers

These are markers representing those who will in some way be affected by the outcome or who will in some way know if something has changed. As representative markers these can indicate how well the constellation is progressing. With family constellations, for example, markers for the client's children are very useful barometers, particularly if the client has identified one as being particularly affected by the issue. In an organisational or problem-solving constellation, 'the customers' or 'the goal' are particularly valuable. Some examples of good barometers:

- The goal (as in a coaching or problem-solving constellation)
- The unknown good solution
- A partner of the client who is not present but would benefit from a good conclusion
- A future version of the client
- The client's children, particularly if there is one identified as having some connection with the issue, or if they are sick, troubled or 'troublesome'
- A good friend of the client who would want the client to do well in their life
- The customer/beneficiary (in an organisational constellation)

Chaper 25

The Genogram

Genograms have been used by many people to elaborate a person's understanding of their family ancestry. A genogram is a simple diagram rather like a family tree, with symbols that can be added to indicate important deaths (e.g. early tragic deaths), marriages, missing children and so on. When I am running a small group, say 10 or less, I often invite the group members to draw a genogram including at least five generations, paying particular attention to those people they know less or very little about. I encourage them to give these lesser-known people a place in the chart. This very often produces quite startling results that may move on to setting up a constellation. In her workshops Ursula Franke often draws a genogram on a flip chart during the initial interview with her client.

Another thing I invite people to do is to include symbols for societal events that affected their family. These might be wars, migrations, persecutions, industrial or technological revolutions or other big events that have affected members of their families. A typical genogram might look like this:

Figure 21

EXAMPLE OF A GENOGRAM

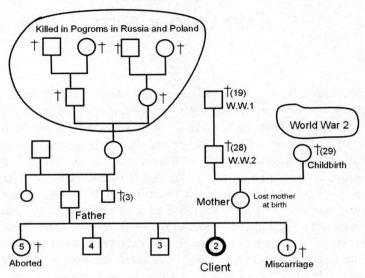

† Deceased before natural time.

It is not necessary to include everyone. It is more useful to include those people who you think might have had some impact on the system that connects with the client's issue.
With thanks to Ursula Franke - verbal teaching.

Section III
Areas of Special Interest

Chapter 26

Structured Constellations

Cappuccino Constellation
(Francis, 2007)

Uses: when time is extremely short. Called a Cappuccino Constellation because it should be possible to complete the constellation in the time it takes to drink a cappuccino!
Elements: Focus[68] + the minimum number of those needed (a maximum of 2 or 3 in total)
Process: The sequence of events in this Constellation is:

- Brief interview and selection of elements
- Clarify that for each element there is a very short time for them to show what is needed (principle of time expanding or contracting according to what is needed)
- Set up the constellation and ask for significant information.
- Invite representatives (if using people) or client (if using objects) to make whatever movements there might be

---

[68] In the Solutions Focused Systemic Structural Constellation *(Sparrer, 2007)* the client's representative is called the Focus, meaning that the representative represents that part of the client that is involved with the issue.

- Understand that this will be unlikely to show a resolution, but will show the next step.
- Close the constellation and consult with the client.

The Café Constellation
(a different form of the Cappuccino Constellation)

This constellation takes place in a café or other public place. Unlike the Cappuccino, it does not have to be quick; several cappuccinos can be consumed during the constellation. I include it to stimulate your creativity in using constellations. It is best used for less personal, more problem solving issues, because of the public place.

Uses: particularly useful in that it can be done just about anywhere, using whatever resources are available. For example in a café one could use salt and pepper pots, cups, sugar cubes etc. or visualisation. It can provide quick and useful information; but be cautious working in this way if there is any likelihood that it may trigger strong emotional reactions.
Elements: whatever is needed for the issue.
Process: as with tabletop constellations, or even short visualised constellations.

Time Line Constellation[69]

This constellation can be useful for understanding more clearly the direction in which one is headed. It arises from the observation that all constellations will configure themselves according to time. So, instead of waiting for the constellation to show the time line, we use the time line as the starting point. It is quick and clear, and has many variations.

---

[69] Other facilitators who have used time as a starting point for structured constellations include Sparrer and von Kibéd (*Sparrer, 2007*), Eva Madelung and Barbara Innecken (*Madelung and Innecken, 2003*)

Uses: for determining direction, understanding present diffi-culties in moving forward, drawing on resources, strengths and skills that one already has.

Elements: The focus, elements for resources, strengths and skills (may be one marker to represent all, or one for each important element), future goal, present difficulties (again may be a marker/representative for each or one to represent all)

Process: The sequence of events is:

- Set up a timeline, using string or tape on the floor
- Client designates which is the future and which is the past, and where along the line the present is
- Client places markers for all the elements where they seem to be in relation to the timeline (they don't have to be on the line, but can be anywhere)
- Client (if using markers) or representatives (if using people) then share their experience and the constellation proceeds from there.

Life Path Constellation

The Life Path Constellation is based on a timeline, which can encompass many generations or just the client's lifetime, depending on what the issue is.

Uses: it is a good way of reflecting on one's path through life, and determining whether one is heading in the direction that one wants to. It is also useful to understand what it might be like to be oneself in the future.

Elements: the client + any number of past and future selves as necessary. For example, myself at 80 years old, myself as a small child.

Process: the client can stand on any marker and speak from their experience on that marker.

Intra-psychic Constellation

This is not dissimilar from methods used in other therapies to understand the interactions between intra-psychic aspects of the self. Mostly particularly I am going to give the one devised by Franz Ruppert, but other elements of the self can be used, such as the part of me that feels lost, or the part of me that wants to succeed.

Uses: help with integration of splits within the self.
Elements: In Franz Ruppert's approach the elements used are: the traumatised self, the surviving self, the healthy self. (Refer to chapter 10 for fuller details about these.)
Process: the elements are set up and allowed to move and speak as they will. There may not be a resolution but useful information can be gained, and often some integration takes place.

Pairs Constellation

This is one that I often do in groups to introduce participants to the representative experience. It is good to do this constellation without any information. It requires two people, one of whom is the "client" and the other is the "helper".

Uses: to explore any issue that can be reduced to two elements (people or abstracts). In addition, this can be used to explore an issue without divulging what the issue is to the helper.
Elements:
Any two elements that make up the issue. One of the elements can be the client as herself, while the "helper" represents the other part of the issue. It is also possible for the constellation to be about two elements, neither of which is the client.
Process:
  • The client selects an issue that involves two elements, for example himself and another person with whom he has an issue, or himself and a house he is thinking of buying, or himself and success etc.

- He sets up his helper and then positions himself either as himself or as the other element of the issue.
- Both people wait and attend to their experience
- Both share their experience, may make some movements, and find a place of rest, perhaps making some statements to each other of what feels true.

Problem constellation
(Sparrer, 2007)

Uses: This is a standard constellation for problem solving.
Elements:
- Focus – the focus is that part of the client that carries the problem
- Goal – if there is a problem there must be a desired goal
- Obstacles – without obstacles there would be no problem
- Resources – we assume that the client has the needed resources even if they don't realise it
- Benefit – this is the benefit to the client of staying in the problem state
- Future task – if a problem were solved there might be a future task that would need to be addressed. This can cause the client to stay in the problem state.

Process:
The client sets up the elements and the constellation is processed in the usual way.

Power Constellation[70]

Uses: the point of this constellation is for the client to be able to take freely from the constituent powers. This is not usually possible in the beginning, one or other of the powers being compromised by hidden or unknown (missing) elements.

---

[70] Adapted from a constellation called the Belief Polarity Constellation originated by Sparrer and Varga von Kibéd *(Sparrer, 2007)*

Elements:
A triangle is formed by representatives (markers or people) for three of the following elements depending on the interests of the client:

- Knowledge
- Love
- Truth
- Beauty
- Logic
- Wisdom
- Insight
- Clarity

Process:

- The client defines a question or need and places a marker (or person) for this in the constellation triangle.
- Or she may wish to put in a marker for herself to understand better her relationship to the powers of the triangle.
- The representatives (if people) or the client as representative (standing on the markers) state their experiences in relation to the client's question.
- If a power element reports experiences that you would not normally deem appropriate for that element (for example if a representative for 'unconditional love' experiences herself as small, limited and depressed) the power element may also represent an important missing element. Take another marker and reassign the power element as itself and the second marker as those experiences that seem not to be to do with the power element. This is a similar process to that described under 'role confusion' in Chapter 11.

Skills Appreciation Constellation

This is useful as a support, particularly in an organisational/business frame.

Uses: to clarify which of one's gained skills and experience one is using, and which one is not, and how the skills and experiences relate to each other.

Elements:
- A marker for each of the client's significant skills and experiences in her life.
- A marker for the client.

Process:
- The markers for the skills and experiences are arranged in a row facing the client's marker.
- The client can stand on each marker making statements related to the experience gained, particularly stating what this particular skill has contributed in the past, and how it might continue to contribute in the present.
- Client returns to her marker in front of all of the skills
- Process and movement are followed as necessary.
- Sometimes it is useful for the client to acknowledge each skill/experience and what it adds to her now in her life.

Once you become familiar with these simple structures you will be able to adapt them to your own needs and those of your client as necessary.

Chapter 27

Small Groups and Couples

Small Groups

Many students of constellations, when starting out running a group, may find that the group they get is quite small. I think that below 6 a group is problematic, particularly if the advertised group is for three days... however, you might want to reduce the time and make refunds and still run the group. The smallest group I ever ran was with 3 and we reduced the time to one day. It worked very well and we all got a lot out of it. Generally however, below 6 I usually suggest that participants come for an individual session instead.

Rather than regarding the small group as a problem, I would encourage you to take it as an opportunity for discipline and creativity. The discipline is in ensuring before you set up the constellation that the issue is clear, and in keeping the constellation down to the absolute essentials in terms of elements represented. You could restrict all constellations to two elements, the client and one other (See chapter 26, the pairs constellation). Also you can use the client herself in the constellation rather than using another person to represent the client, and I have also on occasion used myself as a representative on a marker in a small group, much as I do in the individual session.

The creativity is in finding ways of handling a deficiency of people for representative roles. Here are some suggestions for managing additional roles in a constellation:

- Use floor markers, chairs or cushions
- Use your hand at eye level to give another representative a sense of an additional person

- Ask the representatives to imagine a person standing in a certain place
- Use one person or marker to represent multiple roles

Couples

A couple is a very small group, and presents a particular opportunity in the private consultation. Whatever the issue in the couple relationship, both people will have their own view of it, and each can set up a constellation representing that view or both can be involved in one constellation that incorporates all views. It can also be useful to invite both partners to do a constellation (say a table-top one) at the same time, and then 'visit' each other's constellation and discuss it. If I am working with one of the partners, I may well use the other to help with representative roles in the constellation if it seems possible.

It is important when working with couples that the facilitator holds an impartial stance, never siding or seeming to side with one partner over the other. In working with couples sometimes the force to pull you, as the facilitator, into the confused dynamics is tremendous and it does take skill and experience to side step this and remain impartial. It is also important to as far as is possible always hold that both people bring systemic issues to the relationship ... no one is to blame and both are implicated, and at the same time it is also the case that often one person seems to be bearing the problem so to speak. But on deeper investigation this person is usually holding something for the couple.

It is worth remembering that entering into an intimate couple relationship is at once a relief and a challenge. The impulse to come together with another is operational on many levels, the deepest being that complementary need for the other. However what is also true is that we go into relationship for two other primary diametrically opposed reasons: one is the joy of finding someone who replicates in some way what of our past has felt safe and comfortable, what is familiar and similar to us,[71] (relief); the second is that we look to our partner for something different, to redress the many pains and inadequacies that we perceived in our family, to be that other from our past who, finally, will be as we would have liked them to be (challenge). At the same time our partner must provide us with sameness and difference. To make it even more complex the partner is usually doing the same. The most fundamental aspect of the work with couples is to support them to see each other as they actually are, including their family and ancestral context, without illusion. Only when they can each see the other clearly are they able to truly address the poignant question of whether they can agree to that and make something good of their relationship together.

Case Example 18:

A couple came to see me because one of them had been very ill for some time. She had now recovered somewhat and wanted to see what might have been at the core of the illness so that they could make sure it didn't happen again. It turned out that she had been accident-prone all her life, and had had many debilitating illnesses over the years. She also said she had always had a strong fear of death. I suggested that the woman who had been ill place her partner as 'death' somewhere in the room, and then place herself in relation to 'death'. She did this as follows:

Figure 22

71 For someone from an abusive background this familiarity may well be an abusive relationship situation. The person who experienced abuse may only really feel safe in a similar environment and chooses from this position; and yet the disappointment that it isn't also different somehow can be crippling.

The partner representing 'death' looked at the floor and sagged in her body. She said nothing, but looked as though she might fall down, but she didn't. The client looked anxiously at 'death'. She said to me: I thought I would not be able to look at 'death' but actually I find I am curious and want to move towards her.

I suggested she follow whatever she felt as movement in her body. She moved slightly closer, as if to try and attract the attention of 'death'.

'Death' would not look at her although she indicated by an inclination of her head that she knew she was there.

Eventually after quite a long time both people began to turn away from each other ... 'death' started to stand up straight and looked straight ahead into the distance. The client seemed to draw herself up strongly as she looked away from 'death'. There seemed a sense of settledness and resolution. The picture was like this:

Figure 23

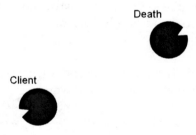

Death

Client

I asked them both if they looked towards anything or anyone. 'Death' said that yes she thought she was looking directly at someone else. I put a marker down in the direction in which she looked. She agreed that that felt better.

The client thought that she was now looking towards her future, and she said she felt much better, she knew 'death' was there, but that at the moment it was not to do with her. We ended the constellation there.

Other strategies that are useful when working with couples are:

- Including a place in the room for the children: this is useful for keeping the couple conscious of this dimension in that their behaviour always affects the children, and children know much more than we think they do about what is going on between their parents. Representatives for children are useful as barometers, informing the facilitator as to how well or not things are going (see Chapter 24). Also it is often very revealing for the parents to stand on a marker for one of their children to understand the effect their difficulties are having on the child.
- The partners stand opposite each other and look at each other; at the same time the facilitator asks each to include in their view behind the other an image of all of the partner's family and ancestors. A ritual here would be to suggest that they say to each other: "I take you as my partner and I include all your family in that taking." This confronts the illusion that I can have this person separate from their roots and family system.

Figure 24 Diagram showing a man and a woman with a space behind each representing their family system.

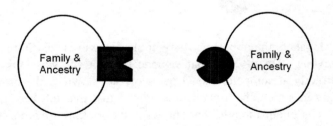

Case Example 19

A woman came to me complaining that her marriage was in jeopardy because her husband's mother was continually interfering and would not leave them alone. When she set up the constellation she placed her husband very close to his mother, just in front of her, and she placed herself quite a long way away, looking towards her husband and her mother-in-law. When she stood on the marker for the mother-in-law she experienced a longing and a wish to reach out and hold the husband in her arms, never to let him go. Back on her own marker she said that she had never seen it this way before, and the experience she had had on the mother-in-law marker was very strong and felt very sad. She has two children of her own, and she said that she suddenly realised what it meant to let your son go to be with another. I suggested that she say something to her mother-in-law and see how it felt. I suggested she say: "I honour you as the mother of my husband. I would not have my good life with him without you, nor my two children, your grandchildren." She said this with tears in her eyes, and said she could feel real love for her mother-in-law. She then went and stood on the mother-in-law's marker. After a moment she drew herself up and said that she felt very good, strong and less needing to hold onto the son in front of her. As she stood there as the mother-in-law she looked moved. I suggested that for a while, every time she saw her mother-in-law or talked to her on the phone, silently inside herself she say the same things, and see how their relationship might change. Some six months later she contacted me to say that her relationship with her mother-in-law was much better.

Another strategy with couples is to use the diagram at the end of Chapter 5 to include the notion of there being some trauma or entanglement in the background of most of us that influences our ability to be in relationship in the present. So on occasion what I suggest to both is to place markers behind them for those who suffered, whose suffering influences how they relate to their partner now. Or I might say to place markers for whatever the systemic trauma might be in their family system. This would look something like this:

Figure 25:
ST = Systemic Trauma

Systemic   Partner 1   Partner 2   Systemic
trauma   trauma

The systemic trauma can be represented by one marker or many, depending on the client's sense of what is needed. This offers each a perspective of the other that is broader. It also gives each partner a greater perspective on what influences and motivates him or her in his or her relationship to the other. It may be that from this there is some mini piece of work that each can do in connection with their own systemic trauma witnessed by the other. I am giving below quite an extended case example to show some of these ways of working.

Case example 20:

I quite often have people come to me who are migrants from Eastern Europe, who have come to the UK to try and make a financially viable life, then meet someone and set up a home with them and have a child.

A couple came to me because the wife had decided she wanted to go back to her country of origin, and she wanted to take their 5 year old son with her. The husband was distraught and found it very difficult to stay in the room as we discussed the dilemma. The wife was also in a bind since obviously she loved her husband and wanted him to go with her back to her country, but he didn't want to go; he didn't speak the language and he had a good job here, and what he was most upset about was not seeing his son as she was insistent on taking him. As we talked the impossible impasse became more and more clear. The wife seemed so set on going home to where her family were; she seemed to be compulsively drawn back, even though she also said that she didn't get on with her mother, her father was dead and most of her siblings were also away from their country of origin like her.

Firstly I suggested one of them choose a marker for the boy and place him somewhere in the room at a good enough distance for him to be safe. They decided between them who should place his marker. When the son had been placed I shared with them that I felt he had been placed too close; that he needed more space from both of them to be able to be present and yet safe from being overly influenced by either. Placing the child as a barometer usually evokes an ability to connect with a wisdom within the child as to what helps and what feels worse.

Next I suggested that they each take as many floor markers as they needed to represent whatever sufferings or traumas they knew of or sensed in their own background that influenced their ability to be present and in relationship with the other at this moment, and then to place them in the area behind where they were sitting (see figures 24 and 25 above). They both sat for a moment and then began to select markers and place them in the space behind. This was obviously very evocative for both, particularly for the woman. They both then sat down and we were quiet for a bit. The woman kept glancing back to the markers behind her and eventually said with great emotion: "That one there is my great grandmother. When my mother was a child the family had to leave our country and become refugees during the war, and my mother always told me of this memory she had of leaving her grandmother behind on the station because she was too ill to travel. They never saw or heard of her again." She went on to talk about how she had such a vivid image of her great grandmother sitting on the platform as her family left even though this was long before she was born, that in some way she had always felt a strong connection with this great grandmother. I suggested she tell her great grandmother: "I am your great granddaughter and I have always known about you and feel in myself how tragic that leaving must have been for you. I have a son of my own, your great great grandson, and I will tell him about you in a good way, and I want you to know that we carry on."

A little later in the session she talked about how her urge to go back to her country felt in some way tied up with remembering this great grandmother and wanting to take her son back to her. For the husband this was very moving to witness and gave him much more information about the underlying reasons for his wife's desire to return home.

We then moved to looking at some of the issues in his background that also contributed to their situation, and at the end I asked each of them to connect briefly with the son to see how he was feeling, and both said that they thought he felt better.

There are two things of interest in this case study: one is that even though I set up a marker for the son, I didn't ask either of them to stand on the marker. I decided that it would not be helpful since neither of them would be likely to be able to be clear enough of their own passion to usefully represent the child and it would just pull the child more into being the focus of the tug-of-war between them rather than being a barometer for the work. I placed the child so that they could be continually conscious of the potential effect of what they were doing in the session on him, and at the end, without asking them to actually stand on the marker I just asked them each to briefly connect with him to see what effect the work might have had. The second is the benefit for both of bringing into sharp focus the context in which they come together, the setting up of whatever unresolved sufferings each system brings to the relationship. It is not necessary for them to even know what these events might be ... but just to follow their instinct is enough.

Chapter 28

Supervision from a Systemic Perspective

I supervise psychotherapists, coaches and counsellors who wish to take a more systemic view of their work, as well as those actually working with constellations. I offer supervision in one-to-one sessions and groups. There are four different potential foci of working with constellations in a supervision context:

1. **Focus on the supervisee and her client as a system:** the relationship between therapist and client. Markers involved: Therapist (supervisee) and Client. Potential additional markers for elements from client's system and also from therapist's family system. This extends the focus of the relationship between the therapist and her client to include the therapist's relationship with the client system (see item 2) and any counter-transference issues (therapist's personal issues that affect her relationship with her client).
2. **Focus on client and client's system:** client's relationship to her system and the supervisee's relationship to the client's system. Markers involved: Client, Client System, Therapist (supervisee).
3. **Focus on helping supervisee to understand how to work with the constellations methodology** with her client. This is for supervisees who work with constellations themselves.
4. **Focus on the relationship between supervisee and supervisor:** Looking at the interrelation of supervisor and supervisee and their systems . . . and how this may affect aspects of the supervisee/client relationship. It is possible here to include a marker for the supervisor should the

supervisor feel that she is not free of counter-transference issues in her consultation with the supervisee.

5. **Focus on the interrelation of client's, therapist's and supervisor's systems**: this takes the supervisor and supervisee into the larger realm of how systems interact and interplay with each other.

As with a client, I believe that if a supervisee brings a case for consultation, then there is definitely something to be worked with, even though the supervisee may not be clear as to what the issue actually is at the outset. The first consideration for me is always the supervisee's relationship to the client. I am less interested in the factual information about the client, but understand that for the supervisee to say something of this eases her into understanding what it might be that concerns her. A way of understanding this relationship between client and the supervisee is simply to set up a marker for each (Focus 1 above), and then invite the supervisee to stand on each and report her experience. The single most common dynamic that I see in this type of constellation is that the therapist marker is far too close to the client. Being 'too close' to the client invites entanglement with the client (counter-transference) and the client's issues (see Chapter 13 on issues of helping). When the supervisee stands on the client marker, if it hasn't been obvious before from looking at the positioning that she is too close, she will know it then. This may lead to an exploration of the parallel issues of the supervisee with her client's issues. For example:

Case example 21:

A regular supervisee of mine brought a case of a woman she was working with who was concerned about her relationship with her daughter. She had been separated from the father of the daughter for many years, and neither mother nor daughter had much to do with the father even though they knew where he lived. He had re-married a woman with children of her own. The woman described her daughter as consistently angry and aggressive with her mother, and the mother felt cowed and diminished by her daughter. The therapist felt stuck, sensing that there was an imbalance of relating between the mother and daughter, but not knowing quite how to proceed.

I suggested we set up a mini constellation of the mother, the daughter and the therapist, (Focus 1 above) which she did. What she set up was a fairly conventional picture of the mother and daughter sitting opposite each other and the therapist sitting between them but away from them, as the third point in a triangle. Having stood on all three markers without adding much information, I suggested we include a marker for the father. When re-visiting the daughter's marker she felt less angry, and sadder. At this point the supervisee (therapist) realised the parallel with her own history, recalling how angry she had been with her mother (whom she had lived with) after her father had left. This had two effects for the supervisee: one was that she understood the impact of the missing father for her client, and secondly she understood why she had been so angry with her mother, realising that it is easier to be angry with the person in front of you than with the person who left.

This Case example prompted me to employ a strategy that I now often use in supervision cases, which is to suggest that the supervisee, in her subsequent sessions with her client, consciously hold a place in the room for the missing or missed person, and see how this might affect her and her client, without saying anything to the client. (This is similar to the notion of the facilitator including the client's family system in her perception of the client.) This holding of a space for the missing sometimes, in time, can translate into actually bringing in a marker for this missed person in the actual therapy session, when the context of the work is right to do so, but in the meantime, ensures that the therapist's consciousness is fully inclusive. In the case above we also discussed the notion of the therapist keeping conscious of her own father in a useful way, and of possibly doing some personal work for herself.

One of the most useful strategies I use in supervision is to have a third chair. For me this third chair is always the client, and at any time I can suggest to the supervisee that she go and sit in this chair and be her client, who has heard all that we have been saying. This is often invaluable, and includes the notion that in some way the client can know what we say in the supervision session.

The second consideration is the supervisee's and the client's relationship to the client system. (Focus 2 above) This 'client system' may, in the specific instance, refer to a person, for example the client's mother, or father, or multiple people such as 'that section of the system that is involved with the client's current issues'. The idea here is to understand, for instance, the best place for the therapist (supervisee) to position herself in relation to the client and the client's system. This is an interesting one, and again requires the supervisee to stand on the client's marker and gain information about where is the best place for the therapist to be. This is not necessarily a physical positioning in the therapy or consulting room, but a positioning that says something about the necessary approach of the therapist in relation to the client addressing her systemic issues, an inner positioning. A common picture we find that feels 'right' to the supervisee standing on the client marker in relation to the client and the client's system is:

Figure 26

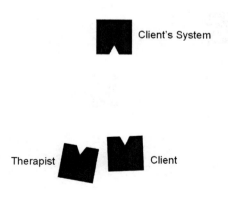

This allows the client to feel supported by the therapist, who looks in the same direction as the client, seeing the client system alongside the client. This positioning is one of collaboration, strength, companionship, comfort, equality, and support and yet not entangled. The therapist can sense the client's emotional process and sees more or less what the client sees. Do not assume that this is always a good position though ... as always it is a testing process. The positioning that feels good gives the supervisee information about how to be with the client in the therapy room. It may be possible for the therapist to represent this symbolically by a slight movement of her chair to a position that represents in a small way what she has seen in the supervisory constellation. Even such a small movement can be a ritual for the therapist; a reminder of a way of being that may be more helpful to the client.

Another common formation that feels good for the supervisee on the client's marker is the following:

Figure 27

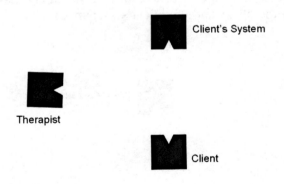

Client's System

Therapist

Client

In this formation the therapist is a witness, and a support to both client and the client's system.

A third formation is one where the client needs the therapist to give support to the client system:

Figure 28

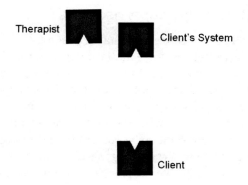

Therapist   Client's System

Client

This formation can be helpful to the client who is confronting issues of guilt and loyalty. In order to express his desire to do something that feels a betrayal of his system, it may help him to see the therapist supporting the system to receive what he wants to say.

The supervisee may also stand on the marker for the system. The purpose is always to understand a better way of being for the therapist in relation to her client and her client's system. Say, for example, the client's system in a particular case is her mother and her mother's mother. To stand on a marker for this part of the client's system may give useful information as to how the supervisee should hold this part of the system in her consciousness. The supervisee might discover a sense of support for the process that the client and the supervisee engage in that had not been evident in the client's description of her mother and grandmother; or a sense of permission to move ahead that the client is not yet in touch with. This often prompts a more respectful attitude to the larger system.

The third focus involves coaching of the supervisee as to how she might set up a constellation with a particular client, which media to use and so on.

The parameters of the supervisor role

In all of the above it is well to stay conscious of what the supervisor is permitted to do. This is fairly commonly understood in the supervision field, but is worth stating here:

It is not the supervisor's job to do the therapy work with the client in the supervision session. That is the job of the supervisee in her sessions with the client. So in all instances of the above it is important to keep within the boundaries of the supervision contract: everything we do is in support of the supervisee's work with the client. The client is never the primary focus of the supervision, the supervisee is: her work, her difficulties, her counter-transference, her systemic entanglements and personal blindnesses, her relationship with her client.

Section IV
And Finally ... Do not be Afraid!

Breathe! You are alive. *Thich Nhat Hanh (1991)*

Do not be afraid:

- To ask the client.
- To ask the representatives (in a group or the client on a marker in the individual context) what needs to happen next.
- To ask the holding circle in a group.
- To pause the constellation.
- To walk away from the constellation and give yourself some space.
- To experiment by including someone or something, or by suggesting someone say something – the constellation will tell you if you are on the right track or not.
- Of not knowing; not knowing leaves space for the others to know and something unexpected to emerge.
- Of confusion – confusion is a necessary stage before clarity.
- Of your own limitations, they are what they are, right now.. in the moment you cannot change that, everyone has them, even the most experienced of facilitators.
- To admit you don't know; people will appreciate your honesty, and it releases everyone from needing to know, thereby allowing something new and unexpected to emerge.
- To stop the constellation because of lack of energy /information/current possibilities.
- To trust (allow without fear).

- To acknowledge when you have misunderstood, got entangled, not known what to do. The client (and the group participants) will value you more for this than if you pretend otherwise.
- To question yourself and your hypotheses.
- To always be open to learning.
- To be part of the collaborative learning experiment that the constellation can be.
- *Not* to set up a constellation.
- To trust the client.
- To trust yourself.
- To breathe!
- ... and to wait ...

Appendices

Appendix 1: Post Traumatic Stress Disorder

309.81 DSM-IV Criteria for diagnosis of Post Traumatic Stress Disorder (309.81)

A. The person has been exposed to a traumatic event in which both of the following have been present:

(1) the person experienced, witnessed, or was confronted with an event or events that involved actual or threatened death or serious injury, or a threat to the physical integrity of self or others

(2) the person's response involved intense fear, helplessness, or horror. **Note:** In children, this may be expressed instead by disorganized or agitated behaviour.

B. The traumatic event is persistently re-experienced in one (or more) of the following ways:

(1) recurrent and intrusive distressing recollections of the event, including images, thoughts, or perceptions. **Note:** In young children, repetitive play may occur in which themes or aspects of the trauma are expressed.

(2) recurrent distressing dreams of the event. **Note:** In children, there may be frightening dreams without recognizable content.

(3) acting or feeling as if the traumatic event were recurring (includes a sense of reliving the experience, illusions, hallucinations, and dissociative flashback episodes, including those that occur upon awakening or when intoxicated). **Note:** In young children, trauma-specific re-enactment may occur.

(4) intense psychological distress at exposure to internal or external cues that symbolize or resemble an aspect of the traumatic event.

(5) physiological reactivity on exposure to internal or external cues that symbolize or resemble an aspect of the traumatic event.

C. Persistent avoidance of stimuli associated with the trauma and numbing of general responsiveness (not present before the trauma), as indicated by three (or more) of the following:

(1) efforts to avoid thoughts, feelings, or conversations associated with the trauma

(2) efforts to avoid activities, places, or people that arouse recollections of the trauma

(3) inability to recall an important aspect of the trauma

(4) markedly diminished interest or participation in significant activities

(5) feeling of detachment or estrangement from others

(6) restricted range of affect (e.g. unable to have loving feelings)

(7) sense of a foreshortened future (e.g. does not expect to have a career, marriage, children, or a normal life span)

D. Persistent symptoms of increased arousal (not present before the trauma), as indicated by two (or more) of the following:

(1) difficulty falling or staying asleep

(2) irritability or outbursts of anger

(3) difficulty concentrating

(4) hypervigilance

(5) exaggerated startle response

E. Duration of the disturbance (symptoms in Criteria B, C, and D) is more than one month.

F. The disturbance causes clinically significant distress or impairment in social, occupational, or other important areas of functioning.

Specify if:

Acute: if duration of symptoms is less than 3 months

Chronic: if duration of symptoms is 3 months or more

With Delayed Onset: if onset of symptoms is at least 6 months after the stressor.

Appendix 2

Trauma Notes

(taken primarily from Rothschild, 2000)

These are notes to help those who work with traumatised clients especially over time as in a conventional psychotherapeutic contract. Rothschild distinguishes various diagnostic types of trauma and, in some cases, her opinion of the therapeutic need (my paraphrasing):

Type I: Single traumatic event. Less attention on the therapeutic relationship, more focus on the trauma.

Type II: Repeatedly traumatised. Differences depend on stability of original background.

Type II (A): multiple traumas + stable background = sufficient resources to separate events. Less need for attention to therapeutic relationship, more focus on trauma.

Type II (B): multiple traumas + less stable background = insufficient resources to be able to separate events. More prior need for good, on-going therapeutic relationship before trauma addressed.

Type II (B) (R) [72]: stable background, complex trauma experience is too overwhelming, resources insufficient to cope. On-going therapeutic relationship helps rebuild resources.

Type II (B) (nR)[73]: never developed resources. Therapeutic relationship may be the whole focus of the therapy.

Type III: Many PTSD symptoms but reports no identifying event. "Prolonged duress stress disorder". Chronic, prolonged stress during developmental years from neglect, chronic illness, dysfunctional family system etc.[74] On-going therapeutic support indicated.

---

[72] Where 'R' indicates that the person has resources but that they are insufficient and need building.

[73] Where 'R' indicates resources and 'n' indicates that the client never had them.

[74] This, of course, would include the transgenerationally transmitted trauma of others.

Rothschild lists the following as <u>10 Foundations for Safe Trauma Therapy</u>:

1. Establish safety within and outside therapy
2. Develop good contact
3. Develop confidence in applying 'accelerator' and 'brake'[75] with client
4. Identify and build client's internal and external resources (support)
5. Regard defences as resources, create more choices
6. Trauma is like a pressure cooker: always work to reduce pressure not increase
7. Adapt therapy to client
8. Have a broad knowledge of theory
9. Never expect one intervention to have the same result with two clients
10. Be prepared to put aside all techniques and just talk

And I would add: keep the person present, aware of the here and now and your presence.

Rothschild also distinguishes the following resources that can be developed over time:

Functional – practical, e.g. to do with safety in therapy room and outside. Contracts.

Physical – strength, agility. Might involve doing some defence training

Psychological – intelligence, humour, creativity, interest

Interpersonal – family and social as a support

Spiritual – any spiritual pursuit that they do.

---

[75] Accelerator means when the client can speed up and brake is when the client needs to slow down because of heightened trauma symptoms.

Appendix 3

Facilitator Style

Diagram to clarify the qualities of two extremes on a continuum of more or less directive style of facilitation.

More Directive

| | Less Directive |

View of constellations process:
Constellation is high static to signal ratio

Qualities:
Less trusting
More active
More controlling
More ordered constellation
Authority lies more with facilitator
Facilitator more visible
Less holding, more managing

Requirements of Facilitator:
More feeling of responsibility for results
Strong need to know what to do next

Challenges for facilitator:
A good outcome relies more on the facilitator
Facilitator more vulnerable to 'failure'

Implications for Constellations Process:
A less collaborative process
Constellation is more ordered and quicker
It may seem more safe, but may not be
Less spontaneous
Possible that important/useful information is missed
The facilitator becomes the authority and their ideas hold sway

View of constellations process:
Constellation is high signal to static ratio

Qualities:
More trusting
Less active
Less controlling
Less ordered constellation
Authority lies more with constellation
Facilitator less visible
Less managing, more holding

Requirements of Facilitator:
Less feeling of responsibility for results
Less need to know what to do next

Challenges for facilitator:
High degree of trust required in self, the process and the representatives
High tolerance of not knowing and uncertainty

Implications for Constellations Process:
A more collaborative process
Constellation can become chaotic and may take more time
It may seem or actually be less safe
More spontaneous
More space for the unknown to emerge
Less likely for important things to be missed
The facilitator is less of an authority and does not need to have ideas

More Directive Less Directive

Implications for Representatives:
Less trusting of themselves
More relying on facilitator to tell them what to do and say
Possibility of important information going unnoticed

Dangers to the work:
Facilitator may fall prey to inflated ego and charisma
Temptation to impose systemic orders instead of negotiating with the constellations energy
At its worst, this can lead to authoritarian and tyrannical behaviour such as bullying
The natural resolving energy of the constellation may be suppressed
Hollow resolution may result
Possibility of re-traumatisation of client or representatives in their own material because representatives discouraged from speaking out
Arrogance and bullying on the part of the facilitator may re-stimulate participants' trauma material

Implications for Representatives:
More trusting of themselves
Less reliant on facilitator to tell them what to do and say
More likely to surface important information as they are encouraged to trust themselves and their experiences

Dangers to the work:
Facilitator may 'disappear' and not hold the space and process sufficiently for safety
Facilitator may relinquish any authority leaving the constellation and representatives in chaos
Possibility of re-traumatisation of client or representatives due to chaotic and unboundaried constellation which may re-stimulate trauma

Appendix 4

Psychotherapy and Constellations

A brief comparison between constellations and psychotherapy may be of interest to some readers. In general I would say that conventional psychotherapy[76] could only gain by absorbing the ideas, perspective and aspects of the methodology of constellations. At the same time the constellations method seems so efficient in getting to the root of the matter, and has such a powerful effect (often needing time for the unfolding of the insights triggered before any other step can be taken), that it is a challenge to some of the basic assumptions that we make in psychotherapy.

The therapy contract

The main assumption that constellations practice challenges is the need for the client to be in a regular weekly meeting contract. This is not to say that there are not people who really do need such continuing support (see Appendix 2), but it does in my view bring it into question as an assumption that it must be that way[77]. There are indeed some clients that I see whom I strongly suggest seek this kind of regular support, but at the same time I have worked in the ad hoc session basis described in the text above with some quite severely abused and fragile people who seem to flourish in an atmosphere where they take such responsibility for when and how often they see

---

[76] I use this term as a means of capturing some of the general ideas and practices that underlie most psychotherapeutic endeavours. Of course the field of psychotherapy is extremely diverse in its theoretical foci and practice, but the issues that I think constellations work challenges or could enhance probably are pretty common to all. It would need a much longer essay to discuss the many variations of thinking in detail.

[77] One of the requirements in the UK of our overall governing body (the United Kingdom Council for Psychotherapy) for psychotherapists to qualify for membership is that you must be seeing at least two clients on a regular weekly basis. Someone practising as I do does not qualify.

me. Perhaps this in fact supports them in their quest for authority and control over their lives.

In the constellations process the therapy relationship is not the main focus of the work as it generally is in conventional psychotherapy. The relationship between the client and the constellations facilitator, while important in that we need to be able to trust each other enough to do some good work together, is not the focus for healing. The relationship between the client and her system as revealed in the constellations process is. This is a shift in emphasis that is demonstrated by how we sit with our client. In a conventional psychotherapy contract we tend to sit directly opposite or, at most, slightly offset. This latter is in recognition that for the client sometimes a directly oppositional placing is too confronting and difficult, particularly in the beginning. She needs some space and freedom to look away. Even so the space between the therapist and the client is deemed to be where the action (so to speak) will take place, where the relationship will be co-created. See examples below.

Figure 29

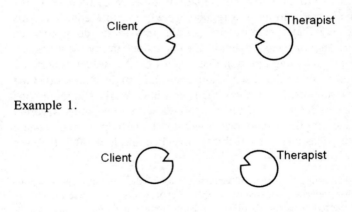

Example 1.

Example 2.

In the constellations practice we tend to sit side by side, perhaps slightly angled towards each other – or with the facilitator slightly back from the client, thereby indicating that it is the client who is the focus, not the facilitator. The client and facilitator are both looking out from their relationship into the space where they know that something is going to happen. The space in front of them represents the vast array of possibilities that may come from the constellation we will do. The client has the space to be with herself while I can wait for her if need be. She doesn't have to look at me, thereby reducing her need to feel obliged to take me into consideration.

Figure 30

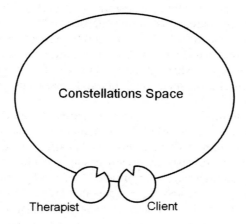

A multi-generational perspective

Psychotherapy rarely looks beyond the client and his parents, whereas in the constellations process we include a multi-generational perspective. If one takes the view that a person is only influenced by events that happen in his own life, thereby excluding the possibility of unconscious influences from several generations back, the context of the work is limited. The perspective that constellations offers (supported by what we experience in the constellation when we put in a representative for someone from the past) allows a far greater context of understanding of the client in front of us. This raises an interesting question: how did we arrive at this rather fixed view of ourselves as only influenced by what happens in our lives? Why is it that we make this assumption? Freud himself referred to "... memory traces of the experience of earlier generations." (1939) And: "I have supposed that the sense of guilt for an action has persisted for many thousands of years and has remained operative in generations which can have no knowledge of that action." (1913) Many other therapists such as Schutzenberger and Boszormenyi-Nagy we know have well understood this perspective of subtle influences across generations ... "traces" as Freud calls them. The psychiatrist John Bowlby, who centralised theories of bonding and attachment between parent and child, proposed an "inter-generational transmission of attachment" (Holmes, 2002), where the attachment ability of the parent was directly related to her own attachment experience with her mother. Although he doesn't specifically state it, this leads to a notion of an attachment ability/style that feeds across many generations.

Generally, at most we assume that our parents' state of being and behaviour do have a major influence on us, and yet is it such a big step to understand that they too have influences that affected their ability to parent us? While current psychotherapy has moved a long way from a culture in some therapies of hyper-critical blaming of parents, encouraging us to vent our rage and accusations, that held us for some time, the constellations' multi-generational perspective that includes the images of trauma and suffering across many generations offers us a perspective filled with compassion and understanding. This in turn allows us more freedom to take what was given to us for what it is, with no blame, dissatisfaction or hurt. Instead of just the 'good-enough mother' we see her in all her context, just as she is. This perception immediately takes us to a deeply spiritual place of understanding that life in itself is the greatest gift.

A wider societal perspective

Furthermore, the constellations process addresses how people are affected profoundly by larger societal events such as wars, persecution, forced migrations, collective shifts in consciousness. Great societal and consciousness transitions such as the Age of Enlightenment and the Industrial Revolution have immense impacts on peoples, communities and families. It is not just the intra-familial events that hurt us, but such memories as of a grandmother, perhaps never met except in stories often told, sitting on a railway station unable to travel with the rest of her family who are fleeing an invading army. The family may never see or hear of her again, but what impact does this ever-present imagery have on the client in front of us, who, like most clients, will work within the framework that we provide? And if that framework does not include an understanding of these across-generation influences they may never arise in the therapy. Surely it is for us as people working with other people to hold as wide a perspective as possible within which the client can decide what is important and what is not.

A methodology to work with across-generational issues

There are those, most particularly from the family therapy tradition (Boszormenyi-Nagy & Spark, Schutzenberger, and probably many other therapists such as Freud and John Bowlby for example), who realised the importance of a trans-generational perspective, but for whom an effective way of working with such issues seemed limited. The methodology of constellations and the representative phenomenon provides an effective way of working with these issues.

Transference and the representative experience

I have already covered this in some detail in Chapter 6, so suffice it to ask a question here that takes the explanation in Chapter 6 a step further: what if transference actually *is* a representative experience? What if we re-framed all that we know about transference within a framework that acknowledged and agreed to the representative experience? How would that change how we thought about transference and thereby how we work? Of course the notion that we are multi-generationally influenced has always been there. . in Freud's early thoughts, in Jung, in John Bowlby's work and in the work of Ivan Boszormenyi-Nagy and other family therapists[78]. Perhaps it faded

---

[78] Since I am discussing constellations and psychotherapy here I have omitted to mention shamanism and the many other forms of working with people that do and have always included a multi-generational ancestral perspective.

from figural view because we did not have a good means of working with it. We were able to speculate and hypothesise, but nothing took us to the direct experience that we seem able to have in the constellation. . except perhaps what we called transference.

Appendix 5

A Brief History of the Influences on the Development of Constellations

For many it has seemed as if the work of Bert Hellinger burst upon the world in a miraculous way; but like all new work and ideas, it has many roots of thought and practice, many forebears. Indeed the research and prior thinking on the transgenerational impact of events, inherited burdens, collective consciousness and interconnectedness are rather greater than we might realise. Sigmund Freud talked of "memory-traces of the experience of earlier generations" (quoted in Schützenberger 1998) and of "the collective mind in which mental processes occur just as they do in the mind of an individual." (ibid) And "I have supposed that the sense of guilt for an action has persisted for many thousands of years and has remained operative in generations which can have no knowledge of that action." (ibid) The other great ancestor of psychology and psychotherapy, Jung, gave us the term "collective unconscious".

In the 1960's and 1970's there was in fact quite a flurry of people who began thinking and theorising about the transgenerational impact of events and cultures within families and the transmission of unresolved conflicts down the generations. These include the French analyst Francoise Dolto and the Hungarian-French psychoanalyst Nicolas Abraham and their followers, and the Hungarian-American psychotherapist Ivan Boszormenyi-Nagy and his co-worker Geraldine Spark. In addition, there were many who focused on the systemic nature of the family, seeing context as crucial to understanding the individual, including Frieda Fromm-Reichmann[79] who worked with Jakob Moreno; Gregory Bateson, Jay

---

[79] Fromm-Reichman was the Dr Fried in the autobiographical novel *I Never Promised You a Rose Garden* by Hanna Green, a classic in the biographical literature of psychotherapy.

Haley, John Weakland, Don Jackson and Paul Watzlawick, and the family therapist Virginia Satir. The latter, along with Jacob Moreno, also pioneered the setting up of family situations using people or objects. Satir's family reconstruction process and family sculptures, and Moreno's psychodrama are the more formal forerunners of the constellations process.[80] Both Moreno's and Satir's work required quite detailed information about family members and a re-enactment of familiar situations within the family. Unlike Moreno, Satir was interested in the greater context, sometimes covering three or four generations and a wide range of social influences.

Moreno proposed the existence of the family and group "co-conscious" and "co-unconscious" as being shared by individuals who are closely bonded to each other. He additionally proposed the use of the concept "tele" (Greek, 'at a distance'). He termed tele as "a 'two-way empathy', a combination of empathy, transference and unconscious 'real communication' ... between people, a communication at a distance." (Schützenberger, 1998)

The notion of the existence of 'uncanny events' in psychotherapy, such as we experience in the constellation, is also not new. As Schützenberger states: "Sometimes the things seen and heard in psychotherapy appear very strange, even to a seasoned therapist." (ibid)

The positioning of representatives with little information and no gestures or coaching of attitude was possibly first used by the German psychiatrist Thea Schönfelder. (Sparrer, 2007)

Hellinger states in his biographical summary (1998) the following influences for his work: his childhood in National Socialist Germany, including his classification by the Gestapo as "suspected of being an enemy of the people" due to his persistent absence from the required Hitler Youth meetings, and his participation in the then illegal Catholic youth organisation; his subsequent drafting into the German army, his experiences of close combat, capture and life in an allied prisoner-of-war camp in Belgium. After the war he entered a Catholic Religious Order at 20 and then worked for 16 years as a missionary with the Zulu people in South Africa. He gained insight

---

[80] For a fuller account of those involved in the family therapy and systemic perspectives of the Palo Alto school and others see Anne Ancelin Schützenberger's book *The Ancestor Syndrome (1998)* from which much of my historical understanding is drawn.

into the role of ritual and ceremony through both, and a deepening sense of respect for parents and ancestry from the Zulu people (during his time with them he learned the Zulu language and immersed himself in their culture and beliefs).

After 25 years within the Catholic church he decided to leave and proceeded to study psychoanalysis, then studying with Janov (Primal Scream), Ruth Cohen and Hilarion Petzold (Gestalt Therapy). He was further influenced by Eric Bern's Transactional Analysis, Ivan Boszormenyi-Nagy's book "Invisible Loyalties", and by training with Ruth McClendon and Leslie in family therapy, which is where he states he "first encountered family constellations" (1998). There was additional work with Thea Schönfelder, Milton Erikson's Hypnotherapy, Neuro-Linguistic Programming, Frank Farelly's Provocative Therapy, Irena Precop's Holding Therapy, and he attended at least one workshop with Virginia Satir (Weber in Morgan, 2009). Underlying all of this was the thinking of Martin Heidegger and Martin Buber.

Appendix 6

Suggested Reading List

This list is not comprehensive in the sense that there are other books on the subject of family and systemic constellations. This list is a start and includes those books that I consider essential.

Love's Hidden Symmetry, What makes Love work in Relationships
Bert Hellinger with Gunthard Weber and Hunter Beaumont, 1998. Zeig, Tucker & Co.

Acknowledging What Is, Conversations with Bert Hellinger
Gabriele ten Hovel, translated by Colleen Beaumont, 1999. Zeig, Tucker & Co.

Insights, Lectures and Stories
Bert Hellinger, 2002. Carl-Auer-Systeme Verlag

Trauma, Bonding & Family Constellations: Healing Injuries of the Soul
Franz Ruppert, 2008. Green Balloon Publishing

Miracle, Solution and System: Solution-focused systemic structural constellations for therapy and organisational change
Insa Sparrer, 2007. Solutions Books

Invisible Loyalties, Reciprocity in Intergenerational Family Therapy
Ivan Boszormenyi-Nagy & Geraldine M. Spark, 1973. Brunner/Mazel

The Ancestor Syndrome, Transgenerational Psychotherapy and the Hidden Links in the Family Tree
Anne Ancelin Schützenberger, 1998. Routledge

In My Mind's Eye, Family Constellations in Individual Therapy & Counselling
Ursula Franke, 2003. Carl-Auer-Systeme Verlag

The Art & Practice of Family Constellations, Leading Family Constellations as Developed by Bert Hellinger:
Bertold Ulsamer, 2003. Carl-Auer-Systeme Verlag

The River never Looks Back, Historical and Practical Foundations of Bert Hellinger's Family Constellations
Ursula Franke, translated by Karen Leube, 2003. Carl-Auer-Systeme Verlag

Entering Inner Images: A Creative Use of Constellations in Individual Therapy, Counselling, Groups and Self-Help
Eva Madelung & Barbara Innecken, 2004. Carl-Auer-Systeme Verlag

Family Constellations: Basic Principles & Procedures
Jakob Schneider, 2007. Carl-Auer-Systeme Verlag

References

Ainsworth, M. (1973) *The Development of Infant-Mother Attachment.* In Caldwell, B. M. And Ricciuti, H. N. (eds.), Review of Child Development Research (Vol. 3). University of Chicago Press, Chicago, USA.

Arkoudis-Konstantara, H. (2004) *The Use of Figures for Constellations in Individual Sessions.* The Systemic Solutions Bulletin (now known as the Knowing Field International Constellations Journal) Issue 5, December 2004. London, UK.

Barker, P. (1992) *Regeneration.* Penguin, London, UK.

Blum, R. (1993) *The Book of Runes, Commentary by Ralph Blum.* Eddison Sadd Editions Limited, London, UK.

Bolte Taylor, J. (2006) *My Stroke of Insight: A Brain Scientist's Person Journey.* Self-published, Bloomington, USA.

Booth Cohen, D. (2008) *Family Constellations and the Soul* in The Knowing Field International Constellations Journal, Issue 12. Frome, Somerset, UK.

Boulton, J. (2006) *Towards an Understanding of the 'Why' in Constellations.* The Knowing Field International Constellations Journal, Issue 8. Frome, Somerset, UK.

Boszormenyi-Nagy, I. & Spark, G. M. (1984) *Invisible Loyalties: Reciprocity in Intergenerational Family Therapy.* Brunner/Mazel, Levittown, PA, USA.

Broughton, V. (2004) *Constellations in Individual Sessions: Review of Two Books and General Discussion,* in The Systemic Solutions Bulletin, Issue 5. Dunton, Bedfordshire, UK.

Broughton, V. (2006) *Constellations in an Individual Setting,* in Self & Society, Vol. 33 No. 4. London, UK.

Broughton, V. (2006) *Constellations Work in Supervision,* in Therapy Today, Vol. 17, No. 9. Lutterworth, Leics, UK.

Broughton, V. (2008) *Book Review and Discussion of Miracle, Solution & System: Solution Focused Systemic Structural Constellations for Therapy & Organisational Change by Insa Sparrer* in The Knowing Field International Constellations Journal, Issue 11. Frome, Somerset, UK.

Broughton, V. (2008) *Constellations, Psychotherapy, Standards & Associations... No, No, No!* in The Knowing Field International

Constellations Journal, Issue 12. Frome, Somerset, UK.

DSM-IV-TR, (2004) American Psychiatric Association, USA.

Dimitrov, V & Dimitrov, J. B. *Fuzzy Logic: A Key to Shared Wisdom*, paper published online at: http://www.zulenet.com /VladimirDimitrov/pages/fuzlog.html.

Francis, T. (2007) *Constellations at Work: Organisational Constellations Learning Forum*. Privately published, Chester, UK.

Franke, U. (2002) *In My Mind's Eye: Family Constellations in Individual Therapy and Counselling*. Carl-Auer-Systeme Verlag, Heidelberg, Germany. Translated from original German edition: *Wenn ich die Augen Schliesse, kann ich dich sehen* (2002) by C. Beaumont. Carl-Auer-Systeme Verlag, Heidelberg, Germany.

Franke, U. (2003) *The River Never Looks Back: Historical and Practical Foundations of Bert Hellinger's Family Constellations,* Translated from original German edition: *Systemische Familienaufstellung* (2001) by K. Leube, Profil Verlag, Munich, Germany. Carl-Auer-Systeme Verlag, Heidelberg, Germany.

Freud, S. (1939) *Moses and Monotheism*, in *The Complete Psychological Works of Sigmund Freud* (1953). The Hogarth Press, London, UK.

Freud, S. (1913) *Totem and Taboo* in *The Complete Psychological Works of Sigmund Freud* (1953). The Hogarth Press, London, UK.

Grove, D.J. & Panzer, B.I. (1991) *Resolving Traumatic Memories: Metaphors and Symbols in Psychotherapy*. Irvington Publishers Inc., New York, USA.

Hanh, Thich Nhat (1991) *Peace is Every Step: The Path of Mindfulness in Everyday Life*. Bantam Books, Random House, London, UK.

Hellinger, B. (1997) *Touching Love: Bert Hellinger at work with Family Constellations* transcript of two videos of the same name, translated by H. Beaumont, C. Beaumont and J. ten Herkel-Chaudhri. Carl-Auer Systeme, Heidelberg, Germany.

Hellinger, B. with **Weber, G. & Beaumont, H.** (1998) *Love's Hidden Symmetry: What Makes Love Work in Relationships*. Zeig, Tucker & Co, Phoenix, Arizona, USA.

Hellinger, B. & ten Hovel, G. (1999) *Acknowledging What is: Conversations with Bert Hellinger*. Translated by C. Beaumont. Zeig, Tucker & Co Inc, Phoenix, Arizona, USA.

Hellinger, B. (2001) *Short Lectures During a Workshop in Taiwan.* Available from www.hellinger.com.

Hellinger, B. (2001) *Christian/Jewish German/Jewish Healing in the Soul,* Lecture at 3rd International Congress for Family and Humans Systems Constellations, Würzburg, Germany 1-4 May, 2001.

Hellinger, B. (2002) *The Alpha and The Omega.* Systemic Solutions Bulletin, Issue 3, London, UK.

Hellinger, B. (2002) *Insights: Lectures and Stories.* Translated by J. ten Herkel. Carl-Auer-System Verlag, Heidelberg, Germany.

Hellinger, B. (2003) *The Orders of Helping,* paper in German at www.hellinger.com, translated and edited by S. Tombleson and J. ten Herkel.

Hellinger, B. (2003) *The Art of Helping,* Systemic Solutions Bulletin, Issue 4. London, UK.

Hellinger, B. (2003a) *Psychotherapy and Religion,* in The Systemic Solutions Bulletin Issue 4. London, UK.

Hellinger, B. (2003) *To the Heart of the Matter: Brief Therapies.* Translated by C. Beaumont. Zeig, Tucker & Theisen Inc, Phoenix, USA.

Holmes, J. (2002) *John Bowlby & Attachment Theory.* Brunner-Routledge, Hove, UK.

Hunter, V. (1991) *John Bowlby: An Interview,* in Psychoanalytic Review 78, (2).

Karpf, A. (1997) *The War After.* Minerva, London, UK.

Krishnamurti, J. (1995) *The Book of Life: Daily Meditations with Krishnamurti.* Harper, San Francisco, USA.

Laszlo, E. (2007) *Science and the Akashic Field: An Integral Theory of Everything.* Inner Traditions, Vermont, USA.

Levinas, E. in **Suurmond, JJ.** (1999) *Beyond Buber: Gestalt Therapy in the Light of Levinas* in The Gestalt Journal, Fall 1999. The Centre for Gestalt Development, New York, USA.

Levine, P. (1997) *Waking the Tiger: Healing Trauma: The Innate Capacity to Transform Overwhelming Experiences.* North Atlantic Books, USA.

Liebermeister, S. (2006) *The Roots of Love: A Guide to Family Constellation: Understanding the ties that bind us and the path to freedom.* Perfect Publishers, Cambridge, UK.

Mahr, A. (2006) *Systemic Constellation Work (scw): A Brief Summary,* unpublished paper. A. Mahr.

Madelung, E. & Innecken, B. (2004) *Entering Inner Images: A Creative use of Constellations in Individual Therapy, Counselling, Groups and Self-Help*. Carl-Auer, Heidelberg, Germany. Translated from original German edition: *Im Bilde Sein* (2003) by C. Beaumont. Carl Auer, Heidelberg, Germany.

McTaggart, L. (2001) *The Field*. Element, London, UK.

Morgan, B. (2008) *Spotlight on Bert Hellinger,* Interview in The Knowing Field International Constellations Journal, Issue 12. Frome, Somerset, UK.

Morgan, B. (2009) *In the Spotlight: Gunthard Weber and Judith Hemming*, The Knowing Field International Constellations Journal, Issue 13. Frome, Somerset, UK.

Moore, T. (1992) *Care of the Soul: How to add Depth and Meaning to Your Everyday Life*. Judy Piatkus Ltd. London, UK.

Payne, J. (2005) *The Healing of Individuals, Families & Nations: Trans-Generational Healing & Family Constellations*. Findhorn Press, Scotland, UK.

Rabin, M. J. (2006) *A Better World, Interview with Bert Hellinger*, in The Knowing Field International Journal Issue 8. Frome, Somerset, UK.

Rothschild, B. (2000) *The Body Remembers: The Psychophysiology of Trauma and Trauma Treatment*. W W Norton & Co, New York, USA.

Ruppert, F. (2008) *Trauma, Bonding & Family Constellations: Healing the Injuries of the Soul*. Green Balloon Publishing, Somerset, UK. Translated from original German edition by S. Tombleson, O. Fry and A. Chalfont, edited by V. Broughton: *Trauma Bindung und Familienstellen* (2005) Pfeiffer bei Klett-Cotta, Stuttgart, Germany,

Schneider, J. (2007) *Family Constellations: Basic Principles and Procedures*. Translated b C. Beaumont. Carl Auer Systeme Verlag, Heidelberg, Germany.

Schützenberger, A.A. (1998) *The Ancestor Syndrome: Trans-generational Psychotherapy and the Hidden Links in the Family Tree*. Routledge, London, UK.

Sgroi, M. (1988) *Vulnerable Populations Volume 1: Evaluation and Treatment of Sexually Abused Children and Adult Survivors*. Lexington Books, Mass. USA.

Shay, J. (2002) *Odysseus in America: Combat Trauma and the Trials of Homecoming*. Scribner, New York, USA.

Sheldrake, R. (1995) *Morphic Resonance & The Presence of the Past: The Habits of Nature*. Park Street Press, Vermont, USA.

Somé, M. P. (1993) *Ritual: Power, Healing and Community*. Windrush Press, Oxford, UK.

Sparrer, I. (2007) *Miracle, Solution & System: Solution-focused systemic structural constellations for therapy and organisational change*. Solutions Books, Cheltenham, UK. Translated from original German edition: *Wunder, Losung und System* (2006), Car-Auer-Systeme, Heidelberg, Germany by S. Onn, edited by V. Broughton.

Stam, J. J. (2006) *Fields of Connection, The Practice of Organisational Constellations*. Uitgeverij Het Noorderflicht, Groningen, The Netherlands.

Suurmond, J.J. (1999) *Beyond Buber: Gestalt Therapy in the Light of Levinas*, in The Gestalt Journal, Vol. XXII, No. 1. The Centre for Gestalt Development Inc. New York, USA.

van Kampenhout, D. (2001) *Images of the Soul, The Workings of the Soul in Shamanic Rituals and Family Constellations*. Carl-Auer-Systeme Verlag, Heidelberg, Germany.

Wilbur, K. (2000) *A Brief History of Everything*, Shambala Publications, Boston, USA.

Wilhelm, R. (1971) (translator). *The I Ching or Book of Changes*. Routledge & Kegan Paul Ltd, London, UK.

Zohar, D. & Marshall I. (1994) *The Quantum Society, Mind, Physics and a New Social Vision,* Flamingo, an imprint of HarperCollins Publishers, London, UK.

Index

Lightning Source UK Ltd.
Milton Keynes UK
UKOW030016190612

194657UK00014BA/64/P